# The American Search for Peace:

## MORAL REASONING, RELIGIOUS HOPE,
## AND NATIONAL SECURITY

# The American Search for Peace:
## MORAL REASONING, RELIGIOUS HOPE, AND NATIONAL SECURITY

ESSAYS BY JAMES F. CHILDRESS, J. BRYAN HEHIR,
DAVID HOLLENBACH, S.J., JAMES TURNER JOHNSON
JOHN P. LANGAN, S.J., ROBIN W. LOVIN,
HAROLD SAUNDERS, AND GEORGE WEIGEL

*WITH CONVERSATIONS REPORTED BY ALBERTO R. COLL*

EDITED BY GEORGE WEIGEL AND JOHN P. LANGAN, S.J.

GEORGETOWN UNIVERSITY PRESS / WASHINGTON, D.C.

10  9  8  7  6  5  4  3  2  1


Library of Congress Cataloging-in-Publication Data

The American search for peace:  moral reasoning, religious hope, and
    national security  /  George Weigel and John P. Langan.
        p.    cm.
    Revised papers presented at a seminar held 1987-1988.
    1. Peace--Religious aspects--Congresses.   2. United States-
-National security--Congresses.   3. Religious ethics--Congresses.
4. United States--Foreign relations--Philosophy--Congresses.
5. United States--Military policy--Religious aspects--Congresses.
6. Religion and international affairs--Congresses.   7. Just war
doctrine--Congresses.   8. Pacifism--Religious aspects--Congresses.
9. United States--Foreign relations--1945- --Congresses.
I. Weigel, George.   II. Langan, John P., 1940-      .
BL65.P4A44    1991                    172'.42--dc20                    90-25416
ISBN 0-87840-507-0 (hard).  --  ISBN 0-87840-519-4 (pbk.)

# CONTENTS

# PREFACE

Back in the days when he was director of the Woodrow Wilson International Center for Scholars, James Billington, the eminent Russian historian now serving as Librarian of Congress, liked to tell the story of a Wilson Center advisory board meeting attended by Dean Rusk. Billington had, as he tells it, conducted a kind of intellectual show-and-tell, explaining to the board at some length the large number and undoubted importance of the books produced by the Center's fellows and staff during the previous year. Members of the board were duly impressed, with the exception of Dean Rusk. When it came his turn to speak, the former Secretary of State and Rhodes Scholar, in his quiet Georgian way, said that he was very interested in all of this publishing: but could Jim Billington assure him that it was worth all those trees?

There is certainly too much "academic" publishing going on in America today. And so people who write, edit, and publish books like this one ought to think about the Dean Rusk Test: is it worth all those trees?

In this case, I think I can speak for my colleague John Langan as well as for myself in saying that our consciences are clean: because of the quality of the individual essays in this volume; because of the vigor of the "conversations" that follow each essay; indeed, because of the very nature of the intellectual exercise that produced the book—about which, a few prefatory words are in order.

The first half of the 1980s saw an explosion of moral argument about U.S. national security policy: in the academy, throughout the religious community, in the prestige and popular media, and in parts of the U.S. government. Whether the policy issue was nuclear weapons and strategy, or the ends and means of U.S. policy in Central America, questions of "ought" were regularly entangled with questions of "is" in the ongoing debate over America's right role in world politics. The churches of mainline Protestantism and the Roman Catholic Church were fully engaged in the argument, often in tandem with secular political lobbies and pressure groups; evangelical Protestantism was slower to get into the fray, but by the mid-1980s was duly enmeshed in sundry controversies. This volatile mix of intellectual and political activism led, in turn, to several major church documents in the middle years of the decade: the 1983 pastoral letter of the Catholic bishops, "The Challenge of Peace: God's Promise and Our Response"; the 1985 study guide of the Presbyterian Church (USA), "Presbyterians and Peacemaking: Are We Now Called to Resistance?"; the 1986 pastoral letter of the bishops of the United Methodist Church, "In Defense of Creation"; the 1986 *Guidelines* document of the National Association of Evangelicals' "Peace, Freedom, and Security Studies Program"; and the 1987 report to the Episcopal Diocese of Washington, "The Nuclear Dilemma: A Christian Search for Understanding."

That the new religious activism on the nuclear weapons issue had its impact on the course of U.S. policy seems, to me, indisputable: although the impact was not perhaps what the activists had hoped it would be. For one significant result of the antideterrence agitations of the early 1980s, many of which were organized through the American religious community and sustained intellectually by the arguments of moral theologians and ethicists, was the Reagan administration's commitment to the Strategic Defense Initiative—a program widely regarded as undesirable (to put it gently) by the very activist community which did so much to prepare the political-cultural ground for it. The question of strategic defense, of course, soon intersected with the question of the possibility of radical change in the Soviet Union (a world-historical development unforeseen by both religious and intellectual activists and the relevant governmental authorities), and what had once seemed a two-sided debate soon began to more closely resemble three-dimensional chess as practiced by Mr. Spock in "Star Trek."

I was a combatant in these intellectual and political wars myself, but in spite of that (or, more likely, because of it), it seemed to me that there was something deeply troubling about the morality-and-national-security-policy debate as we entered the last triennium of the decade. The complexity of the issues involved grew exponentially, but that was, in a sense, the least of our problems. More seriously, people of undoubted intelligence and sophistication were talking past each other (and, in some instances, shouting past each other). The community of scholars was drifting apart from the community of policy makers: in part because of nasty rifts within those communities themselves. These difficulties meant, in turn, that some basic issues weren't being very satisfactorily addressed.

How did one think, with moral and strategic sophistication, about the different modalities of "intervention" in a world that virtually everyone conceded was increasingly interdependent?

The classic categories of the just war tradition had clearly been stretched by the new weapons technologies; but had there been sufficient argument, down to first principles, about the just war canons themselves and their current "place" in the national security system of the United States?

Pacifism had reemerged as a significant voice in the debate; but had the weaknesses of pacifism's past been fully digested by contemporary pacifists (and nonpacifists, for that matter) committed to the nonviolent resolution of international conflict?

Deciding, immodestly, to try to do something about all this, I looked for partners and found them in Father John Langan, S.J., and his colleagues of the Woodstock Theological Center. With generous funding from the newly minted United States Institute of Peace, we—the James Madison Foundation, which I then headed, and Woodstock—began the two-year intellectual exercise whose formal results you now hold in your hands. What did we try to do? What was different about our continuing seminar? How, to go back to the beginning, did we meet the Dean Rusk Test?

The first distinctiveness of the "American Search for Peace" seminar was its throroughly ecumenical character, in both theological and political terms. A review of the seminar's cast of characters (listed at the end of the book) supports the claim, I think, that this was perhaps the most thoroughly "integrated" exercise of its sort organized in the 1980s.

We had Protestants (mainline and evangelical), Catholics (radical, liberal, and conservative), Jews (of various religious observances and moral schools), and some devout (so to speak) secularists.

We had former officials of liberal Democratic administrations, moderate Democratic administrations, and conservative Republican administrations.

We had soldiers (of sundry ranks) and we had pacifists.

We had State Department people and Defense Department people. We had officials of the Executive Branch and senior congressional staffers.

We had people who had spent not inconsiderable time over the previous years in public controversy with each other.

The result of this mix was conversation that ranged from the sturdily workmanlike to the corruscatingly brilliant. (Those who participated, for example, in the conversation launched by Father J. Bryan Hehir's paper on intervention and Charles Krauthammer's critique of the paper were in no doubt, by the end of the seminar, that they had just been part of the most scintillating discussion to take place in Washington—and quite possibly in the United States—that day.) Bringing those conversations, and the papers from which they arose, to a wider audience is one answer to the Dean Rusk Test.

The second distinctive quality of the "American Search for Peace" seminar was its focus on basic issues at the intersection of moral reasoning and national security policy. We worked, quite deliberately, "off the headlines." Our immediate concern (which perhaps marked us as an endangered species in Washington) was not to exert influence on this-or-that. Rather, we tried to bring the accumulated wisdom of the past to bear on the question of creating an adequate moral framework for today's debate on national security policy. The participants in the seminar were fully aware of what had to be decided, in the short term, by our colleagues in government. But those decisions were not the entry-point for our work. So we may hope, and with good reason, that these essays and conversations have a longer shelf life than the usual run of policy studies. We are dealing here with issues as old as Thucydides, but the issues have an immediacy that leaps, daily, from the newspapers on the breakfast table. Closing the gap between the wisdom of the past and the exigencies of the present seemed a good thing to do. And that is our second answer to the Dean Rusk Test.

Finally, the "American Search for Peace" seminar had a special quality because of the interaction we deliberately fostered between scholars and policy makers, in the hope (not altogether unrequited) that we might shake up the certainties of each group. Some of our academic participants were, quite probably, amazed to hear (and from one of the principals involved) about the moral discussion, at the very highest levels of governmental decision making, that preceded the U.S. intervention in Grenada. Some of our participants from the policy community were, quite probably, surprised to learn that academic theologians and philosophers had something more than an abstract, ivory tower view of the pressures, constraints, and possibilities of office. Thus the seminar and its conversations evolved in a stimulating dialectic between moral *reasoning* and national security *policy making*. We illustrated existentially, if you will, the truth of Aristotle's dictum that politics is an extension of ethics. And that, to sum up, is our third answer to the Dean Rusk Test.

Given this rationale for the seminar, it should come as no surprise that we wanted to capture, in this book, the conversations of our seminarists as well as the formal papers prepared for our discussions. Some readers may be surprised, or perhaps even dismayed, to find that the conversations which follow do not always "resolve" the issues being debated. The premise of the seminar, though, was taken from Father John Courtney Murray, the eminent American Jesuit theologian and social ethicist, who used to argue that achieving *disagreement* was a real accomplishment, since so much of what passed for disagreement was really confusion. To "achieve disagreement" meant that the relevant empirical facts of a case had been agreed upon, as had the moral norms and analytic frameworks applicable to the case. Then, and only then, Murray believed, could real *argument* begin. If our seminar helped "achieve disagreement," it did a fine thing indeed.

Between the actual meetings of the seminar (from February 1987 to December 1988) and this book there stands, of course, the Revolution of 1989. Does that remarkable series of events render the seminar's work of antiquarian interest only? I think not. Because we were determined to focus on basic moral and strategic issues (and, in fact, managed to do so, as the conversations demonstrate), the proceedings of our work were less likely to have been overrun by history. Indeed, the kinds of issues explored by the seminar—the relevance of the just war canons, the meaning of "intervention," the internationalist/isolationist debate over national interest and national purpose, the role of negotiations in world politics—are arguably of increasing importance and urgency in the world that will follow the Revolution of 1989.

Therefore, the essays that follow are, essentially, the essays presented in the 1987-88 seminar, refined by modest revisions made for the sake of clarity by the authors at the editors' request. In order to maintain continuity between each paper and its attendant conversation, we did not ask our authors to add codas to their essays in order to bring their papers "up to date," so to speak. Because they deal with enduring issues, these papers are already "up to date," and we hope they will continue to shed light up darkened alleys for years to come: in the academy, but also in the policy community, where the immediacy of Richard Weaver's claim that "ideas have consequences" has been sharply brought home by the extraordinary happenings of late 1989 and early 1990.

A few brief words of acknowledgment and gratitude are in order. The "American Search for Peace" seminar was made possible by a grant from the United States Institute of Peace. USIP chairman John Norton Moore, president Samuel W. Lewis, and then-grants director Kenneth Jensen were stalwart friends of the project. My colleague in the work of the James Madison Foundation, Amy L. Sherman, was responsible for the organizational details and the minutes of the seminar, tasks she performed with her usual competence and good cheer. Christopher Ditzenberger, my associate in the work of the Ethics and Public Policy Center, helped prepare the manuscript for publication. Thanks, too, to Father John Breslin of the Georgetown University Press and his staff for their confidence in the book and their help in bringing it to publication.

The members of the Woodstock Jesuit Community opened their gracious home to us for the seminar, and on behalf of all the participants, I would like to thank these men again for their hospitality, courtesy, and friendship.

Special thanks must go to Dr. Alberto R. Coll, recently of the Naval War College but currently serving as Deputy Assistant Secretary of Defense, for his fine work in preparing the conversations that follow the essays. If this book rises above the norm in academic publishing it is in large part because of these conversations: and having them here, in the book, is in large part due to the work of Alberto Coll.

The members of the seminar were splendid colleagues and I thank them for their participation, but I must save my last word of gratitude for my partner in this enterprise, John Langan, whose intelligence, decency, and good humor were indispensable throughout the project. *Ad multos annos*, as we Catholics used to say.

This book, and the project from which it grew, are now yours. Welcome to the conversation.

GEORGE WEIGEL

*Trinity, 1990*

GEORGE WEIGEL

# The National Interest
# and The National Purpose:
# from Policy Debate to Moral Argument

## I. A PECULIARLY AMERICAN QUESTION:
## NOTES FROM THE HISTORY OF A CONTROVERSY

### Matters of "is" and "ought"

The question of the "national interest" and the "national purpose" (or, as some would insist, "national interest *versus* national purpose") poses itself in a distinctive way in the United States. The reasons why have to do with the nature of the American experiment. The great Jesuit public theologian, John Courtney Murray, defined the peculiarity of the American experiment and the way in which that peculiarity bore on America's historical position in the modern world, in these terms:

> It is classic American doctrine, immortally asserted by Abraham Lincoln, that the new nation which our Fathers brought forth on this continent was dedicated to a "proposition."
>
> I take it that Lincoln used the word with conceptual propriety. In philosophy a proposition is the statement of a truth to be demonstrated. In mathematics a proposition is at times the statement of an operation to be performed. Our Fathers dedicated the nation to a proposition in both these senses. The American Proposition is at once doctrinal and practical, a theorem and a problem. It is an affirmation and also an intention . . .
>
> Neither as a doctrine nor as a project is the American Proposition a finished thing. Its demonstration is never done once for all; and the Proposition itself requires development on penalty of decadence . . .

*1*

In a moment of national crisis Lincoln asserted the imperiled part of the theorem and gave impetus to the impeded part of the project in the noble utterance, at once declaratory and imperative: "All men are created equal." Today, when civil war has become the basic fact of world society, there is no element of the theorem that is not menaced by active negation, and no thrust of the project that does not meet powerful opposition. Today, therefore, thoughtful men among us are saying that America must be clearly more conscious of what it proposes, more articulate in proposing, more purposeful in the realization of the project proposed.[1]

Murray's elegant analysis and language ring as true today as they did in 1960, when *We Hold These Truths: Catholic Reflections on the American Proposition* was first published. The distinctiveness of the American nation is not, finally, its native religious, racial, and ethnic pluralism; nor is it the country's remarkable economic energy. The distinctiveness of the United States is that it is a political community founded, not on blood, or faith, or race, or the accidents of geography and colonial history, but on an *idea*: which Lincoln, following Jefferson, expressed with admirable succinctness—"all men are created equal." That idea (the doctrine, in Murray's terms) gave rise to a distinctive kind of project in political community: the project of republican self-government through representative democracy. The project "side" of the American Proposition raises its own questions about the conduct of America's business in the world.[2] But it is the doctrinal dimension of the proposition that concerns us here. What has it meant, for America's encounter with the world, that the American polity is founded on the doctrine that "all men are created equal"?

In the argument over that question, it has been of considerable importance that Jefferson made a universal claim in the Declaration of Independence. The American Founders did not claim that all English colonists (or, more likely, all white men of property who were not Roman Catholics or Jews) living on the eastern seaboard of North America were created equal. They claimed, simply and flatly, that all men were created equal. Moreover, they implied, this claim was in principle one that could be known and honored by all, since it derived, not from a particularistic religious or philosophical tradition, but from the very structure of human being in the world. "Nature and Nature's God" had created all men equal.

The American Founding, then, had to do with more than the assertion of a new "is" in the world; the "is" that the Founders asserted—the new nation to which they pledged their lives, fortunes, and sacred honor—rested on an "ought." Fact and value, interest and purpose if you will, have been inextricably mixed up in American self-understanding from the very beginning of the nation.[3]

That mixture of interest and purpose gave rise to a distinctive form of nationalism. As Charles Krauthammer has put it, "Our nationalism is unlike others, in that our very nationhood is bound up with and is meant to give expression to the idea of freedom."[4] There has been, in other words, a kind of missionary or evangelical current in American self-understanding from the outset; and that current would inevitably bear, given appropriate historical circumstances, on America's role in world politics. Over the first hundred years or so of our national life, the evangelical current expressed itself in the settlement of the North American continent and, to a lesser extent, in the Monroe Doctrine. The latter was itself a mixture of purpose and interest: Monroe undoubtedly believed that the Western Hemisphere should be free of European colonial control, but it is equally true such an arrangement was to the commercial and security advantage of the United States. (Given the military weakness of the young country, the Monroe Doctrine may also be thought an early example of American cheekiness in world politics.)

## The "older morality"

America was, then, in Chesterton's apt phrase, "the nation with the soul of a church." But if we are to understand the unfolding of the argument over "national interest" and "national purpose" in the twentieth century, we have to recognize that the United States was a nation with the soul of a very particular church. Or, in reality, churches: for its first one hundred fifty years, America was a nation with a generalized Protestant soul. *Kulturprotestantismus*, as Peter Berger has designated the phenomenon, was the semi-established national faith through which the moral problem of national interest and national purpose was read.[5]

This *Kulturprotestantismus* had embedded in it (whether it knew it or not, and it usually didn't) a particular understanding of "morality" with four dominant characteristics, once dissected by John Courtney Murray as follows:

> Its style was voluntarist; it sought the constitution of the moral order in the will of God. The good is good because God commands it; the evil is evil because God forbids it. The notion that certain acts are intrinsically good or evil, and therefore forbidden or commanded by God, was rejected. Rejected, too, was the older intellectualist tradition of ethics and its equation of morality with right reason . . .
>
> In its sources the older morality was scriptural in a fundamentalist sense. In order to find the will of God for man it went directly to the Bible . . . [whose] words [were] to be taken at their immediate face value without further exegetical ado . . .

In its mood the old morality was subjectivist. Technically it would be called a "morality of intention." It set primary and controlling value on a sincerity of interior motive; what matters is not what you do but why you do it. And it was strong on the point that an act is moral only when its motive is altruistic concretely, when the motive is love. If any element of self-interest creeps in, the act is corrupt and sinful.

Finally, in its whole spirit the older morality was individualistic . . . it believed in a direct transference of personal values into social life; it would tolerate nothing less than Christian perfection as a social standard. Its highest assertion was there would be no moral problems in society, if only all men would love their neighbor.[6]

When, after 120 years of hemispheric isolation, the United States emerged as a power to be contended with on the world stage, this was the "morality" or structure of moral reasoning (better, moral sensibility) that was publicly available for thinking about national purpose and national interest. This "older morality," as Murray described it, fit nicely with the simpler understandings of America's evangelical purpose in the world that marked the first two American eruptions into world politics. No doubt Alfred Thayer Mahan's theories influenced men like Theodore Roosevelt and Henry Cabot Lodge in their enthusiasm for the Spanish-American War; but it was the persistence of Spanish colonialism in a rebellious Cuba, and, perhaps even more, the simple moralism summed up in William Howard Taft's sense of America's "civilizing" mission in the Philippines, that carried the country. No doubt balance of power considerations in Europe made the American entry into World War I unavoidable; but it was the war to "make the world safe for democracy" that the Congress endorsed and the people applauded, and that drove men to the recruiting stations.

Despite a last-gasp, generation-long effort to continue avoiding the issue, America was inextricably bound up in world politics, not only as an exemplar but as an actor, after World War I. What we did had its effect (as in the Dawes Plan); what we didn't do also had its effect (as in the weakness of the League of Nations and the general lassitude of the democracies in the face of rising totalitarianism). Could the structure of moral understanding and sensibility that had carried the nation to this point—the "older morality" with its voluntarism, fundamentalism, subjectivism, and individualism—carry the nation any further?

## Pastor Niebuhr objects (as does Professor Morgenthau)

That proposition seemed increasingly dubious to the cadre of theologians and ethicists gathered around the lodestar of Reinhold Niebuhr in the 1930s. Niebuhr had, himself, once been an exponent of a more sophisticated, liberal Protestant form of the "older morality." But the "social question" at home, and the rise of totalitarianism abroad, seemed to him and to others to pose the issue of morality and public policy (in international terms, of national interest and national purpose) in a considerably sharpened form.

By the 1930s, the "older morality" had decayed into (or, perhaps, reached its inevitable terminus in) the kind of soft moralism exemplified by Charles Clayton Morrison of the *Christian Century*, Kirby Page of the Fellowship of Reconciliation, and Frederick Libby of the National Council for the Prevention of War.[7] Pacifism was the universal unguent for the chafings of international politics; wars would cease when men refused to fight. That some men seemed determined, nevertheless, to fight did not really register with interwar liberal Protestant pacifists, who could always find some rationale (the "merchants of death," the injustices of the Versailles Pact, the great powers' exploitative attitude toward China) for the aggressions of the Japanese, the Italians, and the Nazis. If we would but change our sinful ways, their aggression would cease. (In its more sophisticated form, as once argued by Reinhold Niebuhr's brother, H. Richard Niebuhr, the argument was for "the grace of doing nothing"—"The only effective approach to the problem of China and Japan lies in the sphere of an American self-analysis which is likely to result in some surprising discoveries as to the amount of renunciation of self-interest necessary on the part this country . . . before anything effective can be done in the East." This "inactivity of radical Christianity" was "the inaction of those who do not judge their neighbors because they cannot fool themselves into a sense of superior righteousness." For so long as "self-interest" was America's primary motive, it couldn't do much that was useful about the problem of Japanese militarism—which, unlike other pacifists, H. Richard Niebuhr quite understood as an evil.)[8]

Reinhold Niebuhr's attack on interwar moralism was primarily a theological critique, although Niebuhr also drew out its policy implications. What primarily exercised Niebuhr was the idolatry of idealism. The "older morality" had forgotten the doctrine of original sin: which meant it had forgotten that pathos, tragedy, and irony were the very warp and woof of human life. Thus the failures of idealists like Morrison, Page, and Libby were not simply at the level of policy; they were religious failings. Their voluntarism had led them to think they held a monopoly on the discernment of "God's will," which they identified, in one-to-one correspondence, with their own political objectives. Their fundamentalism, subjectivism, and individualism had led to a profound confusion between the ethics of interpersonal relationships and social ethics.

Their radical perception of an "ought" to be pursued in the world had blinded them to the "is"-ness of things. Their dealings with the world as they wished it to be, rather than as it was, constituted a religious, as well as policy, failure.

Niebuhr proposed to replace the "older morality" with his own form of "Christian realism." Beginning with *Moral Man and Immoral Society* (1932), Niebuhr repudiated, "in the name of Protestantism itself . . . the historic liberal Protestant quest for the Kingdom of God" as a this-worldly possibility.[9] The "dream of perpetual peace and brotherhood for human society will never be fully realized," Niebuhr insisted.[10] And yet "society remains man's greatest fulfillment," as well as "his great frustration."[11] Niebuhr's position in *Moral Man and Immoral Society* was not, contrary to some popular interpretations, that society and politics were somehow outside the universe of moral discourse. Rather, Niebuhr wanted to establish social ethics as a distinctive form of moral reasoning. That, he argued, was the precondition for avoiding the sentimentalism that he had rejected in his erstwhile liberal Protestant colleagues.

Faced with the rise of totalitarianism in the late 1930s, Niebuhr had come to understand, as his biographer Richard Wightman Fox puts it, that "the cardinal human flaw was . . . not ignorance but pretension." The positive, political side of this Niebuhrian reclamation of the doctrine of original sin was Niebuhr's appreciation for democracy. That most famous of Niebuhrian aphorisms—"Man's capacity for justice makes democracy possible; but man's inclination to injustice makes democracy necessary"—rested on Niebuhr's chastened belief that democracy created conditions for the possibility of the moral development of the human community, even as it gave the individual a measure of protection against the pretensions of messianic politics.

Niebuhr's theology of Christian realism also gave him the basis on which to reject his brother's "inactivity of radical Christianity." Reinhold could not agree, on theological grounds, with H. Richard's conclusion that "it is better not to act at all than to act from motives which are less than pure, and with the use of methods which are less than critical (coercion)," as Reinhold once described his brother's position. Absolute disinterestedness, Reinhold argued, was impossible for those who had taken responsibility for history. The goal of politics was not love, but justice: and the pursuit of justice meant asserting "right against right and interest against interest until some kind of harmony is achieved." No doubt a "measure of humility and love" was necessary in politics. But this could only "qualify the social struggle in history." What was required, in this world as it is, was an "ethically directed coercion in order that violence be avoided," for "so long as the world of man remains a place where nature and God, the real and the ideal, meet, human progress will depend upon the judicious use of the forces of nature in the service of the ideal" of the beloved community (as Josiah Royce had described the horizon of human striving in the world). Thus the trouble with pacifism was not that it misidentified the Gospel imperative. Pacifism's mistake was to apply the absolute ethic of unconditional love to history in ways that contributed to more, rather than less, violence. Christian love, Niebuhr wrote in 1940, could not be thought of as some sectarian perfectionism over against the world, but as "responsibility for the weal and woe of others."[12]

Niebuhr's theologically grounded attack on moral*ism* was complemented by the political science and policy analyses of Hans Morgenthau and George Kennan. Like Niebuhr, Morgenthau and Kennan wanted an America active in world affairs. What they feared was an America active according to the canons of Wilsonian idealism and the "older morality." The philosopher Charles Frankel recognized that, like Niebuhr, Kennan and Morgenthau were animated by moral considerations. Kennan, wrote Frankel, was not "repelled merely on practical grounds by the American tendency to lecture others on the moralities. The tendency . . . has cut him to the moral quick: he has seen it as a breach of basic principles of tolerance and respect for others." The rationality that Morgenthau urged in the design and conduct of foreign policy was "a moral norm, not simply a technical imperative"; it was "an instrument for reducing human pain and not only for achieving tactical victories."[13] Thus the issue fell, not between "moral" idealists and "amoral" realists, but between different understandings of what constituted moral action and historical possibilities.

Frankel identified six major themes in the realist position as developed by Morgenthau and Kennan in conversation with Niebuhr:

1. General principles are to be held frankly suspect in foreign policy. Kennan in particular (perhaps in reaction to the uses to which his containment doctrine was put) argued against the American tendency to "seek universal formulae or doctrines in which to clothe or justify particular actions." Wise policy would take precise decisions tailored to meet specific, discrete circumstances.[14]

2. Moral principles are a particularly dangerous form of general principles, since to the danger of universalism they add the further perils of zealotry and utopianism. If every policy decision involves a choice between ultimate right and ultimate wrong, there is no possibility of maneuver or compromise, and individual issues are magnified beyond their particular importance. "Ideological fever" is to be rigorously avoided.[15]

3. The parchment barriers of treaties, and the flashier forms of international diplomacy (conferences, verbal proclamations of peace, etc.) should be viewed with a robust skepticism. Kennan, for example, criticized

the "legalistic-moralistic" approach to foreign policy which, "instead of taking the awkward conflicts of national interest and dealing with them on their merits with a view to finding the solution least unsettling to the stability of international life," prefers to "find some formal criteria of a juridical nature by which the permissible behavior of states could be defined."[16]

4. The ethics of interpersonal relationships cannot be transferred to the order of politics without doing grave damage; and the reason for this has to do with the nature of the political act. Morgenthau gave this theme its starkest formulation in 1946:

> Neither science nor ethics nor politics can resolve the conflict between politics and ethics into harmony. . . . To act successfully, that is, according to the rules of the political art, is political wisdom. To know with despair that the political act is inevitably evil, and to act nevertheless, is moral courage.[17]

5. Foreign policy must take human beings as they are, not as we would like them to be. When sin enters the political order, Niebuhr taught, it does its gravest damage by masking egotistical and pretentious drives behind universalistic moral claims. Yet if men would "scale down their moral demands, they might develop a foreign policy capable of accomplishing modest but decent purposes and of avoiding major disasters."[18]

6. The state system is essentially Hobbesian, over the long haul. Peace is the exception; war, in its various forms, the rule. Conflict is the permanent fact of life for the diplomat, as disease is for the physician. Conflict can be eased, temporarily ignored, palliated, and in some limited instances cured. But the nature of international public life is such that the resolution of one conflict often serves to open up another, perhaps unexpected, conflict. In such circumstances, the guiding criterion for policy must be "national interest," which, as defined by Morgenthau, meant "the concept of interest defined in terms of power."

It may seem, on first glance, an amoral concept. And yet, as Morgenthau put his case in *Politics among Nations*, distinctive understandings of both politics and morality were at work here. For the concept of "national interest defined in terms of power" also

> . . . sets up politics as an autonomous sphere of action and understanding apart from other spheres, such as economics (understood as interest defined as wealth), ethics, aesthetics, or religion. Without such a concept a theory of politics, international or domestic, would be altogether impossible, for without it we could not distinguish between political and nonpolitical facts, nor could we bring a measure of systematic order to the political sphere.[19]

## Ironies without end

Classic realism of the Morgenthau/Kennan/Niebuhr school was given a new technological/rationalist twist during the Kennedy administration. In his 1962 Yale University commencement address, President Kennedy suggested that the real problems of the modern age were not philosophical or ideological (and thus inextricably bound up with questions of meaning and value), but rather technical and managerial.[20] Where theologians, chastened by twenty years of reading Reinhold Niebuhr, now feared to tread, systems analysts, it seemed, were eager to rush in.

The debate over U.S. involvement in the Second Indochina War—an involvement intensified by the Kennedy administration's commitment to extended containment and its eagerness to apply the technical/ managerial ethos to the problem of counterinsurgency warfare—brought explicitly moral language and argument back into the American foreign policy debate. Morgenthau, Kennan, and Niebuhr all eventually opposed the Vietnam War on pragmatic or prudential grounds. But what deeply affected the public discourse over America's purpose and interest in world affairs was the moral passion of the Vietnam era "resistance" movement.

Opposition to the American war in Southeast Asia evolved through three stages in the teaching centers of American public life (the literary/ intellectual community, the religious institutions, the prestige media, the universities): Vietnam was first criticized as a policy error; then attacked as an exercise in immorality; and finally condemned as a reflection of the illegitimacy of the American experiment itself.[21] This radical moral judgment led, in the early 1970s, to a neo-isolationism that reversed the terms of classic, interwar isolationism: no longer was it argued that involvement in the sordid affairs of the world would damage the purity of American democracy; now it was a racist, imperialist, militarist (later, sexist) America that was too dangerous for the world. The analytic categories used to argue this case may have been typically drawn from the vulgarized Marxism of the New Left; but the New Left was itself an effort to regain a place for moral argument in the public square, from which it was thought to have been driven by the realism of Morgenthau and the technocratic/managerial elite of the Kennedy administration.

And thus, in an irony that was truly Niebuhrian in quality, the efforts of the realists led, by a roundabout route, to a new form of the moral*ism* they thought they had routed in the wake of Hitler and Pearl Harbor.[22] We may take as the symbolic reference point for the full-blown emergence of the new moral*ism* the 1972 Democratic Convention and particularly the acceptance speech of Senator George McGovern, who managed to combine both neo-isolationism and moralism in the antiphon, "Come home, America." (There is a further irony here: the passion of the anti-U.S.-war-in-Vietnam exponents reflected an inarticulate agreement that America should be "different," should have a purpose beyond self-interest. The collapse of the judgment that America was "different" led to neo-isolationism, as the positive judgment had once led to traditional isolationism.)

The great Constitutional scholar Alexander Bickel was once asked, during this period, what had ever happened to morality in public life. It threatens to drown us, Bickel replied, to his interrogator's confusion. That seemed to be the case to Richard Nixon and Henry Kissinger as well, who set about, in explicit counterpoint, to conduct a foreign policy based on the classic principles of realpolitik.[23] But this first post-Vietnam effort to resurrect a form of realism in response to the new mora*lism* of the neo-isolationists was itself swamped in the moral and political tides of Watergate—which scandal led, in turn and by another Niebuhrian irony, to the election of a president who (quoting Reinhold Niebuhr, no less!) combined both Wilsonian mora*lism* about the national purpose with themes drawn from the neo-isolationism that had achieved a kind of privileged status in the activist Democratic Party.

The Carter administration was full of such paradoxes for those interested in the question of national interest and national purpose. The president's programmatic foreign policy speech, delivered at the University of Notre Dame in 1977, warned that the nation's "inordinate fear of communism" had led to grievous policy errors in the past; redefined the axis of the world *problématique* in North/South, rather than Cold War, East/West terms; and stressed the limits of America's capacity to shape the flow of history—themes dear to neo-isolationism. On the other hand, the Carter administration's human rights policy was, theoretically if not in actual practice, Wilsonian in the breadth of its assertion of American purpose and interest.[24] Moreover, the president had campaigned on a platform that promised a government "as good and as honest as the American people"—as clear a reversion to the older morality as was imaginable.

Events in Iran and Afghanistan led to policy recalculations in the Carter administration; but the intellectual reaction to the new/old mora*lism* and neo-isolationism of the post-Vietnam years had formed even before the Carter administration took office. The 1975 Jackson/Vanik Amendment, which tied "most favored nation" trading status for the Soviet Union to a relaxed Soviet policy on Jewish emigration, was a reassertion of purpose against interest, and of ideological politics against realpolitik, during the Nixon/Kissinger/Ford period. Daniel Patrick Moynihan's incumbency as U.S. ambassador to the United Nations in 1975-1976 gave further definition to what was becoming known as "neoconservatism"; America should, Moynihan urged, become the leader of the "party of liberty" in world affairs, through a kind of Wilsonianism without tears that avoided illusions about international organizations.[25]

President Carter's defeat by Ronald Reagan in 1980 seemed to augur the triumph of the neoconservatives, on many of whose themes candidate Reagan had drawn. Those themes had been given theoretical formulation in the latter half of the 1970s by activist intellectuals such as Irving Kristol (arguing that an ideological age required an ideologically based foreign policy), Norman Podhoretz (arguing that the American national character demanded that "some higher purpose" be served in our dealings with the world), Jeane J. Kirkpatrick (recovering the category of "totalitarianism" for the discourse), and Michael Novak.[26] The "party of liberty" theme was transformed into specific policy proposals by President Reagan in his 1982 address to the British Parliament in Westminster Hall (which led to the creation of the National Endowment for Democracy), and was further specified in Reagan's 1985 State of the Union Address, in which the president proclaimed what Charles Krauthammer would come to call the "Reagan Doctrine"—"overt and unashamed American support for anti-Communist revolution" in Third World locales such as Afghanistan, Angola, Nicaragua, and Ethiopia.[27]

The Reagan Doctrine has not only been challenged from the left, by the neo-isolationists; it has also generated a resurgent realist school, which shares the neoconservatives' vigorous anticommunism and distaste for neo-isolationist perceptions of world realities, but is wary to the point of disbelief that good ends will result from the Reagan Doctrine's explicitly moral reassertion of American purpose in the world. The result has been what one participant in the intellectual combat, Charles Krauthammer, describes as a "three-cornered debate."[28] But it is a debate in which the dialectic of purpose and interest remains unresolved—indeed, posed as harshly as ever before.

### A circular argument, or a perennial one?

The argument over national purpose and national interest, which inextricably involves questions of the role of moral reasoning in foreign policy, has thus come through five cycles in the last two generations. The older moralism of the interwar period was displaced by the realism of Niebuhr and Morgenthau, which was in turn displaced, during and after Vietnam, by a resurgent new moralism clothed in neo-isolationist garb. Neo-isolationist themes remain influential in the teaching centers of American public life, and in the national Democratic Party; but they have in turn been challenged with some measure of success, both intellectually and electorally, by neoconservatives and the Reagan Doctrine. That effort has, in its turn, led to a revived realism that shares the neoconservatives' critical judgment on the world view of the neo-isolationists, but does not share the larger vision and purpose of the Reagan Doctrine.

How to maneuver (conceptually and geopolitically) in the dialectic of purpose and interest seems, on the evidence of this brief survey, to be a question with a distinct fascination for American intellectuals and policy analysts. The argument also seems to have a recurring character; after the fifth turn of the wheel, one wonders whether we have been getting anywhere in these debates. Have we in fact been caught in a circular argument from which little wisdom has been or can be derived? Or is the argument genuinely a perennial one, in which each generation's approaches to the classic questions build on the wisdom of previous intellectual combatants? This seemingly endless debate has led, one might argue, to a measure of political wisdom; it has helped the nation to devise wiser policies (or, more minimally, it has helped the nation understand the folly of policies past). But has it led to moral wisdom? Has the moral argument advanced significantly?

## II.   *STATUS QUAESTIONIS*:
## THE KRAUTHAMMER / TUCKER EXCHANGE

An answer to this last question comes into clearer focus through a more detailed review of the last cycle of the debate, and specifically the argument between neoconservative Charles Krauthammer (creator of the phrase, the "Reagan Doctrine") and Robert W. Tucker, exponent of the new realism.

In a *New Republic* essay published on March 4, 1985,[29] Krauthammer argued that the Vietnam era breakup of the liberal internationalist consensus had led to two new forms of isolationism. The familiar "left isolationism" found in, say, the national Democratic Party, was an isolationism of means, though not of ends. It did not "retreat from the grand Wilsonian commitment to the spread of American values." But it had radically circumscribed the means to that end. "Force is ruled out, effectively if not explicitly . . . And for those 'on the wrong side of history,' as the left likes to say, force is not only wrong, it is futile."[30]

A new form of "right isolationism" had also developed: nationalistic, unilateralist, committed to a selective disengagement from certain arenas of conflict in the world so that the balance between American ends and means could be reset and the nation thereby recover a greater freedom of action. Right isolationism was an isolationism of ends: "it will provide means, but only for a constricted set of interests, principally those required for American security, narrowly defined."[31] Krauthammer saw, in Secretary of Defense Caspar Weinberger's stringent conditions for U.S. military involvement in the Third World, an expression of this "right isolationism." Against both forms of isolationism, Krauthammer proposed the purposeful interventionism of the Reagan Doctrine.

Robert Tucker had his disagreements with Krauthammer's terminology: Did the Democrats really propose to abandon Western Europe and Japan? Caspar Weinberger certainly did not. In what sense, then, were the Democrats and Weinberger "isolationist"? But the gravamen of his attack was on the purpose/interest equation:

> . . . [Interventionists like] Charles Krauthammer argue that our nationalism is unlike all other nationalisms in that we stand for an idea—the idea of freedom—that transcends the narrow confines of national interest. Accordingly, we should be prepared in foreign policy to commit ourselves to the pursuit of freedom, subject only to our now reduced means. To do less, they believe, is for the nation to betray its idea of itself . . .
>
> There is in this vision no acknowledgement of the self-interestedness that marks all foreign policy, including this nation's policy. There is no awareness evident here that in state relations the perils of concern have been at least as great as the perils of indifference, and that given the disparities of power among nations this will doubtless continue to be the case. There is no apparent appreciation of the tragic limitations that attend foreign policy, given even the noblest of intentions.[32]

In his response to Tucker's critique, Krauthammer also pushed the debate away from the interventionist/isolationist terminological bogs, and on to the issue of purpose and interest. "In the end," wrote Krauthammer, "I suspect that what divides Tucker and me is not so much the definition of isolationism as its wisdom. I argue that our intervention abroad should be driven not just by considerations of realpolitik or the requirements of mere physical safety, but by ideology, the ideology of freedom . . . Tucker finds this view misty-eyed and imprudent."[33] Since Tucker does not wish to be pegged an "isolationist," he must defend America's "core alliances" with Western Europe and Japan; but on what grounds does he defend these? Tucker suggested that we defend our core allies because "we do not want to be shut off from societies that begot and that continued to nourish our cultures and institutions." Krauthammer was unpersuaded by this "group therapy theory of alliances," against which he preferred "Wilson's or Truman's democratic idealism." The real nub of the Tucker/Krauthammer disagreement lay, however, not in contrasting theories of the nature of America's core alliances, but in the nexus of purpose and interest: "Tucker's brand of realpolitik," according to Krauthammer, "denies that foreign policy is the realm of values. It is the realm of prudential calculations of safety."[34]

Tucker's counter to Krauthammer's response began with the isolationism issue, considered first as a matter of sensibility ("as between the two fundamental dispositions in foreign policy, isolationism and interventionism, I incline to the former"), but once again moved to more fundamental matters. Tucker's "isolationist" sensibilities (if such they can be called) were not, he wrote, "a matter of temperament" alone. Rather, his preference "responds to the belief that nations can do and have done one another more harm through their 'concern' than through their indifference." Moreover, Tucker argued, "I certainly have no objection to our foreign policy being informed or animated by the values of freedom. Who does? But it is quite another matter to pursue freedom for others who do not have it at the cost of our blood and treasure. At issue here is not the defense of freedom, whether our own or our allies, but its universalization and particularly the price we should be willing to pay for its universalization."[35] Krauthammer had not, according to Tucker, suggested a calculus for relating purpose to interest; he had merely asserted that the two were in fact one on the question of the pursuit of freedom in the world.

In the final round of their exchange, Krauthammer argued that Tucker had, in fact, accepted the notion of an ideologically based, activist foreign policy, since Tucker described his rationale for the U.S. security commitment to Western Europe and Japan as "an aversion to totalitarianism and a desire to see the success of freedom." But what Krauthammer insisted was that "the principle [i.e. international activism on behalf of freedom and against totalitarianism] be prudently and consistently applied to other parts of the world. If freedom and not consanguinity is the reason to defend Europe, then the same principle should logically extend to the Third World as well."[36]

Tucker's final response attempted to refine the notion of "interest" and its relationship to the purposeful American pursuit of freedom in the world:

> In contrast to Mr. Krauthammer [Tucker wrote], I do not believe that physical safety apart, the promotion of freedom should be the only major interest of policy. Between insuring our physical security and promoting freedom, there are a number of other interests that must surely lay claim to our power—the interest in international order being only the most obvious. . . . I can find no persuasive reason why a foreign policy animated by freedom must therefore pursue it everywhere, especially when such pursuit may prove quite costly in the end. . . . My unwillingness to do so need not mean that I am simply indifferent to whether others enjoy freedom. It does mean that a concern for others must have distinct limits not only because of the limited power at our

disposal but because the promotion of freedom cannot be the only, or even the dominant, interest of policy.[37]

After five rounds of debate, then, where stands the argument between Charles Krauthammer's defense of a foreign policy based on ideological purpose and Robert Tucker's preference for the more constrained criteria of "interest(s)" as generally defined by Morgenthau? Both men agree that there is, in the nature of the case, an ideological component to U.S. foreign policy. But where Krauthammer believes that our ideological commitments ought to furnish the basic content of the definition of our "interests," Tucker remains unpersuaded of this toughened form of Wilsonian and Truman Doctrine idealism on two grounds: first, its dubious record in history ("nations can do and have done one another more harm through their 'concern' than through their indifference . . ."), and second, its alleged insensitivity to the prudential claims of interest. Tucker is, in short, considerably more skeptical than Krauthammer that "interest" and "purpose" are so readily served simultaneously. Between the world of fact and the world of value, Tucker seems to be suggesting, there is a gulf that can be occasionally bridged, but never closed.

One senses, at the end of the Krauthammer/Tucker exchange, that while the policy argument may have been somewhat advanced through five rounds of debate and at least a minimum of terminological clarification, the *moral* argument remains in something of a rut. At a certain point, one begins to think that Krauthammer and Tucker are talking past each other, and that the root causes of their disagreement are not being engaged. Both reject the moral*ism* characteristic of Wilsonian idealism in its original form. Tucker seems to remain satisfied with a classic realist approach to the moral question; would the Tucker cited disagree in principle with Morgenthau's claim that the centrality of the concept of "interest defined as power . . . sets politics as an autonomous sphere of action and understanding apart from other spheres, such as . . . ethics, aesthetics, or religion"?

Krauthammer's activism of ideological purpose would not rest comfortably on such a realist base; but Krauthammer has not elaborated a moral understanding of the relationship between purpose and interest. Given the moralistic excesses of the Vietnam era (whose resultant neo-isolationism is Krauthammer's prime target), Charles Krauthammer would hardly wish to jettison the Niebuhrian critique of idealism in its entirety. But his own proposals seem to require a moral doctrine (or, better, concept of moral reasoning in foreign policy) that transcends, even while it includes, the Niebuhrian sensibility. Charles Krauthammer correctly senses that the root of his disagreement with Robert Tucker is over the relationship of moral norms to foreign policy. Still, Krauthammer has not, yet, provided us with a concept of moral reasoning, capable of relating purpose to interest without a collapse into sentimentality and moral*ism*.

But John Courtney Murray has.


## III.  THE NATURAL LAW OPTION

Murray's famous story of his introduction to the "morality and foreign policy debates" in the early 1950s bears repeating:

> My introduction to the state of the problem took place at the outset of the decade in a conversation with a distinguished journalist who is now dead. In public affairs he was immensely knowledgeable; he was also greatly puzzled over the new issue that was being raised. His first question revealed the source of his puzzlement. What, he asked, has the Sermon on the Mount to do with foreign policy? I was not a little taken aback by this statement of the issue. What, I asked, makes you think that morality is identical with the Sermon on the Mount? Innocently and earnestly he replied, "Isn't it?" And that in effect was the end of the conversation. We floundered a while in the shallows and miseries of mutual misunderstanding, and then changed the subject to the tactics of the war going on in Korea.[38]

In his interlocutor's question about the Sermon on the Mount, Murray saw a capsule summary of the "older morality" in its voluntarism, fundamentalism, subjectivism, and individualism. In the 1950s, it was hard to maintain that this "morality" had much to do with foreign policy; that much had been learned from the experience of the 1930s, and the realist critique. Thus, experienced men simply divided the order of politics (or at least international politics) from the order of morality. Still, this didn't seem entirely satisfactory; the question of "morality and foreign policy" kept recurring.

The realist critique, as expounded by Niebuhr, had itself made a cut at an answer to the question of "morality and foreign policy." Murray thought that the realist critique of the "older morality" had been "not only just but also successful." What had the newer, "realist," morality taught? It had taught policy makers to "reckon with the full complexity of man's nature and of human affairs." Against the older morality's absolutism, it stressed the importance of each historical situation. Against fundamentalism, it stressed the importance of the consequence of one's acts. Against the older morality's confidence in judgment, the newer morality stressed the irony, tragedy, and pathos of history. Against the older morality's clear-cut distinctions between "right" and "wrong," the newer morality stressed "ambiguity." And finally,

. . . against the self-righteous tendency of the older morality, the new theory teaches that to act is to sin, to accept responsibility is to incur guilt, to live at all is to stand under the judgment of God, which is uniformly adverse, since every act of moral judgment is vitiated by some hidden fallacy, and every use of human freedom is inevitably an exercise in pride.[39]

The "older morality" and the "newer morality" seemed in dire opposition; and one could be grateful for the attack on sentimentalism that Niebuhr and his colleagues had mounted. And yet, Murray argued, there was an important similarity between the "older morality" and the "newer morality": their "common rejection of the whole style and structure of natural-law morality."[40] This had led both of them to a common set of conundra, which time and again recurred in the debate over morality and foreign policy: the problem of the "gulf between individual man and collective man"; the problem of "self-interest"; and the problem of power. Murray regarded each of these as a "pseudo-problem."

The problem of the "gap" between the moral claims that could be made against an individual and the moral claims that could be made against a collectivity did not occur "within the tradition of reason—or, if you will, in the ethic of natural law."[41] Neither the attempt to apply interpersonal ethics to politics, nor the appeal to "an unresolvable dichotomy between moral man and immoral society"[42] was very useful. Both were based on a "defective theory" of society and the state. In the "tradition of reason," on the other hand, society and the state were natural, not simply remedial, institutions with public, not private, purposes: justice, freedom, security, the general welfare, and civil peace. Given these distinctive *public* ends, social ethics had its own distinctive norms and methods. To confuse those norms and methods by identifying them in an absolutist sense with the structure of moral reasoning appropriate to personal or family life was "inherently fallacious" and made "wreckage not only of public policy but of morality itself."[43]

The tradition of reason also resolved, Murray believed, the question of "self-interest" which had so tortured the older morality, and which the newer morality unsatisfactorily addressed by its appeal to the sinfulness of all political action.

Murray admitted that he, too, was bothered by the question of national interest: "but chiefly lest it be falsely identified in the concrete, thus giving rise to politically stupid policies." But since Murray did not identify the morality of an act exclusively with the intentions of the actor, he was "not at all troubled by the centrality of self-interest as the motive of national action."[44] That motive was both necessary and legitimate, given the distinctive and inherent purposes of organized political life.

There was, however, one reservation. Murray would not admit the interpretation of self-interest as *raison d'état* in its absolutist form. The tradition of reason did not accept the distinctively modern concept of the state's absolute sovereignty. It required, in the modern world, that national interest be conceived as a valid *motive*, but only as a proximate or relative *end*, of America's action in the world. Political action, even in the realm of international public life, was under a moral imperative to work toward the five ends of society and the state noted above. There were inherent limits to the final achievement of these purposes in international life, to be sure. But a realistic appraisal of limits need not lead to an ideology of realism: for, "the national interest, rightly understood, is successfully achieved only at the interior, as it were, of the growing international order to which the pursuit of national interest can and must contribute."[45]

Crafting the concrete policies that would incarnate this concept of interest and purpose was an exercise in casuistry that would be "endlessly difficult," Murray conceded. But that task of practical reason should not be compounded by false and unnecessary theoretical agonies ("whose roots are often in sentimentalism")[46] about the moral relationship between national interest and national purpose.

The problem of "power" was also a pseudo-problem, at least as theoretically misconceived by both the "older" and "newer" or "realist" moralities. Here, too, the practical issue was enormously complex, particularly in an age in which both nuclear weapons and Leninist totalitarianism posed profound threats to civilization. But these difficulties in the order of practical wisdom should not distort the more basic theoretical argument, as happened when a circular argument ensued between the older morality's claim that power was prideful and therefore bad, and the newer morality's reply that the abandonment of power was irresponsible and therefore worse. The natural law tradition, on the other hand, rejected both the Leninist dictum that "the state is a club" *and* the moral queasiness about power that seemed a hallmark of liberal Protestantism and its secular heirs.[47] Politics *was* about power: power understood as the ability to achieve common purposes through a wide range of publicly available instruments. There were limitations on the morally appropriate use of these instruments, the basic distinction being between "force" and "violence":

> Force is the measure of power necessary and sufficient to uphold the valid purposes of both law and politics. What exceeds this measure is violence, which destroys the order of both law and politics . . . . As an instrument, force is morally neutral in itself. The standard of its use is aptitude or ineptitude for the achievement of the obligatory public purposes.[48]

The casuistry here, too, would be "endlessly difficult," particularly when the moral theorist's "refusal to sanction too much force clashes with the soldier's classic reluctance to use too little force."[49] But the theoretical point should be clear: the function of power, in whatever guise it took, violent or nonviolent, was to serve the community, which was "neither a choir of angels nor a pack of wolves." It was simply the human community in its efforts to maintain a margin of safety between itself and barbaric chaos. Toward that end, the state was a necessary instrument which had to embody both reason and force.

Murray was not a utopian in these matters; he did not expect the final vindication of the tradition of reason in this world. But neither was he a cynic:

> The historical success of the civilized community in this continuing effort of the forces of reason to hold at bay the counterforces of barbarism is no more than marginal. The traditional ethic, which asserts the doctrine of the rule of reason in public affairs, does not expect that man's historical success in installing reason in its rightful rule will be more than marginal. But the margin makes the difference.[50]

The historical American argument over "morality and foreign policy," over the relationship between national interest and national purpose, has virtually always been an argument about applications: its orienting question has been, *How* should foreign policy be guided by moral principles? Murray's work suggests that the question has been misposed—and thus the problems deriving from it may be less insoluble than they often appear. The real question, Murray suggests, is this: "What is the moral doctrine by whose norms foreign policy is to be guided?"[51]

Murray's reformulation of the problem has important ecumenical and interreligious implications today. The phrase "natural law" continues to grate on some ears, particularly among those who find in "the tradition of reason" too weak an account of the abiding effects of original sin. And yet consider these two basic claims of natural law theory: There is a fundamental trajectory to creaturely existence (in explicitly Christian terms, from and to God as Creator, Redeemer, and Sanctifier) from which we can derive universally binding moral norms; we can know this trajectory from experience and reflection, and while our knowing of it is illuminated and strengthened by grace, this knowledge is in principle available to all men of good will. Are we really that far here from what other moral theorists seeking an alternative to situationalism or biblical literalism have described as "general revelation" or "common grace"? No promiscuous synthesizing should be allowed in these matters. But there are suggestive convergences of moral intuition at play here, convergences whose exploration is of great importance for addressing the problem of publicly accountable moral argument in the American public square.

The natural law option may not convince Robert Tucker, but it ought to establish the basic point of disagreement between Tucker and Charles Krauthammer, which is a disagreement over the nature of moral reasoning and its function in the policy process. Tucker conceives of moral reasoning on an algebraic model, and charges that this kind of rote simplism inevitably does damage in the complexities of an anarchic world. Tucker's charge must be attended to. Yet the net result of Tucker's formulation is to radically sunder the orders of morality and politics. Another conception of moral reasoning is possible. In the "tradition of reason," theoretical clarity about principles and practical wisdom about their application are both important. There is no need for a bifurcation of "morality" and "foreign policy," of "national interest" and "national purpose" here. There is only (only!) the difficult and endless task of working the casuistry so that the margin of safety between civilization and barbarism expands rather than contracts.

Here, too, is the contribution that Murray and others offer to Charles Krauthammer. Krauthammer's formulation of a new internationalism is cast in both historic and practical terms; America should lead the party of liberty in the world because that is how we have conceived our national experiment, and because that is what will guarantee the safety of the experiment in a world persistently hostile to democratic values. A modern natural law ethic would add to this sketch both a moral rationale that transcends the particularities of American history and the exigencies of the present world-historical moment, and a defense of the casuistry by which ends and means can be related in *morally* appropriate ways as America actively works to shape world politics.

The natural law option, in other words, offers, not middle ground, but new ground, ahead of the present spectrum of debate on "the national interest and the national purpose." It drives the discussion from the level of policy debate to the more fundamental level of moral argument.

## IV.  RESHAPING THE ARGUMENT: TWELVE PROPOSITIONS

1. The "national interest" and the "national purpose" are inextricably connected. They are historically connected, in an American context, by the nation's foundational self-understanding. They are practically connected by the structure of the great conflict in today's world.

But most fundamentally, the "national interest" and the "national purpose" are inextricably connected because of the inherently moral nature of politics and the nature of moral reasoning about politics. "Is" and "ought" must both be accounted for in the devising and execution of foreign policy. In shorthand: the "national purpose" and the "national interest" are in dialectical relationship.

2. Those who argue that one cannot be purposeful in this sort of world, whether for reasons of "complexity" or because of the "impersonal forces" of history, have not reflected very deeply on the history of the twentieth century, which is replete with examples of men bending events to their will. Lenin, Hitler, Mao, Gandhi, Churchill, and the founders of the State of Israel provide some of the more obvious examples.[52] In the more morally admirable of these cases (as well as in the more odious), concepts of "purpose" were informed by calculations of interest. The two seem inextricably linked, in historical fact as well as in moral theory.

3. The moral sensibility of American *Kulturprotestantismus* is inadequate to the tasks of moral reasoning and practical action within the dialectic of national interest and national purpose.

4. The realist critique of the American "older morality," as articulated by Reinhold Niebuhr in particular, was a necessary antidote to the manifold flaws of the moral sensibility of American *Kulturprotestantismus*.

5. A Niebuhrian sensibility—an understanding of the inevitable irony, tragedy, and pathos of history; a sensitivity to the problem of unintended consequences; a robust skepticism about all schemes of human perfection, particularly those in which politics is the instrument of salvation; a moral appreciation of democracy—remains essential for those who would think and act wisely in the dialectic of national interest and purpose today.

6. Reinhold Niebuhr's Christian realism was self-transcending: as Niebuhr himself put it, the ironic temptation of realism was to become so soured in its view of the human prospect that it obscured the "important residual creative factor in human rationality." What Niebuhr offers us today is not so much a framework for moral analysis as a set of moral cautions that are essential to practical reason in foreign policy.

7. Niebuhr's critique of soft moralism must be completed, not by a morality of "ambiguity," but by a modern form of natural law theory which is capable of establishing the distinctive nature of moral reasoning about political action; i.e., that is capable of establishing the *moral* distinctiveness of social ethics.

8. Those basic security concerns that comprise the irreducible core of the national "interest" should be understood as a necessary interior moment in the pursuit of the national purpose: which should in turn be understood as the quest for ordered liberty within a structure of evolving international public life capable of advancing the classic ends of politics—justice, freedom, security, the general welfare, and peace.

9. This understanding of "national purpose" should be viewed, to borrow from the philosopher Bernard Lonergan, as a "horizon concept." It can be known, with theoretical clarity, as that toward which our policy should strive. It helps us measure the gap between things as they are and things as they ought to be. But it is not achievable in any ultimate sense of complete finality. Thus the "national purpose," so construed, is distinguished from a simpler, Wilsonian sense of national *mission*, which involved a considerably shorter temporal framework.

10. The dialectic between "national purpose" and "national interest" will remain unresolved. The pursuit of interest without reference to purpose risks what C. Wright Mills once called "crackpot realism"; the pursuit of grand purposes without reference to the responsibilities of the national interest risks utopianism. The temptations of "crackpot realism" and utopianism may be unavoidable. But succumbing to these temptations is not, given the understanding of politics and of moral reasoning in politics, suggested by the modern natural law tradition.

11. The point of connection between these two dimensions of national public life—national interest and national purpose—will be forged, in moral terms, through a casuistry that recognizes both the reality of moral norms and the necessity of applying them to the world through the mediation of the virtue of prudence. To assert this does not guarantee wise policy. It does reduce the danger of stupid policy based on moral- theoretical confusions.

12. Thus politics, even international politics, remains, as Aristotle taught (and Hans Morgenthau denied), an extension of ethics. To deny this leads to the ruin of both public policy and moral reasoning. Given a reclaimed Aristotelian conception of politics, the debate over the "national interest" and the "national purpose" will remain a perennial one (given changing historical circumstances), but it will not fall into the trap of circularity.

## Notes

1. John Courtney Murray, S.J., *We Hold These Truths: Catholic Reflections on the American Proposition* (New York: Doubleday Image Books, 1964), 7. Hereinafter cited as *WHTT*.

2. Cf., for example, Charles Krauthammer, "The Price of Power," *The New Republic*, 9 February 1987, 23-25.

3. This theme has, in fact, been part of our moral culture since the earliest days of the colonial period. Cf. John Winthrop's famous sermon aboard the *Arbella*, "A Modell of Christian Charity," cited in Robert Bellah, *The Broken Covenant* (New York: Seabury Press, 1975), 14-15.

4. Charles Krauthammer, "Isolationism: A Riposte," *The National Interest* 2 (Winter 1985/86), 115.

5. For a definition and description of this *Kulturprotestantismus*, cf. Peter Berger, "The Social Sources of Apostasy," *This World* 17 (Spring 1987), 6-17.

6. *WHTT*, 263-64.

7. On Niebuhr's break with Morrison, cf. Richard Wightman Fox, *Reinhold Niebuhr: A Biography* (New York: Pantheon, 1985), 196. On Page and Libby, cf. Robert Woito, "Between the Wars," *The Wilson Quarterly* (New Year's 1987), 110ff. Cf. also Reinhold Niebuhr, "Why I Leave the F.O.R.," in *Love and Justice: Selections from the Shorter Writings of Reinhold Niebuhr* (Gloucester, Mass.: Peter Smith, 1976), 254-59.

8. H. Richard Niebuhr, "The Grace of Doing Nothing," in *The Christian Century*, 23 March 1932.

9. Richard Wightman Fox, op.cit., 140.

10. Reinhold Niebuhr, *Moral Man and Immoral Society* (New York: Scribner's, 1932), 21.

11. Ibid., 1.

12. Cf. my fuller discussion of Niebuhr in "The Sensibility of Reinhold Niebuhr," *The National Interest* 5 (Fall 1986), 80-89.

13. Charles Frankel, *Morality and Foreign Policy* (New York: New American Library, 1964), 82-83.

14. Cited in ibid., 20.

15. Cf. ibid., 21-22.

16. George F. Kennan, *American Diplomacy 1900-1950* (New York: New American Library, 1964), 82-83.

17. Hans J. Morgenthau, *Scientific Man vs. Power Politics* (Chicago: University of Chicago Press, 1946), 203.

18. Frankel, op.cit., 25.

19. Hans J. Morgenthau, *Politics among Nations*, 4th edition (New York: Alfred A. Knopf, 1967), 5.

20. Cf. the Yale speech in *Public Papers of the Presidents of the United States: John F. Kennedy, 1962* (Washington, D.C.: Government Printing Office, 1963).

21. Cf. Sandy Vogelsang, *The Long Dark Night of the Soul: The American Intellectual Left and the Vietnam War* (New York: Harper and Row, 1974). Cf. also my application of this schema to the American Catholic debate on Vietnam in *Tranquillitas Ordinis: The Present Failure and Future Promise of American Catholic Thought on War and Peace* (New York: Oxford University Press, 1987), 216-36.

22. Cf. my essay "A Long March," in *The Wilson Quarterly* (New Year's 1987), 122-49. Cf. also my essay, "Intellectual Currents in the American Public Effort for Peace 1930-1980," in *The Nuclear Freeze Debate: Arms Control Issues for the 1980s*, Paul Cole and William Taylor, eds. (Boulder, Colo.: Westview Press, 1983). Cf. also the Vietnam chapter in *Tranquillitas Ordinis*, cited in note 21 above.

23. Cf. Henry Kissinger, *White House Years* (Boston: Little, Brown, 1979), 54-65. Interestingly, under the pressures of the new nuclear debate of the 1980s, Kissinger has emphasized the importance of foreign policies that reflect the moral convictions of the American people.

24. Cf. Joshua Muravchik, *The Uncertain Crusade: Jimmy Carter and the Dilemmas of Human Rights Policy* (Lanham, Md.: Hamilton Press, 1986).

25. Cf. Daniel Patrick Moynihan, *A Dangerous Place* (Boston: Little, Brown, 1978), for the evolution of key themes in the neoconservative position.

26. Cf. Irving Kristol, *Reflections of a Neoconservative* (New York: Basic Books, 1983) and "Foreign Policy in an Age of Ideology," *The National Interest* 1

(Fall 1985), 6-15; Norman Podhoretz, *Breaking Ranks: A Political Memoir* (New York: Harper and Row, 1979), *The Present Danger* (New York: Simon and Schuster, 1980), and *Why We Were in Vietnam* (New York: Simon and Schuster, 1982); Jeane J. Kirkpatrick, "Dictatorships and Double Standards," in *Commentary* (November 1979), and "U.S. Security and Latin America," *Commentary* (January 1981); and Michael Novak, *Rethinking Human Rights* (Washington, D.C.: Foundation for Democratic Education, 1981), and *Rethinking Human Rights II: One Standard, Many Methods* (Washington, D.C.: Foundation for Democratic Education, 1982).

27.   For Reagan's speeches, cf. the Government Printing Office series, *Public Papers of the Presidents of the United States*, the 1982 and 1985 volumes. Cf. also Charles Krauthammer, "The Reagan Doctrine," *Time*, 1 April 1985, 54-55.

28.   Charles Krauthammer, "The Poverty of Realism," *The New Republic*, 17 February 1986, 15.

29.   Charles Krauthammer, "Isolationism, Left and Right," *The New Republic*, 4 March 1985.

30.   Cited in Robert W. Tucker, "Isolationism and Intervention," *The National Interest* 1 (Fall 1985), 20.

31.   Charles Krauthammer, "Isolationism: A Riposte," 115.

32.   Tucker, art. cit., 22-23.

33.   Krauthammer, "Isolationism: A Riposte," 117.

34.   Ibid., 117-18.

35.   Robert W. Tucker, "Confusion and Clarification," *The National Interest* 3 (Spring 1986), 108-11.

36.   Charles Krauthammer, "Debate (continued)," *The National Interest* 4 (Summer 1986), 108.

37.   Robert W. Tucker, "Debate (continued)," *The National Interest* 4 (Summer 1986), 109. Tucker's exchange with Krauthammer is of a piece with his critique of just war theory in general, and the Second Vatican Council's Pastoral Constitution on the Church in the Modern World (*Gaudium et Spes*) in particular. Cf. Robert W. Tucker, *Just War and Vatican Council II* (New York: Council of Religion and International Affairs, 1966). Paul Ramsey's response to Tucker, in the essay "Tucker's *Bellum Contra Bellum Justum*," begins with a telling observation:

> A statement of Jacques Maritain has recently become quite a consolation to me. "Moralists," he wrote in *Man and the State*, "are unhappy people. When they insist on the immutability of moral principles, they are reproached for imposing unlivable requirements on us. When they explain the way in which those immutable principles are to be put into force, they are reproached for making morality relative. In both cases, however, they are only upholding the claims of reason to direct life."
>
> For which aspect of the professional work of a moralist Professor Tucker has the greatest distaste, it is difficult to tell. Any attempt to show how moral principles work in political practice in the conduct of war is like trying to "square the circle." The constituent elements of statecraft, Tucker believes, must revolve in a closed circle. The quest to define *legitimate* military necessity or *legitimate* reasons of state is bound, therefore, to eventuate either in the renunciation of statecraft or in the renunciation of morality. (67)

Whatever else may have changed in Robert Tucker's views, the positions identified by Ramsey certainly haven't, and are clearly in play in Tucker's controversy with Krauthammer.

38. *WHTT*, 262.
39. Ibid., 265.
40. Ibid.
41. Ibid., 272.
42. Ibid., 271.
43. Ibid., 272.
44. Ibid., 272-73.
45. Ibid., 273.
46. Ibid.
47. Ibid., 274.
48. Ibid.
49. Ibid.
50. Ibid., 275.
51. Ibid., 279.
52. Cf. Owen Harries, "Neoconservatives and Realpolitik," in *The National Interest* 1 (Fall 1985), 127.

# THE CONVERSATION

Owen Harries opened the discussion by suggesting that George Weigel was too kind to the realists, especially Hans Morgenthau and George Kennan, whose views on the relationship of morality to politics were incoherent and unpersuasive; for it really is impossible to exclude moral considerations from the definition of a nation's interests. But Harries also thought it unwise to lump Robert Tucker with the realists and accuse him of sundering politics and morality. In claiming that the pursuit of freedom should not be the only interest guiding our foreign policy, Tucker was acknowledging that freedom was indeed one of the moral values our statecraft should serve.

In general, Harries argued, the differences between Tucker and Charles Krauthammer revolved around three issues. First, while Tucker agreed with Krauthammer that it was morally and politically appropriate for America to promote freedom through its foreign policy, Tucker tended to see this as only one among many goals. Second, Krauthammer was more confident than Tucker about the ease of carrying out his enterprise and its prospects for success. For his part, Tucker was eager to underline the costs involved, the possibility of failure, and the difficulty of discerning the prudent course of action. Third, Krauthammer's confidence and Tucker's skepticism reflected sharply divergent assessments of two factors: the strength of democratic forces around the world, and the efficacy of American power as a force for advancing freedom. Unlike Tucker, Krauthammer believed that a democratic revolution was sweeping much of the world today. Tucker, on the other hand, emphasized the intractability of the world and its diverse cultural and political traditions; given such a world, there were significant limits to the United States' ability to transform it. Hence, America's own example, and a policy of moderation that might preserve international stability so as to give democratic forces ample time to take root and slowly develop, were the key ingredients to long-term success.

Harries also thought that Weigel's distinction between "interest" and "purpose" was somewhat confusing and largely unnecessary, arguing that it is better to speak simply of interests, some of which have a moral content and some of which do not. A purpose implies an interest and derives from it; to have an interest is also to have a purpose, the purpose of furthering that interest. The realists were essentially correct to argue that international politics revolves around interests and power. But their conclusion that foreign policy was an amoral activity did not follow from their premise. To say that states pursue their interests is not to say that the interests of all states are the same, or have the same moral worth, or are equally devoid of moral content. While some state interests are dictated by necessity or the anarchic conditions of international society, others may reflect the internal character of a particular society. Societies differ greatly in their moral qualities and in the moral values that animate them. The moral character of a state's foreign policy is related to the moral values embodied, however imperfectly, by the society such a foreign policy is intended to serve and protect. In sum, discussion of a nation's foreign policy in terms of interests need not exclude considerations of moral purpose; indeed, such moral considerations reveal themselves as soon as one begins to probe the nature of the interests in question.

Joseph Nye agreed with much of Weigel's paper, but offered several suggestions. First, he argued that Weigel's characterization of the dialectical interaction in American foreign policy between moralism and realism over the last two decades was more accurate as intellectual history than as a depiction of political reality. The shifts that took place in those years were not so much from realism to moralism, but from a moralism of the left to a moralism of the right. The Kissingerian effort to return to realism had been repudiated by both the right and the left. Jimmy Carter then picked up much of his foreign policy ethos from the liberal moralism of the congressional Democrats of the mid-1970s, and this brand of moralism was in turn replaced by the conservative moralism of the Reagan administration.

Second, Nye disagreed that the realists were to blame for getting us involved in the Vietnam quagmire, and from there into the cycle whereby the Vietnam War became not only a policy error but an immoral act expressing the moral bankruptcy of the American experiment. The most prominent realists, such as Kennan, Morgenthau, and Niebuhr, were among the earliest critics of our Vietnam intervention, and they made their case strictly on policy grounds, not on moral ones. One could argue, in fact, that ideology, moralism, and an obsession with historical analogies on the part of people like Walt Rostow and Dean Rusk had been far more responsible for getting us involved in Vietnam, and hence sliding us into the turbulent moralism of the 1970s, than realist arguments.

Third, Nye thought that Weigel had overplayed Tucker's supposed neo-isolationism. The differences between Krauthammer and Tucker had to do with Tucker's realist perception that the focus of U.S. foreign policy should be on maintaining a favorable balance of power, and that this task required strengthening our links with Western Europe and Japan rather than playing "trivial pursuit," chasing after obscure Third World countries. Far from being isolationist, Tucker wants the United States involved in those critical areas of the Eurasian periphery which, though close to the Soviet Union geographically, are tightly bound to us politically, economically, and militarily, and whose technological, political, and industrial creativity are of irreplaceable value to us.

Nye finally suggested that the paper might have sketched, more precisely and extensively, how casuistry should be done. Nye himself would start with the realist premise that security considerations are the basic building blocks of foreign policy. Yet, one needs to go beyond the realists and recognize that the "state of nature" in which international relations takes place has Lockean as well as Hobbesian characteristics. International politics is not solely the realm of necessity; it is also a realm of choices, and wherever there are choices there are opportunities for moral analysis and moral action. Moral values such as order and justice can be balanced against one another, and neither one of them has to be accorded an absolute preeminence. There are situations where order should receive priority, but others where the gains in terms of justice are well worth the costs to order. The kind of unidimensional ethics practiced by the "survivalists" Weigel criticizes should be replaced by a three-dimensional ethical analysis which carefully weighs motives, means, and possible consequences in evaluating a particular policy. This is what casuistry does. The paper's subtitle perhaps might be inverted to read "from moral argument to a sensible policy debate" because this is really the critical process that the country has been missing for the last two decades.

Larry Fabian asked Weigel whether he wanted to transpose John Courtney Murray's thought from his context to ours, or instead take Murray's ideas and creatively transform them to fit into the different context of the 1990s. The Murray of the late 1950s was quite similar to George Kennan in his refusal to see the U.S.-Soviet struggle in Manichean terms, in his advocacy of a policy of containment that was measured and balanced, and in his neglect of the Third World. The balance and adjustment among Murray's fivefold moral obligations would look very different today than it did in the 1950s; the prudential calculus required would be much more difficult, and the rightness of its outcome considerably less clear than three decades ago. The difficult question is whether Murray can be taken from his historical context and put in today's.

David Newsom was troubled by three questions raised during the discussion. First, does the United States have a special responsibility toward the world, and is the world prepared to recognize and accept such a responsibility? Second, is the United States simply rationalizing realpolitik in moral categories when it supports a Third World movement in the name of freedom and democracy, even though its real objective is the containment of Soviet power? Third, when we announce our intention to project our morality abroad, are we raising expectations that are beyond our power to fulfill? Are we incurring obligations toward many people whom the United States may wind up deserting?

This last issue, as relevant to the Bay of Pigs Cuban exiles of 1961 as to the Nicaraguan *contras* twenty-five years later, was one with which he said he had considerable personal experience, having been present as a U.S. diplomatic officer in five different Third World revolutions, and having had to deal with numerous individuals whom the United States had led to believe it would support but had then abandoned to their fate. It was not enough to argue that if only the United States could muster its national will, it need not abandon its allies around the world. Those who advocate the kind of expansive foreign policy favored openly by Krauthammer and implicitly by Weigel are under a moral obligation to calculate well ahead of time whether there will be enough national support for the high degree of U.S. intervention required to follow through on our rhetoric.

Michael Novak turned the group's attention to a question every thoughtful policy maker should ask: where do we, the United States, want to be twenty-five years from now? In groping for an answer, we must not lose sight of the critical role of ideas in history, the power of ideas to acquire a life of their own and transform political institutions and expectations. Two ideas were especially relevant to the present discussion: liberty and moral judgment. Liberty was an idea central to the American experiment, and its meaning within that experiment had been shaped not only by the Founders and their immediate Whig predecessors but by the Whigs' own intellectual ancestors, including Thomas Aquinas, Cicero, and Aristotle. This is why Weigel's introduction of John Courtney Murray into the discussion was of critical importance. Murray helped to clarify the Catholic and classical roots of the Founders' understanding of liberty, and in so doing could help us understand the implications of that concept for our role in the world.

For the Founders, liberty was not an abstract value but a set of habits and institutions. As much as Thomas Jefferson wished Simon Bolivar well in his attempt to imitate the American colonies' experiment in republican liberty, he thought that the South American nations lacked the habits and institutions necessary for liberty, though he believed that in time they might develop them. The Founders' understanding of liberty as a set of habits and institutions can be immensely helpful to present-day Americans in determining which liberation movements abroad are likely to succeed in establishing genuine regimes of liberty and are therefore deserving of our support.

An exploration of the meaning of "moral judgment" was also important to Weigel's, and this group's, intellectual enterprise. There was
much more to moral judgment than simply elaborating all the reasons for
and against a particular course of action, and then adding them up to see
what the balance was. A first step toward moral judgment was to engage
in the kind of process (described by Nye) of weighing motives, means
and consequences. But it would also be useful to recover older philosophical understandings which recognized moral judgment as a complex
process involving the mediation of various intermediate steps of moral
reasoning and evaluation, and embracing considerations even more
comprehensive than those outlined by Nye.

Going back to the discussion's earlier themes, William O'Brien suggested that Weigel needed to anchor his wide-ranging exploration of
America's interest and purpose in promoting freedom around the world in
a more specific, historical principle central to American foreign policy for
many decades: resistance to aggression. Through the Truman Doctrine,
the formation of NATO, and its Korean intervention, the United States
articulated this principle as central to international law and morality *and* as
beneficial to its interests; and, unlike the British and the French in the
thirties, America succeeded in creating an effective system of collective
security against aggression. Aggression had to be resisted because it was
unlawful and morally wrong, and because a world in which aggressors felt
free to carry out their designs was not safe for American interests or the
American way of life. Opposition to aggression was thus a valuable bridge
between American purpose and interests, and one that would be both
intellectually and politically easier to build and maintain than a generalized notion of promoting freedom around the world.

In response, James Woolsey remarked that one of the most interesting
developments of the 1980s was that the United States, through the
Reagan Doctrine, went considerably beyond its older position of defending the status quo. By aiding insurgents in Cambodia, Angola, and
Nicaragua, the United States was engaging in policies that it earlier
would have labeled aggressive or revolutionary. The American neoconservatives behind the Reagan Doctrine, prepared as they were to use
American power to promote Western freedom and democracy, wanted
the United States to become a revolutionary power promoting radical
change around the world.

O'Brien replied that what disturbed him about the revolutionary logic
of the Reagan Doctrine was that, by undermining or downplaying the
preeminence of the principle of nonaggression, it could cause damage to
the fragile edifice of international law so assiduously supported by the
United States over the last four decades. The United States was a chief
architect of the United Nations Charter, and in Korea, Vietnam, and

elsewhere it had invested a great deal of blood and treasure to show that aggression did not pay, that force was an unacceptable instrument of change in international relations. To back away from this, even implicitly, would send the wrong signals to many around the world, and would leave the United States without the future authority to act as the world's policeman against aggression.

Responding to both Woolsey and O'Brien, Newsom argued that both of them saw an American moral obligation to contain Soviet power as the chief moral foundation of U.S. foreign policy. The problem was that the world did not accept the legitimacy of such a notion. Even our close allies had refused to join us, or had joined us only with great hesitation, in the numerous crusades we had launched since 1945, including Korea, Vietnam, and the spate of Third World interventions in the 1980s. Newsom also warned that discussions of the United States' moral responsibilities in places such as Afghanistan, Cambodia, Angola, and Nicaragua were quite inadequate unless they took into consideration the difficult and varied complexities that differentiated those situations: specifically, the origins of the civil war in question, the degree of Soviet power involved, the opportunities for U.S. leverage, and the support of allies and other states for our policy.

Newsom also argued that, while American foreign policy sometimes may be oriented toward supporting the status quo, the international impact of American institutions, ideas, and rhetoric has been and continues to be revolutionary. Secessionist Kurds in northern Iraq will quote Woodrow Wilson's Fourteen Points and ask American diplomats why their country is so indifferent to the Kurdish quest for self-determination; dissidents in many parts of the world will brandish American symbols and ideals on behalf of their revolutionary struggles. Contrary to what one might conclude from the official position of American foreign policy, the United States was de facto a revolutionary force in much of the world.

In conclusion, John Langan noted that Weigel's paper addressed two different aspects of the debate on the moral dimensions of American foreign policy. One aspect was the structure of American society and its impact on America's moral character and values, on America's view of its international moral responsibilities, and on the interaction of various moral and intellectual currents in American history. The other equally important aspect of the debate was the structure of morality itself. Here were critical issues such as the relationship of moral theory to practice, the importance and limitations of consistency in moral behavior, and the relationship of interest to purpose—and of both of these to moral obligation.

Unraveling these debates, Langan concluded, requires an understanding that ethicists and policy makers often have different notions of the role of moral principles in political life. For ethicists, a moral principle is something akin to the Decalogue: a clear, declarative norm, with the unquestionable authority above and beyond the specifics of a given debate. Policy makers, on the other hand, tend to view moral principles not so much as independent entities with an inner integrity of their own, but as things which are useful or relevant insofar as they have a relation to specific issues of concern to them. Whereas the ethicists tend to probe a principle as a thing in itself, the policy makers focus on the context in which that principle operates in the policy world.

JOHN P. LANGAN, S.J.

# Moral Reasoning and National Security

## I.   A PRELIMINARY VIEW OF THE CONFLICT

In Florence, in the great Franciscan church of Santa Croce, many of
the most illustrious sons of the city and of Italy are buried. On my first
visit there I came across a monument to Niccolo Machiavelli, perhaps the
most controversial of all the sons of Florence. I was intensely curious
about what was said in the inscription on the monument, since I wondered what could be said that would be both respectful of the accomplishments and character of so wily and unflattering an observer of
political humanity, and at the same time appropriate to a church cele-
brating the mystery of the cross and the spirit of St. Francis. When I
made out the inscription in a dimly lit section of the nave, I was filled
with admiration for its justice and tact, its honesty and concision. It was
simple: *Tanto ingenio nullum par elogium.* "For such great talent there is no
adequate praise." There was neither recrimination nor justification,
neither pious concealment nor defiant applause.

The figure of Machiavelli is, we may agree, a particularly difficult and
important one for our shared reflections on moral issues in national security policy. There is, of course, an enormous amount of scholarly literature
about Machiavelli and the interpretation of his works, about the relationships of development and consistency among his various writings, about
the tensions between his own political activity as a Florentine republican
and advisor to Italian princes and his theoretical reflections, about how he
is to be placed in relation to the Renaissance and to medieval and modern
ways of understanding, about his attitudes to classical antiquity and
Christianity (the principal sources of ideas about morality and politics not
merely for him but for nearly all major political thinkers down to the nineteenth century). Without relying on any one resolution of these rich and
instructive scholarly disputes, I would like to focus for a moment on one

particular interpretation of Machiavelli, that offered by the distinguished British philosopher and intellectual historian, Sir Isaiah Berlin. Berlin makes the point that Machiavelli's secularism is not disturbing to "the contemporaries of Voltaire or Bentham or their successors,"[1] but that what shocks observers down to our time is something rather different:

> Machiavelli's cardinal achievement is, let me repeat, his uncovering of an insoluble dilemma, the planting of a permanent question mark in the path of posterity. It stems from his *de facto* recognition that ends equally ultimate, equally sacred, may contradict each other, that entire systems of value may come into collision without possibility of rational arbitration, and that not merely in exceptional circumstances, as a result of abnormality or accident or error—the clash of Antigone and Creon or in the story of Tristan—but (this was surely new) as part of the normal human situation.[2]

Berlin does not present Machiavelli as a theorist of pluralism or relativism; for that would surely be anachronistic. Rather, he presents him as a knowing and committed partisan, choosing for the grandeur of antique Rome over the sacred visions of Jerusalem. His insistence on the incompatibility of these two sets of ideals sets him at odds not merely with Christians and Jews but also with Plato, Hobbes, Rousseau, and Marx.[3] His insistence that this dichotomy was not to be overcome by reason but was to be accepted as an object for choice implied the denial of one coherent moral universe and the rejection of rationalism in the practical ordering of our lives in society. This rationalism Berlin sees as present in Plato and Aristotle, in the Stoics and the Epicureans, the European rationalists and empiricists of the modern age. Machiavelli's denial of it was indeed "a profoundly upsetting conclusion."[4] In Berlin's interpretation, it accounts for the upsetting effect of Machiavelli on our moral consciousness and for the "desperate effort to interpret his doctrines away, to represent him as a cynical and therefore ultimately shallow defender of power politics, or as a diabolist, or as an embittered political failure . . . or in any of the numerous other roles that have been and are still being cast for him."[5]

Berlin's view is that the conflict between the pursuit of greatness for the state and the pursuit of moral excellence or goodness as this has been envisioned by Platonists, by Christians, and by Kantians is one that cannot be overcome. The goals are different, and the actions that each goal requires are in contradiction to the norms laid down for the effective pursuit of the other. The practical world in which we have to live is simply not coherent. It is the merit and genius of Machiavelli that he not merely saw this inconsistency but that he also had the courage to make his understanding plain to others and to be faithful to his insights despite the opprobrium which they were bound to excite.

Now it cannot be easy to demonstrate the consistency of two such projects as the attainment of true virtue and the preservation of American national security.[6] This consistency can be asserted in political speeches, can be evoked by appeals to divine Providence, can be hoped for and prayed for by those who struggle to reconcile the demands of personal conscience and public office. But a demonstration showing that in all possible circumstances no action necessary to protect the security of the United States will be in violation of the norms of morality and that no morally obligatory action will damage the security of the United States does not seem to be attainable. One can, I will admit, do a certain amount of fiddling with definitions with a view either to alleviating or eliminating the problem.[7] But it seems to me, and I would think, to many reasonable and experienced observers, that we do confront the possibility of conflict (more or less intense, more or less avoidable) between these two worthy and important goals. Our understandable and morally respectable desire not to encounter situations of conflict between these goals, with the consequent anxiety and reproach that they generate, may be an appropriate part of the concern that Christians express when they pray—"and lead us not into temptation."

The possibility of tragic choices and of actions which seem worthy of condemnation from the standpoint of one party to a conflict and laudable from the standpoint of another seems to be part of the human situation. When we affirm this, we come close to the point that Berlin is making in his interpretation of Machiavelli, even if we are reluctant to accept Berlin's views about a radical pluralism of values and about the incompatibility between the demands of political virtue and the requirements of the higher types of philosophical and religious morality.[8] We may in some sense be both more agnostic and more hopeful than Berlin is. We are in practice much more likely to adopt a pragmatic policy of being faithful to our responsibility to protect our national security and vital national interests and of being insistent on our own moral integrity and on the meeting of moral obligations by our colleagues and fellow citizens. We can do this without making demands for strict formal consistency; and we are the more likely to feel that we are right in adopting this pragmatic posture precisely because, for most of us, the commitment to work that protects the national security and vital interests of the United States itself functions as a moral commitment. In practice, we are more likely to be concerned with specific conflicts between courses of action that seem to be required by national security considerations and the specific roles and responsibilities that we hold at a given time, on the one hand, and the traditional dictates of common-sense morality. In these specific conflicts, for instance, between deception to protect secret material and truth telling, we can normally work out more or less satisfactory solutions and hope for a reconciliation of values over the long term or at a higher level of generality.

Of course, it is also possible to adopt a somewhat less elevated and theoretical attitude to these matters. Schooled to a large extent by our brothers and sisters the economists, we have come to affirm that we live in a world of conflicting values, that there will inevitably be trade-offs among these values, and that it is unrealistic and utopian to expect anything very different. This approach to the problem captures some important aspects of our experience of difficult decisions, but it is still likely to leave us uncomfortable. There are two reasons for this. The first is that it seems that moral values are not the kinds of things that should be traded off against other values. When we begin thinking and talking this way, we may already have sold the pass. The second is that this approach overlooks the possibility that morality comes into the picture precisely after we have made our judgment about the best balance we can achieve among various nonmoral or premoral values.[9]

The force of these difficulties and how we may resolve them will, I hope, become more apparent as we examine some of the sources of tension between our commitment to preserving national security and our general obligation to do the morally right thing. Doing this will require us to reflect on what we mean by morality. This is a subject which was under particular scrutiny by moral philosophers about fifteen years ago as part of the process by which a turn was made from the emotivist and prescriptivist analysis of moral language which took personal attitude and commitment as bases for the affirmation of moral first principles to a presentation of moral philosophy which stressed the social context of moral principles and which scrutinized the way in which these principles could be used to develop socially acceptable resolutions of important problems in the professions and in society at large. The focus on formal aspects of the concept of morality brought to light certain common features which any action guide or set of practical directives claiming to be a morality must have.

In addition to these common features, I shall also discuss some central features of morality as this is commonly understood in our culture. I shall also indicate corresponding features of our thinking about national security questions which seem to be at variance with these features of morality. This comparative examination should provide us with some reasons for the plausibility of Berlin's thesis that these two ways of thinking are in fundamental conflict. In a further section of the paper, I will try to indicate some paths toward reconciliation.

## II. MORALITY AS A SOCIAL INSTITUTION AND AS A WAY OF THINKING

In what has been probably the most influential text in moral philosophy over the past twenty-five years, Professor William K. Frankena of the University of Michigan offered the following listing of factors included in what Bishop Butler had earlier referred to as "the moral institution of life":

> (1) certain *forms of judgment* in which *particular* objects are said to have or not to have a certain moral quality, obligation, or responsibility; (2) the implication that it is appropriate and possible to give *reasons* for these judgments; (3) some *rules, principles, ideals,* and *virtues* that can be expressed in more *general judgments* and that form the background against which particular judgments are made and reasons given for them; (4) certain characteristic natural or acquired *ways of feeling* that accompany these judgments, rules, and ideals, and help to move us to act in accordance with them; (5) certain *sanctions* or additional sources of motivation that are also often expressed in verbal judgments, namely, holding responsible, praising, and blaming; (6) *a point of view* that is taken in all this judging, reasoning, and feeling, and is somehow different from those taken in prudence, art, and the like.[10]

It should be plain that morality as thus conceived is a reality that is both intellectual and emotional, that can be a matter both of rational argument and personal commitment. It is also, as Frankena points out, a social reality. He observes:

> Morality in the sense indicated is, in one aspect at least, a social enterprise, not just a discovery or invention of the individual for his own guidance. Like one's language, state, or church, it exists before the individual, who is inducted into it and becomes more or less of a participant in it, and it goes on existing after him . . . As first encountered by the individual at any rate, it is an instrument of society as a whole for the guidance of individuals and smaller groups. It makes demands on individuals that are, initially at least, external to them.[11]

Emphasis on the social or intersubjective character of morality takes us away from proposals to regard morality as a matter of purely personal commitments made by isolated individuals toward an understanding of morality as a shared form of life. At the same time, in a culture as individualistic and pluralistic as our own, it stirs up a series of questions: Which society has or presents "morality"? What is the relationship between "morality" and the various codes and action guides that we find in our own society and in the societies with which we come in contact?

Why should I as an individual accept the morality of a society that is likely to be sexist, racist, bourgeois, anthropocentric? Why should I as an individual be concerned about appropriating or joining this social institution at all? These questions and the ease with which we formulate them point up the power of relativistic and individualistic attitudes in our culture and remind us of the necessity we are under in our present divided and shifting culture of explaining to people why the institution of morality is indeed necessary and binding.[12]

We can grasp the same point if we reflect for a moment on the notion of authority in morality. If Frankena's claim about morality being society's instrument for the guidance of individuals and smaller groups is correct, then morality must be authoritative. But our society is deeply divided about who or what properly exercises moral authority; and significant numbers of individuals make it clear by their comments and their actions that they do not regard morality (at least morality as commonly understood in our society) to be binding for them. As a philosopher, one may doubt whether it is possible for relativists and amoral individualists to state these views coherently and to live by them in a consistent fashion.[13] But it seems to me that both teachers of morality and persons concerned for the shaping and direction of our social and political institutions have to take these positions and attitudes seriously and to recognize the difficulties they present for the practice of morality and for the stability and influence of the moral component in our culture. This is a problem on Wall Street and in the Pentagon, in Silicon Valley and in Foggy Bottom, in the world of "L.A. Law" and of "Hill Street Blues," in Harvard Yard and on Capitol Hill.

Morality is not only a social institution; it is also a certain way of thinking which finds expression in the social institution. Frankena, following on the views of David Hume and on the more recent work of Kurt Baier, characterizes the moral point of view in the following terms:

> (a) one is making normative judgments about actions, desires, dispositions, intentions, motives, persons, or traits of character; (b) one is willing to universalize one's judgments; (c) one's reasons for one's judgments consist of facts about what the things judged do to lives of sentient beings in terms of promoting and distributing nonmoral good and evil; and (d) when the judgment is about oneself or one's own actions, one's reasons include such facts about what one's own actions and dispositions do to the lives of other sentient beings as such, if others are affected.[14]

Frankena's concern, like that of many other moral philosophers, is to rule out private expressions of preference and hunches or intuitions or taboos which are not open to rational scrutiny and public argument or which are designed to exclude certain classes of persons from consideration; e.g. women, Jews, Indians, blacks, the Nietzschean herd, the bourgeoisie, Muslims, "Wogs," "gooks," etc. Not every position that people may want to propose as a guide for action can count as a morality. Furthermore, moral proposals are to a certain extent conditioned by our factual knowledge about what the likely consequences of the recommended actions are for the lives of other persons and sentient beings. The legitimacy of feeding people mushrooms and not toadstools depends on matters of fact which we know and which we have a responsibility to know.

## III.  MORALITY AND NATIONAL SECURITY THINKING IN CONTRAST AND CONFLICT

Having reviewed in a general and abstract way the concepts of morality and the moral point of view, we are now in a position to look more specifically at some of the features of morality which are commonly thought to be at variance with the kind of thinking present in debates over national security policy.

First, there is a widespread tendency to think of morality as primarily a matter of universal norms and to contrast these with the working out of particular problems in establishing national security policy, a working out which may require the transgression of one or more of the universal norms. It is indeed true that universal judgments and norms play an important role in the institution of morality. But it is misleading, I suggest, to imply that general norms and principles play no part whatsoever in thinking about national security issues. Concerns for the balance of power, for the faithful keeping of agreements, for the protection of allies, for the shaping of political perceptions in a favorable direction, all provide the basis for universal or general normative principles of statecraft. Strategic thinking in military matters is, as Michael Walzer has trenchantly argued, itself a normative discipline.[15]

Two points may, however, be granted. The first is that the professional specialists in moral analysis and in policy arguments are commonly drawn to different levels of generality in their discourse. Most strategic debate is drawn to focus on the conclusions which are to shape national policy; it is only intermittently, when a profoundly paradoxical instrument such as nuclear deterrence comes to be the center of attention, that more fundamental and general issues are dealt with at length in an explicit way. For the most part, national goals and normative principles are left as the objects of an unexamined consensus.

Second, the norms and principles of strategic thinking and statecraft are treated as rules of thumb rather than as universally binding principles conformity to which is a necessary condition for the correctness of action or of a proposed solution. When we move back to examine whether something similar holds true in our moral thinking, we move into an area of fierce controversy. Those Catholic moral theologians who are commonly referred to as "consequentialists" or "proportionalists" (Schüller and Böckle in Germany, Fuchs in Rome, McCormick and Curran in the United States), along with a great majority of Protestant theologians and of British and American moral philosophers, would adopt a position similar to that taken by W. D. Ross, who distinguishes between prima facie and actual duties.[16] For Ross, a principle stating a prima facie duty is absolute; there are no situations in which the telling of an untruth, the taking of a life, the breaking of an agreement is prima facie right. But there can be situations in which a course of action with these negative elements can be justified. As principles of actual duty these universal norms are not exceptionless.

This is a conclusion which is unacceptable to Kant, to many contemporary Catholic moralists (Anscombe and Finnis in Britain, Grisez in the United States, John Paul II in Rome), and to a great many people in our culture who are working with a kind of common-sense deontology. It is useful to recall that neither Aristotle nor Aquinas argued for understanding morality as a system of exceptionless universal rules. Aristotle observes that in individual cases the determination of what is right "rests with perception."[17] Aquinas considers a case derived from Book I of Plato's *Republic*, involving a man who leaves a weapon on deposit and, in a disturbed condition, demands its return.[18] He says:

> All hold that it is true and right that we should act intelligently. From this starting point it is possible to advance the specific conclusion, that goods held in trust are to be restored to their owners. This is true in the majority of cases, yet a case can crop up when to return the deposit would be injurious, and consequently unreasonable, as for instance were it to be required in order to attack one's country. The more you descend into the detail the more it appears how the general rule admits of exceptions, so that you have to hedge it with cautions and qualifications. The greater the number of conditions accumulated, the greater the number of ways in which the principle is seen to fall short, so that all by itself it cannot tell you whether it be right to return a deposit or not.[19]

The crucial point that Aquinas makes here is that the concrete norm, however many qualifications may be added, is never exceptionless and is not self-applying. If something like this is right, then presenting the contrast between moral thinking and national security thinking as a contrast between exceptionless universal norms and ad hoc adjustments independent of principles is surely wrong.

A second way in which a sharp contrast is often made between moral thinking and policy thinking on national security issues has to do with the difference between impartiality and adversarial awareness. Impartiality in moral thinking is akin to universality in that it requires us not to make exceptions to universal norms on the basis of our own interests or preferences. It does not require that rules be exceptionless, but in its broadest form it does require that we take the interests of all into account, at least in principle. I contrast this broad form of impartiality with more specific forms of impartiality which we strive for in the different situations of legal adjudication, diplomatic negotiation, and various conciliation processes for the settlement of disputes. We recognize the shape of the issues in a given dispute, whether this be between husband and wife, labor and management, Texaco and Pennzoil, Argentina and Chile; and we know roughly what it is like to aim at impartiality in evaluating and settling such a dispute. This is not to say that achieving impartiality and convincing the parties and other observers that one is impartial are easy tasks. It is considerably harder, however, to grasp what it means to achieve impartiality with regard to human beings and their claims in general. Such impartiality is not to be identified with indifference or apathy. The usual expectation is that it is to be combined with benevolence so that judgments and outcomes will be produced that are both fair and favorable.[20] The absence or temporary suppression of benevolence is one of the striking features in the famous judgment of Solomon in 1 Kings 3.

In both Kantian and utilitarian approaches to ethical theory there is an aspiration to universal impartiality. This serves as a control on the open and covert assertion of selfish desires. In utilitarianism, the pleasures and pains, the gains and losses of all are to be counted in determining the rightness of an action or of a rule. This does not require an equality of outcomes; in fact, many philosophers have argued that it is a major defect in utilitarianism that it allows excessively great disparities in outcomes. Rather, what it means is that there must be an equal regard for the interests of all in setting up the basic framework. This is a point that should be borne in mind when we assess attempts at evenhandedness or assertions of "moral equivalence" between two sides in a dispute, which are current formulations expressing the desire for impartiality. Instead of focusing on principles and the basic framework, such approaches usually take the status quo as a starting point for judgment and then aim at achieving equal outcomes either in praise and blame or in a settling of points in dispute. Such a procedure may be pragmatically necessary and justifiable, but it is not adequate to the demands of moral understanding.

One approach that can be interpreted as combining broad and narrow forms of impartiality is the Golden Rule, which can be found in both Jewish and Christian forms and in other cultures as well. This too is a device intended to exclude partiality for oneself in arriving at moral judgments and practical decisions. It can be applied in particular cases and can also be adopted as a general norm for handling all specific conflicts.

What stands in contrast to impartiality in national security thinking is an adversarial attitude. The superpowers are, it is generally agreed, engaged in an *agon* or contest for power and influence, a contest which involves the possibility and threat of hostile military activity against each other and the intermittent use of force against the allies or protegés of the other superpower. As a result, adversarial modes of perceiving, thinking, and reacting have come to be taken for granted in a great deal of our thinking about national security matters. The enemy of my enemy is my friend, even if this friend violates universal norms that I myself regard as correct and binding. Or, as Churchill put the matter in a specially memorable way, "If Hitler invaded Hell, I should feel obliged to put in a good word for the devil in the House of Commons." What damages the other side or puts it at a disadvantage must be favorable for us. Harming the adversary, at least when this does not harm ourselves or other interests that we value, can then come to be viewed as a desirable outcome in itself. Such a frame of mind clearly opens the way to justifying actions that are normally subject to moral condemnation.

But we should remember that adversarial thinking and attitudes can take more or less strong forms and can give varying weight to different factors in a complex situation. The basic limit that just war theory sets to adversarial attitudes is that they should not degenerate into hatred of the enemy, that is, simply willing evil for our adversaries. War is, of course, a situation in which adversarial attitudes are appropriate and are often extremely powerful. It is also a situation in which it is necessary and may well be justifiable to inflict serious harm on national adversaries. Actions undertaken in an adversarial frame of mind need not be immoral; but, from the moral point of view, they should observe limits which are expressed in norms which are intended to protect the long-term welfare and rights of all. The pressures to transgress these norms are in the present adversarial situation very real. In particular, counting harms to the enemy as gains for oneself can lead to a biased and self-serving application of such norms as the principle of proportionality in just war theory. The problem of containing adversarial attitudes within moral limits is particularly acute when the adversary that we confront makes it very clear that he does not share the general form of our moral awareness (as in the case of communist attacks on the notion of "bourgeois morality") or that he does not respect specific and highly valued norms such as the immunity of noncombatants (as in attacks by Islamic terrorists or the Viet Cong). Such challenges from enemies are particularly likely to bring us to a purely adversarial frame of mind.

It is also worth remembering that national security thinking need not be adversarial in a simple dualistic pattern. During the years since 1945, we have to a large extent grown accustomed to think both in terms of the superpower rivalry between the Soviet Union and the United States, of the blocs and alliances they have formed, and of the ideological struggle between communism and the free world. But if we think back to Europe before 1914 and forward to the possibility of a multipolar world order, we can see the need for patterns of thinking about national security issues which will be less closely linked to straightforward calculations of gains and losses for well-defined adversaries. A more fundamental and paradoxical transformation of the adversarial situation is found in the contemporary development of nuclear deterrence, which establishes close interactive connections between catastrophic harm to the adversary and catastrophic harm to ourselves.

A third major area of contrast between thinking from the moral point of view and national security thinking has to do with differences in motivation. This is not an easy contrast to draw, since many philosophers from the time of Plato on have attempted to show either that the moral life is the true fulfillment of fundamental and necessary human aspirations or that certain basic elements of the moral life will be chosen by rational agents concerned for their own well-being. Both these lines of argument are attempts to deal with the problem of persuading selfish persons to revise their understanding of their self-interest in such a way that they will agree to abide by some moral constraints.

Some philosophers and theologians, especially those influenced by Kant, have dismissed these arguments as involving a fundamental misconception of the nature of morality.[21] But if we look at the matter more broadly in terms of beliefs and attitudes that are widespread in our culture, I think that there is a pretheoretical distinction that very many people would make between actions intended to advance personal interest or the interest of a specific and limited group to which one belongs (e.g., the union, the corporation, the profession) and actions undertaken out of a disinterested desire for the good or a sense of obligation to do what is right or out of obedience to the will of God or love for one's neighbor. In this view, the test of whether one is rightly or "morally" motivated is whether one is willing to regard as right and obligatory and to perform actions that have negative consequences for one's own well-being and interests. "Greater love than this has no man, that a man lay down his life for his friends" (John 15, 13). We expect moral action in its fullness not merely to be the morally right thing but to be done out of a desire for the morally good, a desire that is willing to contemplate the sacrifice of other values and interests;[22] and we expect some such motivation to be present in the morally good person. We expect moral action to be not egoistic or self-regarding, but altruistic or other-regarding in its motivation.

It is, of course, a matter of serious dispute among philosophers and social scientists whether such action is really possible or whether there is need for some conceptual redefinition of the problem. But what seems to be clear to nearly all is that, however difficult it may be for individual human beings or small communities of generous individuals to act in this way, it is vastly more difficult for large groups (such as corporations, unions, and classes), for entire societies, or for governments to act in this way. This is a point which was memorably insisted on in Reinhold Niebuhr's early book, *Moral Man and Immoral Society*. If one accepts this general point, there is still room for disagreement about whether the conclusion to be drawn is that large groups and governments will not act for the distinctively moral reasons that can motivate individuals; or that certain categories of actions often described in terms that have a considerable motivational component (such as conversion, generous action, self-sacrifice) are not really open to them; or that they will consistently fail to do the right thing when this conflicts with their understanding of their self-interest; or that even if they are occasionally capable of acting rightly against collective self-interest, they will not be able to do so in a reliable fashion which can sustain policy over time and which can contribute to fashioning a stable order. These are all plausible readings of the contrast in moral responsiveness between individual and society that Niebuhr works with. Awareness of the power of collective egoism, whether this takes the form of nationalism or class consciousness or religious fundamentalism, is probably even higher today that it was when Niebuhr wrote. Liberal Protestant hopes for national conversion and for national policies that would correspond in a straightforward way with the Sermon on the Mount are feeble, at best, and have an aura of unreality and inappropriateness.

The Platonic doctrine of an isomorphism between justice in society and justice in the individual[23] seems misleading when we look at the differences in the scale of problems and in the kinds of available motivations. But we should remember that while both the state and the large-scale society may lack the flexibility and moral responsiveness of the individual, applying the negative assessments of individualism and selfishness to the state and the larger society may well be a confusion of categories and a sign of confused and misleading expectations. The obligation to morally right action has to respect the nature and limitations of the moral agent. Furthermore, we need to recall that while the larger society or organization may act primarily for its own preservation and growth in accordance with what it understands to be its interest, it is at the same time a focus for loyalty and commitment by free and generous individuals. For it to make sacrifices or accept losses voluntarily is very often to impose burdens on its members and dependents. This is one of the important places where the analogy between group and individual is less than perfect.

In some recent academic discussions, a widely adopted view was that one of the defining features of any morality would be that overriding importance is assigned to it.[24] While this at once suggests possible conflicts with religious action guides,[25] it does have hold of a very important point. We do not generally think that, in cases of direct conflict, aesthetic considerations or considerations of personal convenience and pleasure or even considerations of law should prevail against moral considerations. If a person told us that the cries of the tortured provided an interesting musical background to his reflections, we would think him morally depraved rather than aesthetically sensitive or creative. Or if a person told us that in resolving a problem moral considerations were quite secondary, we would doubt whether he or she understood the meaning of the term, "moral."

On the other hand, if we look at human behavior at large, we may wonder whether moral considerations telling us what we ought to do are in fact overriding. This point is nicely made in a passage of elegant teasing by the Cambridge moral philosopher, C.D. Broad, in the introduction to his classic study, *Five Types of Ethical Theory*.

> Fellows of Colleges, in Cambridge at any rate, have few temptations to heroic virtue or spectacular vice; and I could wish that the rest of mankind were as fortunately situated. Moreover, I find it difficult to excite myself very much over right and wrong in practice . . . A healthy appetite for righteousness, kept in due control by good manners, is an excellent thing; but to "hunger and thirst after" it is often merely a symptom of spiritual diabetes.[26]

Our puzzlement about the primacy of morality springs in part from a confusion between the claim that moral considerations are of their nature overriding in the normative order and the quite different claim that such considerations will, in fact, prevail in the deliberations of individuals and collectivities. From Erasmus to Henry Adams, from de la Rochefoucauld to Garry Trudeau, morally concerned observers of the social and political scene, whether they are focusing on perfumed court ritual or sweaty democratic struggle, have been impressed by the vehemence and ingenuity with which selfishness, greed, the *libido dominandi*, the thirst for revenge, the craving for celebrity, the readiness to lie and to cheat, the yearning for power and position assert themselves. We do not need access to either the literary heights or the misanthropic depths of Dean Swift to understand that moral considerations are not, in fact, overriding in our political lives; the somber realism of *Federalist* 51 is enough. But within even the very cynical there is a conviction that this is not the way things ought to be. What gives point to denunciations of the jungle and the wasteland in human society is the conviction that moral considerations ought to be dominant.

I do not bring this up to make the point that within every realist or pessimist about human nature and society there lurks an impassioned idealist, though that is often true. Rather, I think that if we juxtapose these two points—the philosophical claim that morality is the supreme guide to action, so to speak, the legitimate monarch of our practical deliberations; and the persistent observation not merely of experts in national security matters but also of thoughtful moralists with experience of the world of power and politics, that moral considerations are rarely dominant and are regularly set aside—we can then form a question about whether we ought to follow moral norms and allow moral considerations to dominate our thinking. In a world of wolves, *ought* we to behave like lambs? This question may strike some philosophers as conceptually incoherent, as a question of the general pattern: "Ought we to do what is right?" The answer then has to be affirmative; a person who understands the question sees that the answer is a tautology that cannot be denied: We ought to do what we ought to do.

But the question, if we reflect on it, has to be taken as a serious one. It can be put in less paradoxical fashion thus: In a situation where many people do not accord moral considerations a dominant place in their practical thinking and do not observe moral norms, ought we to do precisely what moral norms require for the different situation in which all or most people do treat moral considerations as overriding and act accordingly? Or to put the matter in terminology that Rawls uses, do the same norms hold for situations of strict compliance and imperfect or noncompliance?[27] These are questions that do not have tautologous answers. I will argue further on in this paper that our answers have to be yes in some cases and no in others. Our answers will vary with the shape of the problem. For in the situation of widespread noncompliance with moral norms, persons with public responsibilities are confronted with a twofold moral task: (a) to preserve their own integrity as moral agents, and (b) to prevent harm to persons and societies whose well-being they have a moral responsibility to protect.

There are two further aspects of the concept of morality as this is often understood in our society that serve as points of contrast with our thinking about national security and interest. Both these contrasts seem to me to rest on an incomplete and thus mistaken understanding of morality. But the views on which they rest are sufficiently widespread that they have to be addressed if we are not to be the victims of confusion. The first of these is the view that moral considerations are essentially private concerns of individuals, which they are free to worry about in their private capacity but which they should not allow to intrude into their treatment of public concerns. The second is the view that morality is properly concerned with the intentions and subjective dispositions of moral agents, whereas public policy and, specifically, national security policy, have to be shaped by concern for consequences.

The conception of morality as a purely private matter has several roots. One is a parallel view of the relation of religion to politics and the larger society. Another is a focus on certain private situations as paradigmatic cases of moral-immoral behavior and also as a central theme for elementary moral instruction and formation. A third is the fear of the destructive consequences of mistaken moral judgments by individuals, consequences that may be destructive for public well-being. A fourth is the widespread acceptance, not merely in academic philosophy but also in a great deal of our popular culture, of a noncognitivist interpretation of moral judgments. Moral judgments are then regarded as emotional intrusions into what should be the rational structure of public discourse on policy matters. Some types of moral judgments are likely to be dismissed as invocations of irrational taboos inappropriate to an enlightened, scientific, and pragmatic society. A fifth is the fear that acknowledging the relevance of moral considerations to policy discourse will produce intrusive inquiries into the private lives of policy makers. For instance, political candidates or White House staffers or cabinet appointees might be rejected on grounds of sexual promiscuity or homosexuality or views on abortion or addiction to drugs or alcohol. And so there is a tendency to say "Away with all these moral and religious hangups." This can be accompanied by the thesis that law and the Constitution provide sufficient protection for the public against the vagaries of individual behavior and possible abuses of power, and so explicit moral considerations are useless and irrelevant.

It is not possible to deal comprehensively with these considerations pushing toward the privatization of morality. But we should acknowledge that they are socially powerful. Nonetheless, if anything like Frankena's analysis of morality as a social institution is correct, then there has to be something profoundly misleading about the privatistic approach. Some suggestions may be helpful on this point. First, a key aspect of the public/private distinction is its connection with the question of authority: who rightly has the power to decide matters? Affirming that there is a moral aspect to public policy issues need not imply that some moral or religious authority is thereby empowered to set the shape of public policy. Such an arrangement would be unacceptable in a pluralistic society; it would also exceed the competence, both legal and cognitive, of those bodies that explicitly devote themselves to teaching on moral questions, such as the various Christian churches and rabbinical assemblies.

The question of what it is right or wrong to do and the question of who properly decides what is to be done should not be confused. To hold that a public issue has significant moral aspects is not to maintain that it should be settled by a particular moral community or group of experts. Second, the distinction between public and private should be understood as a distinction within morality, not as marking a contrast between a realm of private concerns and an amoral arena of public issues that are best resolved in terms of nonmoral considerations of power and interest. The area of public morality has to be understood and shaped in terms of very broad and catholic conceptions so that ample room is allowed for freedom of conscience, for respect for diverse moral and religious traditions, and for the autonomy of various relevant secular disciplines. The invoking of moral considerations is to form part of a process of democratic debate and decision making. When this process functions properly, it is not the imposition of the standards of a particular sectarian group, and it provides opportunities for the correction of idiosyncratic and mistaken moral beliefs.

A second widespread misconception about the contrast to be drawn between morality and national security thinking is that morality is concerned with evaluating the intentions of agents, whereas national security thinking, like statecraft in general, has to be concerned with the consequences or results of policy and particular decisions. There is something to this way of conceiving the matter. In our moral assessments of persons or agents, we do attach a special importance to their intentions and motives, to the frame of mind they were in as they made a given decision. The absence of an intent to do harm, the presence of benevolent intentions are of central importance in the judgments that we form about the potential culpability and the actual moral worth of persons. Even in the political sphere, we may give unsuccessful leaders such as Chancellor Bruening or Neville Chamberlain high marks for good intentions. On the other hand, it is often supposed that an effective course of action on a national security issue may be praiseworthy even if it involves a departure from moral standards of telling the truth and keeping agreements.

Still, it is not merely utilitarianism, but a much wider range of ethical theories which demand in determining the rightness of a course of action that we look to the foreseeable consequences of the action. This is true even when we are dealing with interpersonal relationships on an intimate scale and when we are relying on such recognized principles as the obligation to tell the truth. For a friend or a family member to tell tragic news to a suicidal person, for a physician to announce terminal cancer as a bolt from the blue, for one spouse to spread embarrassing or humiliating facts about the other—for any of these things to be done without some consideration of consequences shows a lack of sensitivity and responsibility. The sensitivity and responsibility needed in such cases are moral characteristics, since they look to the bearing of our actions on the well-being and self-esteem of others. Disregard of consequences, even if accompanied by good intentions, is destructive in both public and private spheres of life. We should also recall that morality in the public sphere is not simply a matter of great institutions and large policy issues; it depends on personal decisions and on interpersonal relationships in various working situations. The basic characteristics and constituents of moral action are not to be thought of as totally different in the two spheres.

Meeting the demands of the moral life, especially for one who has a position of public responsibility, is not simply a matter of having a pure heart and wishing no harm to anyone; it involves reflection and research on the consequences of one's actions and of the policies one advocates, both when they succeed and when they fail. This reflection in public life has to consider not merely consequences as they might be in some ideal world of rational agents, but as they are likely to be in a world of self-interested, imperfectly rational agents with different culturally shaped expectations and quite imperfect information. At the same time we should recognize that an effective but morally flawed action may be satisfactory and even praiseworthy from some points of view, but that its moral deficiencies are likely to diminish its effectiveness in an open and democratic society, even in purely political terms. A Machiavellian leader or state, once perceived as such, labors under great difficulties precisely because such a leader or state forfeits trust and will find it increasingly hard to elicit responses of compliance and cooperation.

A final sort of contrast that is often made between our moral reasoning and our thinking about national security matters has to do with the range and character of the means employed in an effective national security policy. It seems to most observers that such a policy requires a willingness to use both force and deception. In Machiavelli's terms, it requires leaders who are prepared to be lions and foxes. The utility and necessity of force in interstate relations serves as an unquestioned premise for nearly all of those who function as makers of decisions and shapers of opinions in this area of our political life, though there are, of course, vehement and sometimes even profound disagreements about how to handle particular situations and about just when the threat or use of force will produce the desired results. But everyone understands that the Pentagon is a central and in many ways dominant factor in the maintenance of our national security, and no one seriously expects a change in this regard in the near future. The use of deception is, of course, less open and more controversial. Nearly everyone recognizes the difficulties and risks inherent in disinformation campaigns. But there is also general recognition that deception is in certain contexts necessary in order to preserve secrecy and surprise for our own activities and in order to gain intelligence about certain aspects of the activities and intentions of actual and potential adversaries.[28]

It is precisely for these reasons that some would draw the further conclusion that morality and thinking about national security must be kept quite separate. Insistence on such a separation can come from a desire to preserve the purity of moral reasoning and action and to prevent the use of moral considerations to justify the unjustifiable. It can also come from a desire to prevent thinking and action about national security matters from being "sicklied o'er by the pale cast of thought" and to ensure that moral considerations do not have an inhibiting and deleterious effect on the vigorous implementation of what military and political necessity require.

It is certainly true that force and deception present serious problems for the living of the moral life and for any efforts to achieve a coherent set of principles that will be an effective and realistic guide for action in a vitally important area of our national life. But they can only provide the basis for a complete separation between moral thinking and national security policy if we believe that morality forbids us to do harm in any way or that certain kinds of action are so intrinsically immoral that they can never be justified under any circumstances, and that they are likely to be required by a reasonable national security policy.

The first of these approaches might well begin from something like an extension of the first phrase of the Hippocratic Oath: "First, do no harm," or from what Thomas Aquinas lays down as the first and most general precept of the natural law: "Good is to be done, and evil is to be avoided."[29] These are formulations that have an incontestable attraction for all of us, since they are injunctions based on tautologies. But they do not provide much guidance in dealing with those critical situations in which harm simply cannot be avoided and the question is: who suffers it and for what reason? Those are the situations that one of my colleagues in biomedical ethics sought to deal with under the title *Doing Evil to Achieve Good*.[30]

If one takes as correct the general description which Hume gives of our social situation in terms of limited resources and our need to work and cooperate and our limited benevolence,[31] then we will always have a need for norms of justice and for institutions of justice. We will then always be confronted with the possibility of violations of justice and with the need for enforcing just judgments. In this situation a morally based refusal to countenance the possibility of doing harm to others amounts to acquiescence (not approval) in the possibility that others will do harm to ourselves and to innocent third parties. I do not propose here to settle the dispute between pacifists and just war theorists as to what is the range of right or permitted responses to injustice and violence. Rather, I want to maintain two things. First, that responses involving the likelihood of inflicting harm on others are not to be ruled out of the realm of morality on definitional grounds. Second, that we need an understanding of morality which is adequate to justify the inflicting of harm on others and also to restrict both the motives for and the extent of the harm which is to be justifiably inflicted or threatened. This understanding of morality will necessarily be complex and will have elements that are in tension with each other.

What applies to the defense of others applies as well to the defense of oneself; but the responsibility to defend others is a conception that even those who would, for theological or other reasons, be very skeptical of self-defense and self-interest as bases for ethical action may be prepared to acknowledge as a morally significant value.[32] If we believe that there is a duty to come to the aid of others,[33] it seems arbitrary to restrict this to aid against the forces of nature (as, for instance, in the case of the nonswimmer drowning in the ocean) and to rule out the bringing of aid to the innocent against human attackers. The defense of innocent others, if it is to be effective in a violent world, requires a readiness not merely to oppose but even to harm the noninnocent others who are the attackers and oppressors. This readiness may take the form of threats or resistance to attack or punishment; it may be internal to a society, as in the case of police activity and legal coercion, or it may occur between states, as in the case of deterrence and waging war. At the same time, the readiness to consider harming others must not become a desire to harm others, a desire which is rightly condemned as immoral; it must not become active outside the appropriate justifying circumstances; and it must not exceed in amount or duration the harm needed to achieve the justifying objective. There will always remain a certain element of paradox in justifying the infliction of harm on others. There will always remain a double obligation to ensure that the infliction of harm does not make either those who inflict it or those on whom it is inflicted worse as moral persons.[34] There will always be a desire, utopian but omnipresent, unfulfilled but persistent, that we move to a situation in which the willingness to inflict harm is no longer necessary or justifiable. This will be particularly true when the operative moral tendency in society is either utilitarian or perfectionist, since in those cases the infliction of harm is seen as a deviation or subtraction from morally urgent goals.

While the justifications for the use of force and for the readiness to inflict harm on others for the preservation of higher social goods are familiar and enjoy a fairly high degree of acceptance, the same cannot be said of justifications for deception in the protection of national security. An inescapable practical problem here is the difficulty of offering an open justification for deception along with the successful carrying out of deception. Paradoxes inevitably arise when statements of the intention to deceive are made. Insuperable moral objections can be raised to any effort to offer a carte blanche justification for deception in general.[35] Even in the political realm, there are serious costs and penalties when deceptions are uncovered. This is particularly true when deceptions have been elaborated for the purpose of concealing amateurish and illegal policies from the processes of democratic scrutiny.

What can be affirmed, I would argue, is the possibility of offering moral justification in restricted critical situations for deceptions as departures from a prima facie norm of truth telling. This is a specification of the general point made earlier about the universal character of moral norms. In this regard, it is interesting to note that the one specific issue in the conduct of war that Aquinas considers is the question of whether ambushes (*insidiae*) are justified in war and that he gives an affirmative answer, accepting what is an inherently deceptive practice.[36] It is possible that in certain kinds of military and intelligence situations the forms of deception are so conventionalized and so likely to be discounted that they do not constitute a significant threat to the value of veracity for those carrying them out. But it is also possible that deception is then more likely to be used more extensively than is warranted by the values of national security and that it comes to be used as an instrument of bureaucratic infighting, self-protection, and manipulation of public opinion. Like force, deception is not to be regarded as a neutral instrument to be used at the discretion of those in power or sufficiently justified by the good intentions of those who employ it. Despite its pernicious persistence in large areas of our social lives, and despite its short-term attractiveness in many tight situations, it has to be restricted to the best of our ability.

## IV. RECONCILING MORALITY AND NATIONAL SECURITY THINKING

Thus far, I have been preoccupied with reviewing some of the contrasts which many people have drawn between moral reasoning and thinking about national security, and which many have wanted to appeal to in arguing for what amounts to a divorce between the two. In doing this, I have focused, as a philosopher is inclined to do, on certain general features of these two ways of thinking rather than on the historical tensions between realist and idealist approaches to the making of foreign policy. I have also tried to keep one eye on the dilemmas and the awareness of both moral demands and national security requirements that I discern in the professionals who work on national security issues. Now I would like to take up at least in a preliminary way the task of reconciling these two ways of thinking.

The main part of this chapter has been devoted to laying out some of the differences between our ordinary style of reasoning and the kind of thinking that is dominant in discussions about national security. My concern has been to present some of the major differences between these two kinds of practical thinking without proceeding from within the perspective of a particular moral theory and without arguing for the moral justification of a particular conception of national security. This accounts for the paper's emphasis on formal and general considerations. I have also not attempted to argue directly for the reconciliation of these two ways of thinking or for the subordination of one to the other. Those who have read thus far will have noticed, however, various points at which I have tried to revise and perhaps soften the sharp contrasts that are often present in lay discussions of this issue.

For it is my own view that many of these contrasts are too sharply drawn and that often both those who propose to subject national security thinking to moral control and those who wish to exempt it from moral scrutiny are working with an understanding of morality that stresses universal law and private conscience and intention. This way of understanding morality strives to set a distance between an unsullied realm of morality and the painful problems produced by the effort to apply demanding norms while attaining urgent and precarious goals. In this approach one is then free to treat the moral law as a herald of the need for radical and even revolutionary change in the social context, or as a pedagogical reminder of our own inescapable sinfulness, or as an unattainable and therefore irrelevant ideal.

This is not a surprising result if we think about where we put morality and national security thinking on our intellectual and social maps. We place morality near the high peaks of religion and philosophy and the lofty plateau of law in a territory nourished by the streams of personal development and interpersonal relations. We entrust it to the care of the family and the church or synagogue and the academy. We expect its exponents to be learned divines or abstruse philosophers, though we are also keen to have it preached by those who can touch the heart and to have it illustrated by the lives of the devout and the humble. We place strategic thinking on an open and vulnerable plain, like the plains of

Lombardy or the Ukraine, near the mineral deposits of technology and behind the fortifications of military strategy. It is laid out geometrically according to the dictates of mathematics and theoretical economics, but it also supports crops on the flood deposits of history. We entrust it to the guardianship of diplomats, the military, and a more worldly variety of academicians and experts; and we have grown accustomed to seeing it as a realm divided by doctrinal and financial disputes. It is "a darkling plain" where bureaucratic armies "clash by night." Occasional reconnaissances by journalists enable us to survey it in part, and intermittent adjudications by political overseers keep its conflicts within boundaries. Its population is largely unchurched, and its topography is not transcendental. The inhabitants occasionally glance at the moral peaks in the distance; they admire their sparkling, snowcapped purity on clear days, but they do not regard them as scalable.

This metaphorical separation of morality and national security is less abstract and formal than the contrasts that preceded, but it serves to remind us of the different connections and contiguities that we commonly assign to these two different concerns and of the different populations that we expect to be present in them and of their different social roles and expectations. But like all metaphors, it can be profoundly misleading. For what it causes us to overlook is the presence of an important moral component within the national security project itself.

There are, I would argue, three distinct elements in this component. First, there is the moral concern of individual men and women working in this area. Large numbers of them, though not all, are people capable of moral feelings and commitments, searching for moral reasons to justify what they do, earnest in their desire for moral integrity, and anxious about the demands of conscience. They are not simply dwellers in the cities of the plain, absorbed in technical and mundane tasks and self-interested pleasures and profits. Second, there are significant moral factors built into the systems and institutions which are professionally responsible for activities in the national security area. Prominent among these institutionalized factors are the requirements of obedience to legitimate authority and accountability for one's decisions, the concern for international order and law, and the various efforts of the armed services to ensure compliance with the laws of war and the requirements of just war theory.

Third, and most important for the character of our democratic polity and for the shaping of public debate, is the morally compelling character of the ultimate goal. This is, in the words of *The Challenge of Peace*, the letter of the U.S. Catholic bishops, to "prevent nuclear war from ever occurring *and* to protect and preserve those key values of justice, freedom and independence which are necessary for personal dignity and national integrity."[37]

Taken together, these moral factors constitute a major aspect of the making of national security policy and, at the same time, a reason why moral considerations cannot be effectively excluded from our thinking about national security issues. Indeed, it is very difficult to exclude moral considerations on a permanent or consistent basis from any large or significant area of human activity. I remember vividly an occasion when, after I had given a fairly theoretical lecture about morality to a group of government officials, one of them decisively dismissed the relevance and worth of what I had said, observing that morality had nothing to do with intelligence gathering and espionage activities. He then went on to comment that of course there were certain ways in which one simply ought not to treat people. I replied that I would give him "morality" if he would give me "ought."

The key point here is that in any human activity directed to socially significant goals and involving cooperation with other persons there is an inherent moral aspect. As St. Augustine saw long ago, there had to be at least an image or shadow of justice in the dealings of robbers with each other.[38] It has to be understood that such a moral aspect is minimal and does not ensure that those who participate in an activity understand it primarily in moral terms or that they do the right thing. But it does show that the effort of the proponents of realpolitik to eliminate moral considerations altogether is foredoomed to failure.

Further, I would maintain that the moral factors present in the personnel, structures, and goals of the national security community are at least in principle elements of a genuinely moral character. Again, this does not mean that they ensure that actors within the national security world invariably or even regularly do the right thing or that moral factors are always explicit, much less predominant in the shaping of policy. But it does mean that the moral factors are authentic and are capable of inclusion within a correct and authentic morality. They are not merely to be included in a purely descriptive account of what some group of people adopts as its normative code. This is in some ways a personal and existential judgment on my part, though many facts about persons and about the working and deeper tendencies of the American political system are relevant to it; at the same time, it is not an idiosyncratic or eccentric or partisan judgment, since if the question were clearly put, a decisive majority of the American people would, I think, be in agreement.

The presence of a significant and authentic moral component within the thinking of the national security community does not ensure that the task of reconciling moral reasoning and national security thinking is completed or even that it can be completed. Rather it underscores the necessity of this reconciliation if the work of the national security community is to be carried on with integrity—that is, with intellectual consistency and with wholehearted moral commitment.

What does this reconciliation require, particularly in the context of our ideologically divided and religiously and philosophically pluralistic society? Let me make five proposals in answer to this question.

First, there has to be recognition of the legitimate autonomy of the moral point of view as a limiting and critical factor with regard to national security policy. The path indicated by moral judgment can and will diverge from paths indicated by popular or narrow conceptions of the national interest or recommended by the political and military leadership at any given time. This can be expected to occur even in the case of upright men and women whenever intense efforts are devoted to a morally worthy goal and the discipline of the task requires that they overcome resistance. Temptations to do the wrong thing and neglect of morally relevant considerations in the pursuit of a worthy goal do not pre-suppose a prior corruption or moral collapse. One can try to minimize or control these divergences by developing a more elevated or more long-term or more universalist conception of the national interest; but one cannot overcome the possibility of divergence in principle. Morality is debased and subverted when it loses its independence and becomes a fund of ideological rationalizations for those who hold power.

Moral judgments—and in our polity, significant moral judgments—will be made by those who stand outside and perhaps in opposition to the national security community and its activities. While such judgments are often marked by insufficient information and marred by ideological blindness, it would be a destructive mistake to equate the social and political divisions between the national security community and its critics with the contrast between national security thinking and moral reasoning. It has been one of the great achievements of the prophetic tradition in Israel and of the Christian tradition, particularly in its Catholic and Calvinist forms, that it has kept alive the idea and reality of an independent religious basis for raising moral questions about the use of power. It is at the same time important that this not turn into a kind of ecclesiastical or moralistic counterpolitics in which the temptations of the religious to self-righteousness, hypocrisy, and utopianism cause them to minimize the constraints under which political, economic, and military decision makers have to operate and to dismiss the puzzling and painful character of our historical experience.

Second, reconciling moral reasoning and national security policy requires an acceptance of the legitimacy of casuistry, that is, of a mode of thinking about the application of moral norms to concrete situations or cases that will be sensitive to the complexity and variability of situations both in factual terms and in their connections with the broader policy context in which significant value conflicts are bound to be present. Casuistry is a mode of moral thinking which is not unprincipled but which is thoroughly contextual. Without a willingness to engage in casuistry in a disciplined and sustained way there can be little hope of scrutinizing and evaluating the justifications that persons working on national security problems advance to show that their activities are a morally correct response to an imperfect and unsatisfactory situation. In this sense, morality has to be brought down from the lofty pinnacles of theory and principle to the plains of contest and struggle. The task is still to determine what the right thing to do is in a given complex situation, not to provide a moral screen or veil to conceal the morally wrong from critical public scrutiny.

Third, in carrying on the work of casuistry, we should rely on the broad consensus that can be drawn in support of mid-level moral principles and of the values which are present in the working of both democratic and bureaucratic processes (accountability, honesty, respect for the rule of law, opportunity for those affected by decisions to express their views). There is abundant opportunity for dispute about just what courses of action are mandated by those values and about how moral principles are to be applied to particular cases. There is also in the background, of course, a continuing philosophical and theological dispute over first principles of ethical theory. The shaping of the moral dimension of public policy in our pluralistic society with its pressing problems cannot be made to wait on a definitive resolution of the problems of ethical theory. We should, of course, be ready to recognize and evaluate lines of argument drawn from particular theoretical traditions, whether these be utilitarian or Kantian or Thomistic or Humean or Calvinist or existentialist or pragmatist or rabbinical. We can also look to a wide range of philosophical and religious traditions for ways of reconceiving our dilemmas.

But we should not allow the strong tendencies to moral skepticism in our culture to undermine the seriousness and the cognitive standing of our moral concerns. This skepticism can take the form of a relaxed and permissive abandonment of standards or of a biting authoritarianism. Neither of these is helpful to mature discussion about the ways to make hard choices and to meet the moral demands of preserving and improving our society. Three lines of argument can serve as useful pointers to the key areas where we can find principles to employ in the working out of an appropriate casuistry for the moral resolution of national security problems. These are: (a) the affirmation of the core principles of Hebrew-Christian morality in the work of Alan Donagan; (b) the minimalist approach to natural law propounded by the British philosopher of law, H.L.A. Hart;[39] (c) the elaboration of the implications of the individual's activity as an agent claiming rights and affirming obligations found in the work of Alan Gewirth. In any of these approaches, we can find a rational basis for agreement on specific principles which will prescribe some kinds of action and prohibit others. The basis for agreement will not presuppose that we have settled our religious and metaphysical disagreements, and it will not require a general overturning or reconstruction of the moral beliefs and norms of our culture and our major religious traditions. Adopting any one of these approaches does bring with it commitment to certain controversial ways of resolving the questions of ethical theory. Such a step is necessary for the satisfactory development of a comprehensive ethics. But, for the purpose of discussing the moral aspects of public policy, it seems to me that what is important is that these approaches give us a disciplined basis for affirming points of moral consensus, a basis which is not merely ad hoc but which can be shown to be accessible to reasoned reflection and thus contributing to a rational response to moral skepticism.

Fourth, this way of proceeding should lead us to a reaffirmation of the basic principles of just war theory such as the norms of proportionality and discrimination in the conduct of war and other exercises involving the use of force and the norms of just cause, right intention, reasonable hope of success, right authority, and proportionality in justifying the resort to force in the first place.[40] This does not require us to accept particular formulations of just war criteria or to insist that particular ways of conforming to criteria must remain fixed despite changes in the technological instruments of force and in the social-political context. The just war theory is itself a complex historical construction, even though its key principles can be argued to on the basis of fairly simple formal considerations about situations in which it could be necessary and justifiable to inflict evils on other persons. Thus it is not surprising that a scholar such as Stanley Hoffmann manages both to reject just war theory and to reinvent its basic principles.[41] Such changes as the development of nuclear weapons, the rise of guerrilla movements, and the increasing reliance on terrorist tactics by political movements and by governments present severe difficulties for those who are charged with mounting effective responses within the limits set down by just war theory and international law. Moral concern does not require that we adhere to a given formulation of these limits; but it does require that any departure from them be carefully thought out so that lasting harm to our moral integrity and to our core values is not done in the search for a "quick fix." Another way of making this point is to remind ourselves that the just war theory is not simply a fixed body of norms but rather forms a developing tradition, within which thinkers, while respecting and reaffirming its key principles, have felt both free and impelled to develop new responses to new problems.[42]

Fifth, we have to recognize that, whatever theoretical or formal reconciliation between moral reasoning and national security thinking may be proposed, the synthesis will be unstable. This instability is the inevitable result of the complexity of the issues, the serious divisions within our culture about both the place of morality and the use of force, and the different social locations, perceptions, and professional responsibilities of the various participants in the public debate. I make this point not in order to depreciate the worth of our current enterprise but in order to caution against unrealistic expectations and the discouragement and confusion that usually ensue when such expectations are overthrown.

# Notes

1. Isaiah Berlin, "The Originality of Machiavelli," in *Against the Current: Essays in the History of Ideas* (New York: Viking Press, 1980), 74.

2. Ibid., 74-75.

3. Ibid., 70.

4. Ibid., 69.

5. Ibid., 70-71.

6. Alan Donagan, *The Theory of Morality* (Chicago: University of Chicago Press, 1977), chap. 5, argues at length that the system of morality is common or internally consistent, though "its consistency does not admit of formal proof" (149).

7. David Sachs, "A Fallacy in Plato's *Republic*," in *Plato: A Collection of Critical Essays*, ed. Gregory Vlastos (Garden City, N.Y.: Doubleday Anchor, 1971), 35-51, argues that the central argument of the *Republic* to the effect that just men are happier than unjust men relies on such definitional shifts for its plausibility.

8. See also Isaiah Berlin, "John Stuart Mill on the Ends of Life," in *Essays on Liberty*.

9. See writings of Bruno Schüller, S.J., especially *Begrundung sittlicher Urteile*, 2d ed. (Dusseldorf: Patmos Verlag, 1973); and of Richard McCormick, S.J., *Doing Evil to Achieve Good* (Chicago: Loyola University Press, 1978).

10. William K. Frankena, *Ethics*, 2d ed. (Englewood Cliffs, N.J.: Prentice-Hall, 1973), 9.

11. Ibid., 6.

12. The thesis that the morality of our culture is in a state of profound disorder and incoherence is a central thesis in Alasdair MacIntyre, *After Virtue* (Notre Dame, Ind.: University of Notre Dame Press, 1981).

13. This point is made concisely in Frankena, 109-10. It is fundamental to the argument of Alan Gewirth, *Reason and Morality* (Chicago: University of Chicago Press, 1978).

14. Frankena, 113.

15. Michael Walzer, *Just and Unjust Wars* (New York: Basic Books, 1977), 13-16.

16. W. D. Ross, *The Right and the Good* (Oxford: Clarendon Press, 1930).

17. Aristotle, *Nicomachean Ethics* VI, 8, 1142a 25-30.

18. Plato, *Republic* I, 331c.

19. Thomas Aquinas, *Summa Theologiae*, I-II, 94, 4C, trans. Thomas Gilby, O.P. (Westminster: Blackfriars, 1966).

20. Impartiality is a characteristic of the ideal observer theory once propounded by Roderick Firth and Richard Brandt. For an introductory discussion, see Richard Brandt, *Ethical Theory* (Englewood Cliffs, N.J.: Prentice-Hall, 1959), 173-76.

21. See, for instance, the influential essay by H.A. Prichard, "Does Moral Philosophy Rest on a Mistake?" in *Duty and Interest* (Oxford: Clarendon Press, 1929).

22. Thus Aristotle observes that it is not sufficient to do the just thing in order to have the virtue of justice but that one must act as the just man does. "A man is just when he acts justly by choice." *Nicomachean Ethics* V, 8, 1136aB. The motivational point is clearer in Matt. 5:43-47.

23. See Plato, *Republic* II, 368d-369a, where justice in the individual and justice in the state are compared as small and large letters.

24. See, for instance, the discussion of necessary and sufficient features of morality in William K. Frankena, "The Concept of Morality," in *The Definition of Morality*, ed. G. Wallace and A.D.M. Walker (London: Methuen, 1970), 146-73. He points to R. M. Hare, *Freedom and Reason* (Oxford: Oxford University Press, 1963), 168-69 as an important source for making supremacy or overridingness an essential feature of morality.

25. A useful effort at sorting out some of the resulting problems can be found in David Little and Sumner B. Twiss, Jr., "Basic Terms in the Study of Religious Ethics," in *Religion and Morality*, ed. Gene Outka and John P. Reeder, Jr. (Garden City, N.Y.: Doubleday Anchor, 1973).

26. C.D. Broad, *Five Types of Ethical Theory* (London: Routledge & Kegan Paul, 1930), xxiv.

27. See John Rawls, *A Theory of Justice* (Cambridge, Mass.: Harvard University Press, 1971), 145.

28. See John Langan, S.J., "National Interest, Morality and Intelligence," in *Studies in Intelligence* 27 (1983): 57-69.

29. Thomas Aquinas, *Summa Theologiae*, I-II, 94, 2c.

30. Richard McCormick, S.J., *Doing Evil to Achieve Good.*

31. For a contemporary presentation of this notion see Rawls, 126-30.

32. For a line of argument which bases just war theory on our duty in love to aid the neighbor, see Paul Ramsey.

33. For a careful treatment of this topic, see Gewirth, 217-30.

34. Plato, *Republic* I, 335 a-e.

35. See Sissela Bok, *Lying* (New York: Pantheon, 1979).

36. Thomas Aquinas, *Summa Theologiae* II-II, 40, 3c.

37. National Conference of Catholic Bishops, *The Challenge of Peace* (Washington, D.C.: U.S. Catholic Conference, 1983), par. 175.

38. St. Augustine, *The City of God*, IV, 4.

39. See H.L.A. Hart, *The Concept of Law* (Oxford: Clarendon Press, 1961), 189-95.

40. See, for instance, the enumeration of these norms in *The Challenge of Peace*, paras. 85-110.

41. Stanley Hoffmann, *Duties beyond Borders* (Syracuse, N.Y.: Syracuse University Press, 1981).

42. An instructive example of how this may be done is found in the essays in James Turner Johnson, *Can Modern Wars Be Just?* (New Haven, Conn.: Yale University Press, 1984).

# THE CONVERSATION

Bruce Douglass's response to John Langan, "The Encouraging Words from Woodstock: Some Reservations," combined appreciation for Langan's theoretical model with several cautions about its applicability to the current American cultural-political scene. Douglass was reassured, for example, by Langan's insistence that reason plays an inescapable and important part in moral calculation—a once unfashionable opinion in the academy. But Douglass also worried that some of Langan's other "reassurances" were more problematical. How solid, for example, is the moral consensus within our culture? And if, in fact, it's not at all that solid, how can "the moral point of view" provide policy makers with guidance on the advisability of various national security options?

Beyond these reservations, Douglass outlined three criticisms. First, he argued that Langan's "moral point of view" brushed too lightly over major differences about the meaning of morality. Langan's viewpoint is really that of the moderate, reasonable individual who takes seriously the Kantian requirement that moral values be universalizable, as opposed to the moral zealot. It is the philosopher William Frankena, not the Ayatollah Khomeini, whom Langan has in mind. But there are more Khomeinis than Frankenas in the world.

Douglass also cautioned Langan against the temptation to downplay tensions and dissonance within the body of reason-based morality itself. Langan, for example, pointed out three components of moral reasoning in the day-to-day national security decision-making process: a personal concern for practicing the right kind of behavior, respect for accountable and legitimate institutions, and recognition of the authority of morally compelling public goals. Yet Langan overlooked the degree to which the third element can become an instrument for subverting or negating the effect of the other two. Officials will justify immoral conduct or policies in the name of a morally compelling goal. In a wider sense, Douglass suggested, Langan and Isaiah Berlin underestimated both the impact of Machiavelli's critique of the compatibility of morality with other worthwhile goals, and the fragmentation among moral goals themselves.

Second, Douglass thought it was essential to remember that the United States, like all nations, often promotes its interests by damaging the interests of other states. This immorality is endemic to the very existence and projection of national power; that concern for the well-being of others which is one of the basic elements of "the moral point of view" is the exception, rather than the norm, in the elaboration of foreign policy. Langan's reassurances to the contrary could lead us to underestimate the seriousness of this problem, and hence prevent us from recognizing the existence of moral dilemmas in which we may be faced with choosing the good of another country or the world over our own national security interests.

Third, Douglass questioned the feasibility of discovering and nurturing elements of a common moral consensus in our increasingly relativistic and pluralistic culture. The points of disagreement within our society over the moral norms and goals that should animate our national security policy are far more pronounced and numerous than the points of agreement. This public cacophony, quite obvious to the policy makers themselves, is likely to become more intense in the future, complicating immensely—and perhaps beyond hope of solution—the problem of developing in American society a moral consensus capable of guiding national security policy.

In sum, Douglass's reservations seemed to him as significant as Langan's reassurances: Langan's paper provided the beginning, not the resolution, of the search for common ground between moral reasoning and national security.

Robert Gessert offered three suggestions for strengthening Langan's argument. The variety of methods in ethics and the rich diversity in ethical traditions (an ethic of obligation, an ethic of righteousness, an ethic of self-fulfillment) might be spelled out. Langan also needed to tackle the question of whether there was room in the national security debate for a Christocentric ethic; while not altogether successful, the Catholic bishops had tried to deal with this issue in their 1983 pastoral letter on nuclear weapons. Finally, echoing Douglass's earlier point, Gessert noted a multiplicity of dissonant voices claiming to speak for "the moral point of view" in our society. What was one to do, for example, about the different views on the morality of nuclear deterrence held by such Christian institutions as the U.S. Catholic bishops and the Methodist bishops?

In response to Douglass and Gessert, Langan acknowledged that there is no simple solution to the problem of moral disagreement in our culture. On the other hand, some fundamentals remain in place: there is a high level of agreement on the need for serious justification in the taking of human life, and there is widespread agreement on the value of speaking and acting truthfully. Moreover, most reasonable people recognize that the world of high political and military strategy is not value-free. As Michael Walzer has shown, it is a realm in which people regularly confront moral choices, and interpose moral values as they face those choices. Therefore, there are multiple opportunities for moral dialogue, and for the gradual nurturing of the elements of moral consensus.

David Hollenbach argued against framing the problem in terms of morality vs. national security, as if each of these categories were a homogeneous bloc of common assumptions and shared meanings. In the real world, there are different conceptions of national security as well as different definitions of what is morally desirable. National security experts might disagree, for example, on whether Nicaragua's Sandinista regime posed a security threat to the United States. Different answers to that question would reflect different readings of the facts and different conceptions of American security requirements.

Similarly, ethicists might disagree on which moral goals should receive priority in an American policy toward Nicaragua: social equality, human rights, peace, democratic pluralism, or state sovereignty. Advocates of American intervention in Nicaragua emphasize the value of democratic pluralism, while skeptics of interventionist policies cite peace and state sovereignty as important moral goals. Meanwhile, both kinds of ethicists disagree, factually and normatively, on whether Sandinista human rights violations are sufficiently egregious to justify American efforts to overthrow the Nicaraguan government. Ethicists who advocated U.S. intervention focused on Sandinista violations of civil and political rights, while opponents of intervention pointed to Sandinista progress in "economic and social" rights to support their position. Langan's real challenge is the reconciliation of diverse conceptions of national security with a plurality of moral goals and normative visions of the common good.

Larry Fabian thought that Langan's paper assumed a narrow, traditional, and increasingly obsolescent view of national security. In the world of the 1980s and 1990s, our understanding of national security has broadened to include economic and environmental concerns, and there is greater awareness that many threats to national security are best managed, not through bipolar competitive rivalries, but through multipolar processes and strategies that blend competitive with cooperative elements.

Harold Saunders similarly noted the greater currency, among policy makers, of concepts of "common security" which recognize that a state's security interests are best protected within a multilateral framework that also insures the security of others. According to Saunders, there is growing recognition that a country's security problems are best managed through interactive relationships that pay heed to the other parties' own legitimate security needs. Whether the issue is nuclear weapons, the degradation of the environment, or the Arab-Israeli impasse, we are finding that many critical security issues cannot be resolved by the unilateral resort to force, but require the creation of multilateral cooperative relationships and procedures in which the advancement of one state's interests requires the protection of the interests of others. There were thus new opportunities in world politics for bridging the dichotomy of "morality" and "interests."

Taking issue with Bruce Douglass, James Turner Johnson argued that there had never been a very coherent moral consensus in American society, as the debates at the Constitutional Convention and the Civil War proved. Moreover, a consensus on values was probably not as important in holding a liberal society together as were commonly agreed patterns of interaction or procedural rules. The American experience suggests that cooperative moral and political interaction is possible even in the midst of a high degree of disagreement on the definition and scope of some key norms. Johnson also suggested that such a paradigm may be valid at the international level. Contemporary international law is moving inexorably in the direction of creating institutions and patterns of cooperative interaction under the impetus, not of a consensus of values, but of reciprocity and shared interests.

In response, Langan agreed that Douglass's critique implied an ahistorical golden age of a harmonious American moral universe. Nevertheless, Langan insisted, there were far more elements of a moral consensus in today's society than either Douglass or Johnson implied. The widespread deference toward such basic norms as the sanctity of human life and the obligation to be truthful were not insignificant.

For Bruce Weinrod, a key question posed, but not answered, by Langan's paper was: how do we deal with adversaries and friends who do not share our moral principles? Since 1945, the United States had faced a relentless global challenge from an ideological adversary with a different conception of morality. Moreover, as part of its responsibilities to help nurture a world balance of power in favor of the West, the United States had acquired a set of long-term global relationships that often brought us into useful cooperation with friendly authoritarian regimes that did not share our moral values. How do we conduct an alliance with people living in a different moral and religious universe?

Langan conceded that there were no easy answers here. But his own view was that we should be faithful to our own moral commitments and traditions even if the other party, be it friend or foe, is not prepared to reciprocate. The United States may be justified in striking back against Middle East terrorists who attack us, but we should observe the principle of discrimination even if the terrorists do not. A failure to adhere to our own moral standards will undermine, in the eyes of our own people and the rest of the world, the legitimacy of what we are doing—and will also create serious moral difficulties for those whom we ask to carry out our policies.

Responding to William O'Brien's query about what he meant by casuistry, Langan explained that "casuistry" is a method in moral theology which recognizes, as Aristotle did, that universal laws or norms cannot always provide sufficient moral guidance for resolving individual cases. In such situations, the decision maker studies past cases and the principles which have been applied to resolve them; he differentiates those cases from the present one, and looks at the degree to which the principles applied to them may or may not be relevant to the one presently before him; he then decides the case, offering a coherent explanation for the application to the case of those principles to which he ultimately resorted.

In both the Jewish and Catholic traditions, the practice of casuistry implies respect for a legitimate plurality of moral viewpoints. The decision reached is defended as being the most reasonable solution available given the unique context involved, but those who disagree are not regarded as beyond the pale of moral dialogue. The tentativeness involved in casuistry, the emphasis on the variety of circumstances, and the recognition that moral principles are often difficult to apply with clear-cut certainty incline the casuistical method toward pluralism and tolerance. Hence, casuistry lends itself to a pluralistic culture such as the United States, where citizens and public officials will have to make moral decisions concerning national security policy in the context of persistent, and often unresolvable, disagreements.

James Watkins wanted to underline the degree to which good moral reasoning takes into account the expected response of other international actors to our policies. National security policy must embrace in its calculus not only our normative traditions, but the likely responses of others. One of the weaknesses of the first two drafts of the U.S. Catholic bishops' letter on nuclear deterrence was its failure to address seriously the Soviet Union's threat to Western lives and freedoms. The third draft corrected this problem, thereby strengthening the letter considerably.

David Hollenbach agreed with Watkins, noting that Germain Grisez's call for unilateral nuclear disarmament in his co-authored book, *Nuclear Deterrence, Morality and Realism* (1987), illustrates the pitfalls into which ethicists slide when they fail to take seriously, and in their moral calculus, the response of "the other side" to the policies one is recommending. Grisez's preferred policies might well lead to the enslavement or destruction of millions of Americans and Europeans at the hands of a Soviet Union emboldened to act with impudence by the West's self-renunciation of nuclear weapons; but that possibility does not carry real moral weight in Grisez's calculus—which is a real problem.

With reference to the possible reconciliation of morality with national security policy, William O'Brien asked James Watkins if he thought there was a significant convergence between military necessity and morality, between what is militarily sensible for a state to do in a conflict and what is morally permissible. Watkins replied that most of the time there was such convergence. It was difficult to conceive of outrageously immoral deeds in wartime that were either militarily necessary for victory or even very useful in improving one's prospect of victory. As a former Chief of Naval Operations and member of the Joint Chiefs of Staff, he had also been impressed by the degree of seriousness with which many American military leaders took considerations of morality as they debated whether to use military force in specific situations. Even when they concurred that the agreed upon policy was militarily feasible, the president and the joint chiefs still insisted on asking themselves whether it was a *sensible* thing to do. Did the policy make sense, not only militarily and politically, but also morally?

Larry Fabian responded that Admiral Watkins would himself agree that his experience was not representative of the whole military bureaucracy, or of the highest military and political circles, at all times. More specifically, Fabian suggested that we have little knowledge of the actual impact of moral reasoning on the foreign policy and national security policy process. It would be useful if scholars could begin to look at key cases in post-1945 American foreign policy, including critical turning points in U.S.-Soviet relations, and try to ascertain empirically the extent to which moral considerations and moral reasoning shaped, and even decided, U.S. policy debates. James Watkins replied that much depends, of course, on the moral sensitivities of individuals in leadership positions. One cannot predict whether at any particular time there is a critical mass of people in key national security positions who have developed sophisticated habits of moral reasoning. But, Watkins insisted, such people do exist—and do make a difference.

JAMES TURNER JOHNSON

# The Just War Idea
# and
# the American Search for Peace

## INTRODUCTION

The title of the series of seminars on which this book is based, "The American Search for Peace: Moral Reasoning, Religious Hope, and National Security," might well serve to encapsulate the major thrust of just war tradition in Western cultural history. The just war idea is, after all, rooted firmly in moral reasoning, albeit an eclectic form of moral reasoning that mixes natural law, prudential calculation, and an ethic of motivation, and which proceeds from values drawn from the experience of statecraft, reflection on the rights of persons, and religious tradition. The primacy of defense among the classically accepted "just causes" for resort to force serves as a reminder that the just war idea has fundamentally to do with the security of political units against aggression by others; this makes plain that "national security" is not some aberration of the age of nation-states but is a particular expression of the need of any political community to secure and maintain the general good of its members. Religious hope, even in the more secularized versions of just war tradition, informs the vision that human moral agents, acting by their best lights, can avert needless destruction in the interaction of their political communities and can even secure a real, if limited, justice in a world that, this side of the Eschaton, remains a world of sin. More radically, the just war theory has historically been the basis for a number of utopian conceptions of world order that mirror, in this-worldly terms, the Augustinian vision of the City of God.

Finally, just war tradition is profoundly about peace, though it is not solely or primarily about peace in the sense of the absence of armed conflicts among nations. "The end of peace" that is one of the classical criteria of a justified resort to force means the cessation of hostilities between the belligerents, but it means a great deal more. It means the restoration of amicable relations between former belligerents, as Grotius and Locke well knew when, reinterpreting this tradition for the modern age, they took care to spell out the rights of postliminy and the proper interrelation between victors and vanquished. Peace, for just war tradition, means the avoidance of acts of hatred in war, as exemplified by the emphasis on protection of noncombatants and on limited means of force in the *jus in bello* (law of war) of the tradition. And it always fundamentally means internal peace within the political community, for such peace is essential to the continued existence of any such common endeavor.

Yet a question remains: is the just war tradition also "American"? That is, to what extent is this moral tradition embodied in the way Americans think and act, particularly as they think and act toward other nations in the international arena? Are we as a people and as a national entity guided, in any real ways, consciously or unconsciously, by the moral tradition of just war? *Should* we be guided by it, in any case, apart from the question whether we *are* so guided or are not? Finally, if we should seek consciously to employ this tradition in the decisions of statecraft of our own nation, there remains the question of how best to do so: the question of making the tradition relevant to our own historical context and the responsibilities we confront there. The analysis that follows is defined by these questions.


## ARGUMENTS AGAINST THE PRESENCE (AND RELEVANCE) OF JUST WAR TRADITION IN AMERICAN CULTURE


Before arguing the positive case for the presence of just war ways of thinking and acting in American culture, it is necessary to take stock of the signs to the contrary. These are quite serious in nature, and by no means to be explained away lightly; indeed, even though I am convinced that just war tradition is alive and well in American culture, these signs to the contrary point to countercurrents that, in various ways, reveal contrasting aspects of American modes of thinking about our own and other nations and acting out our national presence in the world.

## 1. That American just war tradition is different

A fundamental challenge to the presence and contemporary relevance of just war tradition in American culture is exemplified by Robert W. Tucker's argument in his book, *The Just War*,[1] that there is a peculiar *American* "just war doctrine" which can be discerned from our national history and which is importantly different from the broader moral tradition about which I have been speaking. Set in the immediate context of a criticism of the foreign policy of the Eisenhower-Dulles era, Tucker's analysis is framed largely around the idealistic assumptions he identifies as motivating ideas behind that foreign policy; yet he makes clear that he believes that this is but a particularly stark example of a strain that runs throughout American history. In the broader as well as the narrower context, Tucker's purpose is to argue for realism as opposed to idealism in setting national policy. I shall return to the realism-idealism debate below; for now, the issue is the nature of the "American just war doctrine" that Tucker identifies in order to criticize.

What are the characteristics of this "American just war doctrine"? First, it assumes American ideals and goals to be identical with the good of humanity at large. By extension, where our national goals conflict with those of other nations, it is clear by definition that the others are in the wrong. Second, the United States is an inherently peaceful country that resorts to armed force only when forced to do so by another power. That is, the United States will never be an aggressor but will only use its armed power, however reluctantly and at whatever degree of national sacrifice, to defend our own values which are, as already noted, identified with those of humanity in the aggregate. Third, given the definition, in the first two assumptions, of the high and universal ideals to be preserved and the evil purposes of the enemy who by his aggression threatens those ideals, any and all levels of force that may be necessary are justified to bring about the enemy's defeat and to punish his society for its aggression. In the immediate context of the Eisenhower-Dulles policy era, this conception underlay and justified the strategy of massive retaliation; yet, as noted earlier, the strain is much broader. Tucker comments:

> An extreme reluctance to resort to war has not implied restraint in the manner of employing force once war has been thrust upon us. This lack of restraint . . . has commonly been attributed to the indignation we feel towards the "aggressor" who initially resorted to armed force.[2]

The example he cites to drive home the point is the explanation offered by President Truman for the atomic bombing of Hiroshima.

A similar perspective on American moral attitudes toward war is found in Russell Weigley's *The American Way of War*.[3] Following the German historian Hans Delbruck's distinction between a "strategy of attrition" and a "strategy of annihilation" in war, Weigley makes an extended argument throughout the book for a preference for a "strategy of annihilation" as the "American way of war." What he has in mind is the total elimination of the enemy's war-making power, including both the eradication of his military forces and the destruction of citizen morale. Weigley, like Tucker, makes full use of the World War II example, but he reaches back farther into American history as well: Grant and Sherman in the Civil War; even Washington, who though forced by weakness to fight a war of maneuver and attrition, never swerved from a conception of his purpose as being the total defeat of the British forces.

A third, and for the purposes of the present sketch of positions final, argument that American culture has a different conception of war from that of classic just war tradition is the historical adaptation of a particular reading of Clausewitz in the teaching of strategy at the United States Military Academy after 1865. In part as a response to the lackluster battlefield performance of Union Army generals who had been taught strategic thought via Baron de Jomini's *The Art of War*, a strong statement of a limited-war model for campaiging, the Military Academy changed its curriculum after the Civil War to emphasize the "absolute war" concept drawn from Clausewitz, interpreted to mean that war should always be pressed to the fullest, with the enemy defined as the entire society of the opposing belligerent, and with the utter defeat of that society's ability to make war as its goal.

Apart from these specific examples, I believe a common-sense look around American society would uncover many other cases of the underlying attitude expressed here. To put it in a paraphrase of Tucker's three categories, many Americans no doubt believe in a convergence or even identity between the values and goals of this society and those of humanity at large; many Americans no doubt think of this country as ideally a peaceful giant which attempts to avoid wars except when forced into them by the evildoing of others; and many Americans no doubt share the conviction that in such cases, the right thing to do is to hit the enemy hard and reduce him to nothing as a prelude to rebuilding his society on a democratic model. World War II provides the paradigm; a more recent expression of the paradigm, where overwhelming military force was employed but without overwhelming civilian destruction, is the incident in Grenada. Not only the massive retaliation doctrine of the 1950s but nuclear deterrence doctrine in general also makes sense according to this "American just war doctrine," though it embodies a great many problems from the perspective of the historical just war tradition.

While I am critical of some elements of this position—in particular, the move to embrace totalistic means of war as justified for the protection of values common to American society and to all of humanity—I want before turning to another topic to draw attention to the elements of value in the viewpoint sketched here. First, the identification of American values and goals with those of humanity at large is far from being only an expression of short-sighted hubris and self-righteousness. It is why this nation can afford to be unrelenting in our insistence on the provision of basic human rights in other societies. It is why Americans can maintain a certain confidence in the liberal-democratic model of self-government as opposed to both totalitarian and authoritarian forms. It is why the provision of "life, liberty, and the pursuit of happiness," as well as other protections guaranteed in our Constitution, should be among our exports alongside wheat and the products of high technology.

Second, while it is not always the more moral course to wait for an enemy to strike the first blow, there is a deep moral wisdom in avoiding rash commitments of military force and in the effort to make utterly sure of the enemy's intentions before making military commitments. Not only, though, is this moral wisdom. It is also the most prudent response to America's cultural and political diversity, which need a clear demonstration of concrete evil intent on the part of an enemy to coalesce into the political unity necessary to support a commitment of national military force. The caution expressed here is not alien to that found in the classical just war concern that recourse to armed force be had only as "last resort."

## 2. That America has only an immoral conception of the use of force

This second position radically inverts the first—or at least its first two assumptions. In place of the assumption that American goals and values are those also appropriate for the rest of humanity, this second position views this country's purposes and values as inimical to the good of the rest of the world. America is, as the most extreme version of this position has it, "Amerika": imperialist, overbearing, exploitative, and selfish. In place of the assumption that America generally waits until severely provoked before resorting to military force, this position finds an aggressive militarism driven by egoistic national policies, macho civilian and military leaders, and business interests that press for national military power to be used to protect profitable enterprises, at home and (especially) in the Third World.

Some expressions of this way of reading the American nation's working doctrine on military force are religious, while some are secular;

some are rooted in a convictional pacifist suspicion of the state and a rejection of all war, while some are clearly rooted in political hostility. What they all have in common is a suspicion of American military power and the political goals connected to it. The concept of using this power in a just cause, many would say, has been undermined by the nature of this military might itself. That is the idea of "militarism" as used in contemporary liberal Protestant and ecumenical rhetoric, one of the most visible expressions of this second position.

Ronald Stone and Dana Wilbanks, in the introduction to their edited volume, *The Peacemaking Struggle: Militarism and Resistance*, stated the issue in a way characteristic of this rhetoric, speaking of "belligerent militarism on the part of the U.S.A." linked to an "obsession with national security."[4] The United States, indeed, rather than being at present a just polity, is a "national security state" that, far from serving the common good of its citizens or the world, is preparing "for suicide."[5] The evils and injustices in the world are importantly the root of the arms race as such, and the United States, instead of representing values and purposes that tend toward the correction of those evils and injustices, is a major source of them.[6] Later in the same volume Richard Barnet elaborates further the theme that "national security institutions" have "transformed the government of the United States and its relationship to its citizens,"[7] leading to an attempt to socialize Americans to believe that "the only peace possible is a form of permanent war."[8] It is small comfort for Barnet that the Soviet Union is plagued as well by a "national security" obsession; indeed, this makes global peace only that much less likely. If there is to be justice in international affairs, Barnet does not expect it to come from either of the superpowers, both of which he treats as on a basis of moral equivalency.

Similar themes, assumptions, and arguments are found in other documents; military technology is singled out as villain by the 1979 World Council of Churches Conference on Faith, Science, and the Future;[9] Alan Geyer's widely circulated book, *The Idea of Disarmament*,[10] has the same theme, as does the 1986 pastoral letter of the American Methodist bishops (drafted, incidentally, by Geyer).[11] Stone and Wilbanks' position paper, "Shall Presbyterianism Become a Resistance Church?"[12] faults the United States for being an enemy of *shalom*, peace with justice; again, the villain is "militarism" rooted in an obsessive concern with national security and the acquisition of military power.

The language used in the above is intentionally extreme and meant to be shocking. Its purpose is at least as much evangelism—or, in a word favored in liberal Protestant circles, "prophecy"— as analysis. Yet its existence poses a fundamental challenge to the contemporary presence of just war tradition in American culture. Many, perhaps most, in this camp would assert the contemporary irrelevance of just war ideas, claiming they have no place in a nuclear age; even those who still accept some relevance of just war concepts for analytical purposes regard the United States as being in fundamental violation of these ideas because of its possession of nuclear weapons and its overall "militarism."[13] A similar point, though argued with far less extreme rhetoric, is made by Mennonite theologian John Howard Yoder, who maintains that just war theory in the present context would imply surrender, not fighting, in case of attack on the United States. Yoder also argues, by applying just war criteria as an absolutist set of ethical principles, that the United States has never fought a just war, so that just war theory is not in practice a presence in the shaping of American military policy.[14]

It is not to the point of the present discussion to multiply examples of this position further. Rather, the point is to establish what the position is in general outline, where and how it is being enunciated, and its negative implications for the argument I will make below for the contemporary presence and relevance of the moral tradition of just war in American culture. I have not given examples of every strain of the position described in this section but have chosen one of the more visible and extreme expressions of it. This is enough, though, for us to differentiate this position from the others being discussed and to discern what are the lines of assumptions and argument that divide them.

### 3. That America ought to judge its foreign policy by national interests, not by moral values

This is, of course, the position of political realism, and its particular forms are as varied as the position sketched in the previous section. It is a well-known position, and its attack on "moralism" and/or "idealism" in foreign affairs hardly needs to be summarized one more time. The expression given it by one of its most vocal contemporary exponents, Robert W. Tucker, has moreover already been touched on earlier in this paper. For present purposes, then, I shall focus only on certain major elements in the position and how they relate to the question of the presence and relevance of just war tradition in American culture.

Expressions of realism may be prescriptive or descriptive. The former tend to be intellectual arguments. Morgenthau, Osgood, and Tucker, for example, all advance arguments against the introduction of moral value considerations into the making or carrying out of foreign policy (including military policy). The only exception—a small one—would be where taking account of American moral values is necessary to describe American interests properly. Policy and actions in the international arena should be based on considerations of interests, which in principle are nonideological (that is, nonidealistic and nonmoral, in the realists' terminology). Tucker's own animus against the Eisenhower-Dulles foreign policy, highly visible in his critique of the "American just war doctrine" discussed earlier, proceeded in part from what was to him the illegitimate and dangerous introduction of ideological elements (judgments about American moral purpose as righteous, description of the actions of nations as "good" or "evil") into America's dealings with other nations. He finds the same tendencies—and thus the same problems—in the Reagan administration. From such a perspective, just war tradition is objectionable precisely because of its value component, its emphasis on justice and rightness.

Descriptive realism is somewhat different. It may be expressed as an intellectual argument, but more often it is put forward simply as an observation of fact about the way policy is made and carried out in the context of American government. On this view, what matters above all is the technical, legal, political, or other particular competence of the actors in the policy field; they may bring moral convictions with them to the process of decision making, but it is best if they strip off at the door all elements of these convictions except what makes them persons of integrity. Just war ideas, as an explicit body of moral tradition, thus are to be left outside; governmental decision making is empirically a process that has no room for this.

Prescriptive realism, I suggest, is the intellectual rationale that makes descriptive realism seem "right." At the same time, descriptive realism appeals to an American penchant for deriving the "ought" from the "is," and thus the practical exclusion of moral analysis from policy debates and governmental decisions reinforces the credibility of the argument that this is, after all, the way it should be.

Realism of both sorts clearly responds to important currents in American life. In a morally and religiously pluralistic culture it is a simple fact of political interaction that actors cloak their personal convictions in arguments and actions that are justifiable in terms that can be commonly accepted; thus we may be able to agree on an "interest" if not on a "value" or a "belief." The irrelevance of value considerations is reinforced in an educational system that is highly technicized—for example, as focused on producing competent technicians of the law as of engineering. When such persons enter the policy forum, they have already been socialized to regard moral value considerations as not belonging there, however morally sensitive they may be as private individuals. In a culture that lacks an appreciation for history but instead responds to the present on a case-by-case basis, reflection on the implications of historical cultural values like those contained in just war tradition has every reason to be sluggish, uninformed, and, like a machine that is not often used, creaky and unfamiliar to operate when someone tries to get it going.

There remain, though, some nagging inadequacies in the realist posture. Are not "interests" only "values" by another name? Is taking account of moral concerns in fact identical with the introduction of illegitimate, factionalist ideology? Is it genuinely better to leave the tools of moral analysis outside the door when policy is being formulated or actions are being determined? Is the short shrift given to history an adequate response to the need to be self-consciously aware of the roots and development of our cultural and national identity? And indeed, is it ever enough for citizens of *this* nation to seek consciously to bracket out any role for values in shaping our national presence in the world? While it can be granted that much of the critique that realists have in the past directed at certain forms of idealism in American foreign policy has been on target, this is far from establishing the intellectual case that the best international posture is a value-free one. Realism is a needed corrective to a naive idealism; yet it too has its own way of introducing naiveté into the making and carrying out of policy.

Clearly, there are other currents in the national foreign policy debate than the three discussed above; yet these are major, broad streams with many tributaries. Relationally, they are like points of a triangle: each is different from the others; each opposes the others. What they have in common is that they all challenge, in their particular ways, the proposition that just war tradition is a presence in American culture and that, in contemporary debates over foreign policy in general or military affairs in particular, it has any relevance. In the next section I will argue the case for the presence of this tradition, and in the final section I will argue for its contemporary relevance.

## THE PRESENCE OF JUST WAR TRADITION IN AMERICAN CULTURE

Just war tradition is not a "theory" or a "doctrine" but a *tradition* that is carried in different but related forms by various historical streams within the broader culture. I will sketch the presence of just war tradition in five of these: secular political philosophy, international law, military ethics, military policy, and theology.

### 1. The presence of just war tradition in secular political philosophy

The major figures here include such individuals as Elizabeth Anscombe, Thomas Nagel, Michael Walzer, and Stanley Hoffmann; others can be quickly identified by following the debates on morality and war in the journal *Philosophy and Public Affairs*, which has provided a forum for the working out of a contemporary philosophical version of just war theory and its application to political and military affairs. I will, however, discuss the positions staked out by Walzer and Hoffmann in book-length studies. Hoffmann's *Duties beyond Borders* includes an extended discussion in which a historical version of just war theory is examined only to be rejected, then reinstated in modified form under the rubric of "guidelines which address themselves to the moral issues of modern war."[15] The theory Hoffmann rejects (he calls it "the old 'just war' theory") is identified by him with Christian theology and with the medieval era. It is no longer useful, he argues, because it "was elaborated for three sets of circumstances which are no longer with us":[16]

— a world ruled by Christian princes and in which the church had sufficient authority and power to define and interpret morality;
— wars that "were very different from the present Frankenstein monsters which we call total wars";
— circumstances in which "there was a fairly clear distinction between peace and war" and deterrence theory had not yet come to play a major role in military policy.

Now, whether Hoffmann is correct to identify just war thinking so narrowly with Christian morality and the medieval period, or whether the difference between the circumstances then and now is as significant as he believes, are matters on which I differ profoundly with him; yet this is not the place to debate these issues.[17] The point on which I wish to focus is rather what Hoffmann says next, after rejecting "the old 'just war' theory." What he in fact does is to reconstruct a *new* just war theory (minus the name) that has clear affinities with the one thrown out. What is missing in Hoffmann's analysis is how this way of thinking developed from the thirteenth century to the present, to explain how he, writing in the 1980s, would fall into patterns of moral analysis and judgment so reminiscent of those of the rejected theory. James Childress has argued that just war theory expresses a set of "*prima facie* duties" that are widely accepted in our culture; the classical categories are particular expressions of the way people in Western culture think when they think about morality and war.[18] Hoffmann's contemporary reconstruction of just war theory (minus the name) is a case in point. Let us look briefly at how he carries out this reconstruction.

First, Hoffmann distinguishes between problems of ends and problems of means.[19] This is, of course, exactly the same distinction made in the *jus ad bellum* and *jus in bello* of just war tradition. Second, he seeks to establish the possibility of justification for the use of force in international affairs (traditionally the question of "just cause"), and when he turns out to argue for self-defense, "anticipatory self-defense," and certain "nonselfish causes"—"ends that transcend the (evident) interest of the initiating state"— for nondefensive wars,[20] the historian of just war tradition must be forgiven for interjecting that we have already been this way before along the line of development of a moral tradition of analysis and judgment that reaches back into the classical and Hebraic roots of Western culture. The same is true of other topics drawn from the list of classic just war criteria: right intention (p.61), proportionality of ends (pp. 60, 62), reasonable hope of success (p. 62), the end of peace (p. 61), last resort (p. 62), proportionality of means (p. 60), the rights of noncombatants (pp. 73-74). Hoffmann dwells at some length (pp. 62-72) on the possible justification for military intervention (for example, to correct egregious violations of human rights), and in this he again shows his affinity with the ongoing just war tradition by thus justifying what was classically termed the just cause of "punishment of evil." This is the more striking because of its divergence from what is accepted as just cause by one of the other major cultural streams that carries just war tradition, international law, where there has been a concerted attempt to restrict the justifications for resort to armed force to one: self-defense against armed attack. (See the discussion of international law below.)

Michael Walzer's *Just and Unjust Wars* is a far more thoroughly developed and historically sensitive new construction of just war thinking than Hoffmann's, though both these political philosophers recognize the kinship of their efforts. Walzer does not, however, like Hoffmann begin by rejecting the older just war tradition. Rather, he readily accepts that there are historical foundations, including religious ones, for the moral arguments he makes in the book:

> I want to recapture the just war for political and moral theory. My own work . . . looks back to that religious tradition within which Western politics and morality were first given shape, to the books of writers like Maimonides, Aquinas, Vitoria, and Suarez and then to the books of writers like Hugo Grotius, who took over the tradition and began to work it into a secular form. But I have not attempted a history of just war theory. . . .[21]

Walzer's use of "historical illustrations" as an integral part of his theoretical reconstruction reveals that he views the moral argument he is developing as one with historical depth. It is, moreover, one with a universalistic dimension. Walzer is a political philosopher of the post-Grotius age, and the religious dimension of just war thinking has for him, as for Grotius, been sublimated into a commonalty of perception to be found wherever in humankind one may look. For Grotius, this was the arena of what "nature" allowed in the conduct of war; for Walzer, the common element is the idea that persons everywhere and in whatever time have the ability to recognize evil and the motivation to reject it.[22] What comes out of such individual and cumulative historical judgment is Walzer's reconstruction of the just war idea: a reestablishment of a kind of moral idealism against the realists, a reestablishment of the *jus ad bellum* as a "theory of aggression" and the *jus in bello* as "the war convention," in which the traditional moral categories are developed under rubrics ranging over the whole shape of armed conflict from World War II forward.

Walzer's "recaptured" just war theory has been widely studied. *Just and Unjust Wars* has been a textbook at the U.S. Army War College and West Point, as well as in the 1986 Naval Chaplain Corps Professional Development and Training Course. It would be impossible to assess how many college students have been introduced to it through courses in philosophical ethics or the odd course in other departments. My own thoroughly unscientific sampling of people who have been first acquainted with this book in undergraduate courses suggests that they, life Hoffmann, identify just war theory with a Catholic doctrine of the Middle Ages, and do not think of Walzer's book as an effort to "recapture the just war for moral and political theory." They have clearly not read the introduction to *Just and Unjust Wars*.

## 2. The presence of just war tradition in international law

The accomplishment of Grotius and the other theorists of international law, as Walzer has noted, was to transform the inherited just war tradition from the shape it had taken in the context of medieval Christendom into a shape that allowed it to become a basis of modern international law.[23] Ever since, international law has been a major carrier of just war tradition, though the international law of war is somewhat truncated as compared to the broader moral tradition.[24]

An important benchmark of the international law *jus ad bellum* is provided by the General Treaty for the Renunciation of War (the Pact of Paris or Kellogg-Briand Pact of 1928), of which the United States was one of the initiators and principal sponsors. Signatories to this treaty rejected the first resort to force in the settlement of international disputes. At the time it was promulgated, the Pact of Paris was an effort to strengthen the international arbitration provisions in the League of Nations Covenant to make war less likely as a means of settling disputes. The provision for resort to armed force only in defense after another nation has initiated armed conflict has been carried over into the present major source of the international law *jus ad bellum*, the United Nations Charter. Here, in articles 2 and 51, the right of first resort to armed force is restricted and the right of second defensive use of such force is explicitly affirmed. While this does not go so far as the classic triad of just causes in just war tradition (defense against attack, recovery of property or rights wrongly taken by another, the punishment of evil), the tendency has been to enlarge the legal concept of "defense" to include the other two, as, for example, in the justifications used by both the United Kingdom and Argentina at the time of the Falklands war.

Much more attention has been given in international law to the *jus in bello*, the law of war, than to questions of the rights of states to resort to armed force. Restrictions on the means of war and on treatment of various categories of persons in time of war make up "Hague law," "Geneva law," and ongoing treaty efforts to achieve arms control and limitation. The United States has been a participant in most of the processes that have produced such law, and it has been a signatory to most of the law thus produced. In the most rudimentary prima facie sense, this shows the presence and contemporary relevance of at least this redaction of just war tradition in American culture. Beyond that, the active role various United States administrations have taken over the last century of development of international law demonstrates that the affirmation of just war tradition thus made has been a natural expression of our national sense of international right and wrong.

### 3. The presence of just war tradition in military ethics

Historically, just war tradition has been shaped significantly by moral reflection on the concerns of military professionalism. The medieval chivalric code contributed heavily to the creation of a tradition defining noncombatants as against combatants and attempting to secure the former from the destruction and harm of war. The limited war theory and practice of the Enlightenment era encapsulated the just war concept of proportionality in both its *jus ad bellum* and *jus in bello* senses. In the American military from the Civil War period forward, the military manuals of the law of war have defined an ethic for military personnel that applies just war categories in concrete ways to the sorts of situations likely to arise in wartime. Insofar as these manuals reflect the work of the judge advocate's office, they incorporate just war tradition through the implications of international law.

But there is more to the matter than this. Military professionals have always recognized certain fundamentals to the socialization of a soldier which are expressions in different form of ideas encountered in just war tradition. The protection of noncombatants is more than a nod in the direction of the Geneva conventions; it is a recognition that military socialization should include an effort to inculcate the kind of character that will identify the foe in the role he plays as agent of a hostile force, and which will seek to protect the rights of others in harm's way even at potential cost to oneself. Military discipline, too, implies socialization that turns military personnel away from temptations to plunder and to use their arms as a way of bullying others who are not of the enemy. The rules of engagement—in Vietnam, in Lebanon, in Grenada, in the Persian Gulf—reflect more than law; they reflect a commitment to the underlying values that comprise the broad just war tradition.[25]

## 4. The presence of just war tradition in military policy

I will comment here on the policy debate that took place in late 1984 and early 1985 between Secretary of Defense Caspar Weinberger and Secretary of State George Shultz over the criteria for commitment of American military forces. The immediate context was provided, on the one hand, by the question of the proper role of the American military in Central America and, on the other hand, by the question whether more aggressive use ought to be made of military forces in attempting to combat terrorism. It is my contention that both Weinberger and Shultz, in staking out their respective positions as the administration sought a coherent policy, argued according to just war categories and, in the content they gave to these categories, reflected major conceptual streams in just war tradition. This is not to say that they did so consciously, though the Weinberger position is framed in such a way as to suggest that a listing of just war criteria may have been before the author at the time of the drafting of the defense secretary's statement. Even if there was no conscious effort to adapt the tradition, though, we have already seen in the case of Stanley Hoffmann how the categories and content of this tradition may rise in policy reflection to define the issues and influence policy positions. That is the minimum I wish to claim for the Weinberger-Shultz debate, but that in itself is a significant sign of the presence of just war tradition in American military policy.

The treatment I will give the two positions is necessarily cursory. I am working from Weinberger's statement in his February 5, 1986 report to the Congress[26] (Figure 1, page 84) and from Shultz's in his address at Yeshiva University on October 25, 1984[27] (Figure 2, page 86). Both secretaries aired their views in numerous contexts, but using similar language, during this policy debate; the texts chosen are representative and, in the case of Weinberger's, constitutes an authoritative policy statement: "the Weinberger doctrine." I will begin with it.

First, the Weinberger doctrine is a *jus ad bellum* statement almost exclusively; except by implication it does not directly address *jus in bello* issues. The traditional *jus ad bellum* categories, however, are all present.

The defense secretary's concept of just cause is phrased in the language of political realism; yet like international law, it stresses that force must be defensive to be justified. It does not extend protection to any and all nations that may be threatened by aggression, and so it stops short of what was allowed in classic just war theory; yet this notion of just cause clearly falls inside the bounds of just war tradition.

Right intention, as defined by Weinberger, falls third in his list (it is usually second in traditional *jus in bello* listings) and again uses the language of realism, not that of morality. We do not have here Augustine's ruling out of "implacable animosity" and "the lust of domination"; yet those are already implicitly rejected in realist political thought. Compared to international law, whose *jus ad bellum* generally takes little account of this traditional just war category, the Weinberger statement goes much farther.

Right authority, usually placed third in traditional listings, comes much later in Weinberger's "six conditions," but its importance is nonetheless clear. This doctrine aimed at avoiding "another Vietnam," insisting on public and congressional concurrence before the commitment of force. That is an unambiguous statement of the criterion of right authority.

The Weinberger statement of reasonable hope of success, in its focus on the concept of "winning," says both more and less than the traditional content of this just war category. "Success" may or may not mean "winning," depending on how the terms are defined. In limited war, which approximates the criteria of the traditional *jus in bello*, "success" may mean only prevention of the enemy's success. Thus, for example, the proper extent of defense may be only to turn the enemy back from one's borders and may not include pursuit of the repulsed enemy for the purpose of punishment. This, in one context, is properly described as "winning"; I think of the British objectives and their achievement in the Falklands war or the American ones in the Grenada incursion. In another context, "winning" means something far more apocalyptic; I think of the definition of "winning" as "unconditional surrender" in World War II, or

Figure 1. Six Conditions for Committing U.S. Military Forces
(Weinberger).

*Just cause:*

1. When vital to defense of national or allied interests

*Reasonable hope of success:*

2. With intention of winning

■ sole object of winning

■ forces and resources sufficient to achieve objectives, or not at all

*Right intention:*

3. For clearly defined political and military objectives

■ determine objectives

■ decide strategy

*Proportionality:*

4. With correlation between objectives and forces

■ if national interests require us to fight, then we must win

■ assess and adjust force size and composition as necessary

*Right authority:*

5. With public/congressional concurrence

■ commit American public before American forces

■ cannot fight at home and on the battlefield

*Last resort:*

6. As last resort

■ only when other means have failed or have no prospect for success

■ military force is not a substitute for diplomacy

*End of peace:*

Not explicitly stated but implicit in 1 and 6

of the objectives of Iran, as opposed to the initial goals of Iraq, in the conflict between these two countries. Emphasis on "winning" in the second sense may go beyond the traditional bounds of just war theory into holy war or ideological war.

I will not comment on the remaining "conditions" outlined by the defense secretary except to reiterate that, in my judgment, they reflect both the categories of just war tradition and the historical content of those categories, though the language employed is that of contemporary policy debate.

Similarly, I will not treat the Shultz position, outlined in Figure 2, in its entirety. Again, I find in his statements a reflection, in contemporary language, of the traditional just war categories; while I am less happy about the content he gives to these concepts than I am with that defined by Weinberger, I must still affirm that there is a link here with the content given in just war tradition. Like the Weinberger doctrine, Shultz's is a *jus ad bellum* statement. Here, though, the language used is idealistic rather than realistic, and the conditions, rather than being restrictive of the use of force, tend to define a principled and somewhat elastic allowance of such use. Restraint enters explicitly only through intentionality and what Shultz calls "our decency." Shultz has a great deal more to say about intentionality than Weinberger, and here he is considerably closer to the classic right-intention concept of just war tradition. Shultz's position on right authority represents another perspective on the proper nature and exercise of such authority in the American political framework. His allusion to the example of Hitler gives a different tone to what he says about the proper proportion of ends and degree of force employed. Yet again, we have in Secretary Shultz's position an exemplification of the contemporary presence in the American policy forum of ideas and forms of thought from just war tradition.

## 5. The presence of just war tradition in contemporary American theology

I have left this topic until last in this quick survey of the presence of just war tradition in American culture in order to underscore that, contrary to what many people think, this tradition is not solely or even principally a creation and possession of Christian theology. I have argued this point in two books[28] and do not intend to go over that ground again here. The foregoing has been intended to show the presence and influence of just war modes of thought in various explicitly nonreligious contexts within American culture.

**Figure 2.** The Legitimate Use of Power (Shultz).

*Just cause:*

"To further the cause of freedom and enhance international security and stability."

*Right authority:*

President has such authority; when exercised rightly, people and Congress will support it (case of Grenada cited).

*Right intention:*

"The use of power is legitimate

- *Not* when it crushes the human spirit and tramples human freedom, but when it can help liberate a people or support the yearning for freedom;

- *Not* when it imposes an alien will on an unwilling people, but when its aim is to bring peace or to support peaceful processes; when it prevents others from abusing *their* power through aggression or oppression; and

- *Not* when it is applied unsparingly, without care or concern for innocent life, but when it is applied with the greatest efforts to avoid unnecessary casualties and with a conscience troubled by the pain unavoidably inflicted."

*Proportionality:*

Use of military force to deter aggression or oppression may avoid "The awful necessity of using far greater force later on"—example of Hitler.

*Reasonable hope of success:*

Not treated explicitly: seems to be assumed. Shultz speaks instead of the need to have moral courage "to act in difficult situations."

*Last resort:*

Reluctance to use force is "the mark of our decency. And clearly the use of force must always be a last resort."

*End of peace:*

"We will be a true champion of freedom and bulwark of peace."

*Jus in bello:*

See third "not" under right intention, above.

This said, it is necessary to stress that just war tradition is present also, of course, in contemporary religious reflection on morality and war. That this is where conventional wisdom *expects* it to be means that simply to list American just war theologians would be a prima facie proof of the presence of just war tradition in the religious segment of American culture. The names of these theologians would include John C. Ford, Paul Ramsey, and John Courtney Murray, all from earlier stages in the debate; I would also, as I have elsewhere done, place Reinhold Niebuhr in this context as well, arguing that the position he took in rejecting Christian pacifism in the late 1930s was a just war argument.[29] More recent names would include my own, as well as those of John Langan and David Hollenbach, James Childress and other younger scholars in moral theology and religious ethics. This list would have to include Bryan Hehir, who, as author of the final drafts of the American Catholic bishops' 1983 pastoral on war and peace, explicitly shaped the arguments of the crucial second section of that document around just war principles, and George Weigel, whose *Tranquillitas Ordinis*[30] develops the side of the Augustinian tradition on good statecraft which forms the context for the theological development of just war theory. William O'Brien, who, though not formally trained in theology, often has entered the theological debates, bridges the generational division I have created.[31] All these are examples of positive uses of the specifically Christian stream of just war tradition; it is perhaps no accident that most of the persons named are Catholics. This last, though, is not due to the religious tradition of just war being more specifically Catholic than Protestant; among those American churches that have made explicit use of just war tradition in recent statements are the Lutheran Church in America and the Episcopal Church. Rather, it is because of the methodology of Catholic theological reflection, which is far more historically conscious than is most Protestant theological methodology.

Finally, respect for just war tradition in religious circles can be found even in individuals who, in last analysis, tend to use reasoning from the just war categories to argue against the contemporary relevance of those categories in American policy: I am thinking here specifically of John Howard Yoder and Ronald Stone in the works cited earlier. Stanley Hauerwas might be named to exemplify the critical analysis of Christian just war pacifism as the most properly Christian moral stance.[32]

Granted that just war tradition is present in American culture through religion, *how* is it present? The short answer is that it has been far more in evidence through reflection on the *jus in bello* categories of discrimination and proportionality of means than through the *jus ad bellum* concepts. In the American Catholic bishops' *The Challenge of Peace*, the *jus in bello* is even employed itself to generate a new category in the *jus ad bellum*: nuclear war would be so awful that, for the bishops, "[W]e must continually say 'no' to the idea of nuclear war."[33] Similar reasoning surfaced in religious criticism of American military involvement in Vietnam, and it has been a familiar phenomenon in religious criticism of nuclear weapons.

The use of just war tradition in the religious framework has been, furthermore, mostly reactive; it begins with the political situation and then applies just war reflection to it. As a historian of just war tradition, I know intimately how few other scholars work on uncovering how the historical tradition developed and why it developed as it did. Efforts aimed at exploring the theological basis of just war reasoning and establishing that basis in terms acceptable within the framework of contemporary theology has been only sporadic: I think of Ramsey's effort to define the principle of discrimination in terms of neighbor-love[34] and Langan's revival of natural law theory in his chapter in this volume. Childress's exploration of the moral basis of the just war criteria[35] owes more to philosophy than to theology.

So much for the shortcomings, though I would surely have more to say about particulars if space permitted such detail here. It is one of the historical strengths of this tradition that it has taken shape out of such internal criticism and dialogue.

The usage of just war thinking in American religious circles has also, though, had an undoubted positive effect. Preeminently, it is religious thinkers who have reawakened a consciousness of this tradition, its moral categories, and their content in public debate about foreign policy and military affairs over the last fifty years, and particularly since World War II. Without decrying the significance of the historical work done by the international lawyer James Brown Scott to link just war tradition to the creation of modern international law,[36] I doubt that just war categories would have been recovered by a Walzer or a Hoffmann, or by a philosopher like Thomas Nagel, or by a contemporary international lawyer like Tom Farer, or by a political realist like Tucker, without the recovery and introduction of these ideas into public debate by Ramsey, Murray, the Second Vatican Council, and others in more recent controversies. This has had the effect of countering the simplistic division between realism and idealism, for just war tradition is both realist and idealist, forged in the interaction between moral ideals and political praxis. In short, it has raised the tone of the debate and given it a positive moral content, and the religious sector has been responsible for this.

## 6. The place of just war tradition in American culture

All the above examples of the presence of just war tradition in American culture—secular political philosophy, international law, military ethics, military policy, theology—are cases of the development of this tradition within the particular context set by each of these distinguishable communities of discourse. Each draws from a larger reservoir of ideas than it expresses by itself; yet together they bear witness to that fuller pool of cultural moral agreement. This pattern is characteristic of major moral traditions in general: a tracing of the historical development and contemporary presence of the moral tradition on marriage and divorce, for example, would reveal the same pattern. The preservation and development of moral traditions over time owe much to the work of representatives of various elites constituted as particular communities of moral value within the larger framework of the moral values of the culture as a whole. In practice, those traditions are most easily accessed by analysis of the particular contributions of those elites, and through them it is possible to view the moral attitudes and values of the culture as a whole.

It would be a mistake, then, to infer from the discussion above that just war tradition is present in American culture only within the attitudes and assumptions of certain elites, but not in the moral world of "ordinary" people—people who are not political philosophers, international lawyers, military professionals, policy makers, or theologians. Rather, the presence of this tradition in such a diverse range of communities of discourse argues just the opposite: the perdurance and vitality of just war categories and concepts in American society at large.

In this society, moreover, the concept of "ordinary" people is misleading because of the high degree of intellectual and social mobility. There is a certain obvious truth in arguing, for example, that in the Middle Ages commoners did not share the moral attitudes and convictions of the chivalric class, or the contributions of this class to the development of the coalescing just war tradition. Their moral worlds were accordingly separate and different. But no similar wall of birth, privilege, and socialization divides "ordinary" Americans from any of the communities of discourse discussed above. Indeed, the concept of citizen—as opposed to that of subject to a feudal lord—implies that the best citizen is the one who, as necessary, moves into and out of dialogue with the various specialized centers of discourse found in the society as a whole. Americans may do this individually, but more commonly they do it by membership in one or more communities of value which engage the larger society in specified ways. An American may not be a professional theologian, for example, but he or she may be a participating member of a religious denomination via a local church; an American may not be a professional political philosopher, but he or she may become involved in debates over issues of political philosophy through participation in local or national affairs.

It is significant, then, that just war categories and concepts have entered public discourse through such vehicles as the churches and through public debate over military policy issues such as participation in the Vietnam War and nuclear deterrence. At the level of popular public discourse, reflection on the meaning of categories and concepts drawn from just war tradition is no longer simply the province of theologians and philosophers or policy professionals. The ostensible division between elites and ordinary people dissolves.

This is not, however, to imply that just war categories and concepts are to be found everywhere, or in all places equally strongly or equally well understood within American culture as a whole. It is a truism that America is morally pluralistic, and this pluralism in the case of just war tradition is also attested by the various ways in which that tradition is rendered within the several contexts discussed above. Pluralism by itself, though, is centrifugal in effect, tending to divide and break up a society. If American culture were only pluralistic, it would not be a recognizable culture. That it is results from the strongly centripetal effect of dialogue and reciprocal interaction among the many distinguishable centers of value within the society as a whole.

This implies a responsibility for proponents of categories and concepts from just war tradition within the various elite cultural contexts discussed above: to seek actively to create such dialogue and reciprocal interaction, both with members of other elite groups as well as with the larger American community. Each of these particular groups has a teaching responsibility, to clarify and develop the implications of the tradition as understood in that context; and each has a learning responsibility, to allow its own understanding to be broadened and made more coherent by the insights and conceptions of its partners in dialogue. Historically, this has been how just war tradition has developed within Western culture; it is also a particularly appropriate model for the American context.

## THE RELEVANCE OF JUST WAR TRADITION IN AMERICAN CULTURE: TWO MILITARY ISSUES

Though the argument for relevance could be made through reflection on American history or through investigating just how recent war thinking has affected the tone of public policy debate, I will here argue for relevance first by making an application of just war modes of thought to some contemporary military issues and then, in the conclusion to this chapter, by specific consideration of the implications of just war tradition for the pursuit of peace. The military issues I will comment on are the nuclear-conventional mix in American military forces and the strategic defense initiative (SDI). In neither case will I attempt to be comprehensive but will only raise to view certain particular points significant in terms of just war analysis.

## 1. The nuclear-conventional mix

In *The Challenge of Peace*, the American Catholic bishops wrote:

> Non-nuclear attacks by another state must be resisted by other than nuclear means. Therefore, a serious moral obligation exists to develop non-nuclear defensive strategies as rapidly as possible.[37]

The implications of this comment for the components of American military forces were followed up, however, only in another section of the pastoral and then only in a few brief and very general paragraphs.[38] This is striking because a strengthening of conventional military capability has been under way for several years, both in land forces (especially important in the area of responsibility of the NATO alliance) and in naval forces. It is striking as well, given the adamant rejection of "nuclear war-fighting capability" and "war-fighting strategies" elsewhere in the document.[39] And it is all the more striking in the context of other American religious positions on military forces, particularly the use of the term "militarism" by certain Protestant groups to oppose almost any new military initiatives whatever, other than reductions in force.

What might have been said, from a just war perspective? In the first place, the point might have been made that conventional weapons are inherently more capable of proportional and discriminating use than nuclear ones (though I do not accept the argument, made by the American Catholic bishops and others, that nuclear weapons as a class are inherently disproportionate and indiscriminate; this is to confuse current strategic weapons and strategic targeting plans that include targets in population centers with what is possible with lower-yield weapons of more accuracy, used in smaller numbers and discriminating fashion against targets outside population centers). Given the desire to reduce overall destruction and, in particular, to spare noncombatants as much as possible the destruction of war, this comparative advantage of conventional weapons, as a class, over nuclear ones is of special importance.

Second, the point might have been developed that at least one possible contemporary interpretation of the moral criterion of proportionality of means is that forces should be opposed by similar forces. (This seems to be the assumption behind the bishops' stipulation that "non-nuclear attacks are to be resisted by other than nuclear means.") Since, for example, in Europe the conventional forces of the Warsaw Pact appear, by common measures, to be considerably greater than those of the NATO allies (and since, in the first place, the United States introduced battlefield nuclear weapons into NATO in order to offset the greater conventional strength of the Warsaw Pact forces), there seems to be a moral bias toward increasing NATO's conventional strength while simultaneously reducing battlefield nuclear weapons. Doing this would, however, clearly cost more money and require more military personnel, and the overall cost of such a configuration of military force would almost certainly be greater, not less, than the cost of the present configuration. Should this additional cost be paid? If nuclear weapons are as bad as they are held to be, the answer seems obvious; yet this would create conflict with other goals, such as savings in military expenditures so as to feed the poor. Liberal Protestants tend to resolve this issue by denouncing increased military spending as "militarism"; the American Catholic bishops simply decline to reach a conclusion: "We cannot judge the strength of these arguments."[40]

A third point that might have been made concerns the matter of the "humanization" of contemporary war. The argument is sometimes made that just war theory is irrelevant to modern war, since modern war has become an activity carried on at great distances by actors who are not physically aware of their opponents as fellow humans. In such a context, Vattel's comment that in time of war we should "never forget that our enemies are men"[41] becomes hard to observe; our enemies have become targets on a map of the world or, at most, blips on a radar screen. What I am terming "humanization" here amounts to the impact on moral attitudes of restoring some of the lost ability to distinguish combatants and their functions from noncombatants and theirs; this is, as argued above, inherently easier with conventional forces. It also means, though, increasing the impact on moral attitudes of slowing down a military conflict to the speed of conventional destruction of forces so that the belligerents experience the death and destruction as well as the nobility and heroism of war and have time to react morally to it while it is still under way. That is, if nuclear weapons have, as their opponents (including the Catholic bishops) argue, made war an immoral activity, restoring the primacy of conventional weapons on the battlefield holds at least the promise of restoring the moral dimension that is claimed to have been lost.

Further, there is a just war requirement that war be waged by right authority. If this be carried through to the operational level, a move away from nuclear to conventional forces—again, Western Europe is the usual context to be considered—removes the "use them or lose them" imperative relative to nuclear weapons in forward deployment and thus restores a greater degree of control to the authorities who count as "right" ones in just war terms. In the United States this means the President and the Congress, as well as the chain of military command.

Negatively (aside from the matter of cost mentioned above), the impact of a shift toward conventional forces on the likelihood of war ought to be assessed in any just war analysis of such a prospective shift. There is a prima facie argument that nuclear weapons have deterred war between the superpowers, and that removal of nuclear weapons from the European theater will increase the likelihood of war there. War, in just war tradition, is justified only when its end is to bring peace. If peace can be had without war, that is so much the better, and both the criterion of "last resort" and "the end of peace" are thereby served. The other side of this, however, is the question whether peace is the highest goal. I am convinced that in just war tradition it is not; justice is. Then the question becomes, in just war terms, whether a shift toward conventional weapons will make for a military force more usable to further the cause of justice in the world.

## 2. The strategic defense initiative

The debate over the strategic defense initiative (SDI) has been conducted almost entirely outside the reference points of just war tradition. Debate has focused upon pragmatic questions: its cost, whether the weapons systems contemplated can be expected to work, whether SDI will help or hinder arms control, and whether it will be more likely to bring about nuclear war or to increase deterrence. The concept itself has undergone considerable transformation from President Reagan's original idea of a space-based defensive shield capable of providing umbrella-like protection to American society as a whole, to the later justifications for a less ambitious SDI system as enhancing the existing nuclear deterrent and providing insurance against accidental launches of nuclear weapons or ballistic missile attacks by outlaw states. I suggest that in terms of the concerns found in just war tradition there are five issues in particular that need to be addressed relative to SDI in all its forms.

First, is it *mala in se?* Some critics seem to be claiming that it is because of the negative effect they project deployment of strategic defense weapons would have on deterrence. That is, it is bad in itself because it would bring on a nuclear war. To understand what just war tradition might imply on this, we should look at the category of means *mala in se* in the law of war: they include dumdum bullets, gas warfare, and the torture of captives. Historically, within the broader tradition, poisoning of wells and other means that make a territory unfit for habitation by noncombatants are understood as evil in themselves. Is SDI bad in itself in the same way that these are? I think not; the criterion within just war tradition seems to be whether the means in question cause needless suffering (violating the principle of proportionality of means) or directly cause noncombatants to suffer (violating the principle of discrimination or noncombatant immunity). By these standards, strategic nuclear weapons, as well as some forms or uses of conventional weapons, fall short of the mark, but SDI in whatever form that has been described in the debate does not. Whether SDI is evil in itself ought, therefore, to be considered relative to these concerns and not only relative to speculation about whether it would cause or help prevent nuclear war.

Second, just war tradition requires that new means of war be compared with their alternatives. In this case, SDI should be compared to the present system of deterrence, and the results of the use of strategic defensive means need to be weighed against the results of the use of strategic nuclear weapons. Again, not only *jus ad bellum* concerns are relevant; the *jus in bello* principles of proportionality and discrimination need also to be brought to bear in assessing the morality of strategic defense.

The American Catholic bishops, in their 1988 "Report on 'The Challenge of Peace' and Policy Developments 1983-1988," argue that a proper moral judgment of SDI cannot be made without taking into account the prudential concerns of feasibility, stability, and cost.[42] The second of these themes, stability, has to do with the risk that SDI may cause strategic instability and, in particular, create a "possible shift toward offensive use of this defensive system" and "the further 'tilt' of the deterrence relationship toward pre-emptive strategies during the transition period" in which SDI is being deployed. Neither of these possibilities is certain, and neither has to do with SDI as such, as the bishops admit; yet they argue that these concerns are "central to the policy debate." Central to the policy debate they are; yet they are not properly a part of the moral debate over SDI as such. Judging the moral status of this weapons system in itself requires backing away from the policy debate to look hard at what SDI is in itself, and at how it compares with the strategic nuclear weapons system.

Third, but still on the matter of alternatives, there is the question of the relative value and disvalue of SDI as opposed to those of certain other possible defense postures. This would also need to include some assessment of the likelihood of success of each element compared, as well as of a strategic defense system. A short list of such alternatives includes (a) general disarmament, unilateral or mutual; (b) partial disarmament, unilateral or mutual; (c) standing pat with the current sort of deterrence weapons and strategy; (d) seeking to improve the nuclear deterrent and/or nuclear war-fighting capability (after all, deterrence might fail) by adding more nuclear weapons of greater sophistication to the arsenal (such as low-CEP, low-yield ballistic missiles suitable for limited counterforce warfare); and (e) strengthening conventional means of defense, including civil defense.

In the current climate, though not at the time the SDI concept was introduced, the potential for success of efforts at disarmament is highly promising. Nonetheless, the criterion for moral judgment is not feasibility but whether the path chosen is the more likely to satisfy the fundamental goal of the just war tradition, the protection of values against attack by force. So long as there are arms, there will be need for defense. A scaling down of armaments in itself lowers the threat but does not defend against the threat that remains. It follows that the morally relevant question for SDI is how well it would protect against this threat, especially as compared with a continuation of deterrence (at some level) or other forms of active or passive defense.

Fourth, there is the question of SDI versus the system of deterrence. Nuclear deterrence is highly questionable in just war terms because of its resting so heavily on the threat of retaliation and because that threat, if ever carried out, would produce so much harm to noncombatants, not only in the enemy nation but across the world. In classic just war terms, retaliation would be justified only if it were a "punishment of evil," a concept that perhaps remains morally justified but has, as noted above, disappeared from international law. Taken broadly, so as to include international law as well as other streams of just war thought in Western culture, just war tradition evinces a clear bias toward defense and away from punishment of evil. In just war terms, then, one of the most relevant questions to answer regarding SDI is the extent to which it is genuinely defensive and representative of a tendency to move away from war fighting in the mode of punishment by strategic nuclear strike.

Fifth, there is the issue of "counting the costs," that is, of proportionality of ends. In its *jus ad bellum* sense, any means of force requires to be judged in terms of this total calculus of costs and benefits. SDI is projected to be an enormously costly weapons system. In this context, the so-called "spin-offs" from SDI research become moral counters in judging the value or disvalue of this initiative. Nonetheless, the costs of any weapons system may themselves represent a threat to the values of this society, and embody harm against these values if other means can provide equal protection less expensively.

Obviously, much more could be said, and in particular I might proceed to give, in addition to the brief comments above, my own analysis of these issues and answers to the questions I have posed from out of a perspective in just war thought. The point here, though, is not this analysis or these answers but whether they are relevant in the context of public policy debate. A judgment that they are is a judgment for the contemporary relevance of just war tradition.[43]

## CONCLUSION:
## THE RELEVANCE OF JUST WAR TRADITION
## IN THE CONTEMPORARY SEARCH FOR PEACE

The quest for peace in Western culture has taken three related but different paths.[44] Two of these may be generally characterized as pacifist. The path of sectarian withdrawal from society rejects violence and seeks to create its own perfect community without violence in the midst of an imperfect, violent world, but separated from it. For sectarians, all of society outside their own is marked by evil and strife; nothing humanly possible can change this, and the only moral course is to withdraw, so far as possible, from it. In this withdrawal, and in the community created by those who have withdrawn, lies the only peace that can be achieved in this world. This peace implies rejection of violence, for violence is understood as being one of the marks of the "outside" world. Such sectarian pacifism is usually, though not always, religious, as in the so-called "peace churches" in American society.

The second pacifist path assumes just the opposite about human possibilities in history: that society can be perfected, so that strife will be ended and there will be no occasion for violence. The ideal was stated by Erasmus and developed in the "perpetual peace" theorists of the Enlightenment era; in the contemporary American peace debate it is found in such diverse places as the writings of Jonathan Schell and the World Order Movement. In its ideal expression, this utopian form of pacifism identifies peace with the creation of a universal political order which, by its very universality, represents the end of war. The causes of strife in human history are identified with the nation-state, and the dissolution of states into a universal polity thus removes these causes from history. Once established, then, there will be no reason why the universal society will ever go out of being. Establishing it is, for the utopian pacifist tradition, within the reach of human action; so the quest for peace must imply the rejection of violence in the service of the nation-state, the preference of more inclusive forms of political ordering over any individual state, and the effort to achieve a world political order that will replace all states and thus, by definition, end all armed conflicts between individual states.

The third path in the quest for peace in Western culture is just war tradition, which takes a middle road between the two positions sketched above in its conception of human nature and of what is possible in human history. This tradition seeks peace in the existence of a just social order in which human rights are protected and human values flourish. Where such a social order does not exist, for this tradition there is no genuine peace, for the mere absence of overt violence alone (as in a totalitarian dictatorship, for example, or as in a nonaggression agreement between two unjust societies that preserves the status quo between them) is no real peace. For this reason, just war tradition has classically held that there are certain conditions under which a resort to military force—coupled with restraint in accord with the requirements of justice—may provide the best available way to serve the cause of peace.

This is why, in the thought of Ambrose of Milan in the fourth century, the obligation to intervene to protect an innocent person from an unjust assailant includes the right to use the sword against the evildoer; it is why, in the thirteenth-century reflections on war of Thomas Aquinas, the three justifications for resort to force conceived by the Romans remained apt: recovery of something wrongly taken, defense against unjust attack, and the restraint and punishment of evil; and it is why, in modern international law, the right of self-defense has been preserved for nations and groups of nations even in the face of great pressure to outlaw resort to military force and thus, putatively, to abolish war.

Thinking about peace in just war terms, however, requires a certain pessimism about human nature and prospects for achieving a just social order across the globe. This tradition holds out no utopian vision of a world without strife. It has developed through history around the experience of challenges to justice in human relations—challenges not able to be met except by the use of force. It assumes, at least for practical purposes, that such challenges are going to continue throughout human history, so that the need for a just presence of force to ward off injustice will also remain.

On this understanding of human possibility, then, the concept of peace has several different levels of meaning. The ideal—a just social order in which human rights and values flourish and are protected—may be approached by empirical human societies in history, and it is positively to be sought by political means, though it is not expected ever to be fully achieved over the whole face of humankind and for all time. This ideal of peace serves to provide the reference point for positive statecraft within the framework of the just war tradition. George Weigel has encapsulated this positive thrust of the tradition toward a condition of just peace in the phrase *jus ad pacem*.[45]

This concept of peace also defines the just war conception of when force may be employed justly and what the limits of just force should be. That reference point has meaning, however, only within societies which themselves honor the ideal of a just social order and approach it in their own historical existence. Peace, on this level, refers to the conditions of life inside such societies and to the ability of such societies to deter or defend against challenges to those conditions of life. On the same level, it refers to the ability and willingness of such societies to influence and aid others toward achieving similar conditions for their own citizens—exporting and spreading the *jus ad pacem*. Finally, on a third and derivative level, the concept of peace in just war tradition means the attempt to protect justice, when challenged, by other means than military ones where possible; this is the intention of the tradition's requirement that resort to force be a *last* resort. Yet as already noted, the avoidance of armed conflict itself is not a sufficient definition of peace.

American society, in both its ideals and its empirical reality, embodies a commitment to protect human rights and values and allow them to flourish. When Americans debate how to achieve peace, they should not overlook the peace this society has achieved through its institutions in realization of its national ideals. At the same time, they should frankly measure the relative degree of peace—in the sense of a just social order protecting, preserving, and nourishing human rights and values—found in other societies with which our own is in competition. One point of relevance of just war tradition to the contemporary American search for peace is, then, to remind Americans engaged in that search of a concept of peace that implies not just the absence of war but the positive presence of justice in human relations.

There is, however, more: this tradition offers a view of human nature and of the nature of politics that keeps in center focus the relative fragility of efforts to protect and preserve human rights and values. There *is* evil in the world, this tradition says; sooner or later this evil will mount a challenge against those social orders which have achieved some measure of justice in themselves and in their relations with others. Such challenges may be through armed force, and armed force may be necessary to protect and preserve the values threatened by preserving the integrity and strength of the societies that honor and nourish those values. The proper understanding of the achievement of peace, then, is that it means the creation of such societies and their preservation as just societies, even when that preservation requires military means.

Finally, it is also true that this conception of the nature of peace and its relation to the use of armed force rules out many sorts of uses of such force. Since the emphasis is on the maintenance of justice, on the protection and preservation of human rights and values, there is a clear bias in favor of defense, and in favor of societies that are themselves relatively just. The international law attempt to outlaw first use of force as inherently aggressive while approving second—defensive—resort to force is an expression of this preference, though it tends to oversimplify the tradition by the first use-second use dichotomy. (Preemption by a just state seeking to preserve itself is not morally wrong; defense by an unjust social entity is not inherently right.)

In terms of the just war tradition, American society has an obligation to foster a just peace and supporting political institutions in the world, but correspondingly to maintain the military strength necessary to preserve itself as a society that has achieved a high level of justice for its members and in its relations with other national societies. It may—indeed must, in the last resort—use that strength to protect its own ability to achieve or to protect these goods. In this duality lies the just war conception of peace in history: the successful promulgation of human rights and values and their protection against the challenges of evil.

❖   ❖   ❖

The case for the relevance of any set of ideas at any time in history rests not only on the power of the ideas in themselves to inform and elucidate the issues in question. Relevance also depends crucially on whether these ideas are perceived as able to do so and applied tellingly by those who thus perceive them. The final case for the relevance of just war tradition to contemporary American culture, then, must rest on the abilities of those who employ concepts from this tradition to persuade others of the correctness of their arguments. This is always a task to be done and is never finished; thus, the case for relevance can never be answered in its entirety, once and for all, but must be made anew in every new context.

## Notes

1. Robert W. Tucker, *The Just War* (Baltimore: The Johns Hopkins Press, 1960).
2. Ibid., 35.
3. Russell F. Weigley, *The American Way of War* (New York: Macmillan Publishing Co.; London: Collier Macmillan Publishers, 1973).
4. Ronald H. Stone and Dana Wilbanks, *The Peacemaking Struggle: Militarism and Resistance* (Lanham, Md.: University Press of America, 1985), 4.
5. Ibid.
6. Ibid., 1, 3.
7. Ibid., 81.
8. Ibid., 86.
9. Alan Geyer, *The Idea of Disarmament!* (Elgin, Ill.: The Brethren Press, 1982), 224-30.
10. Ibid.
11. United Methodist Council of Bishops, *In Defense of Creation* (Nashville, Tenn.: Graded Press, 1986).

12. Stone and Wilbanks, "Shall Presbyterianism Become a Resistance Church?" (unpublished, 1986).

13. Stone and Wilbanks, *The Peacemaking Struggle*, 185-95.

14. John Howard Yoder, *When War Is Unjust* (Minneapolis: Augsburg Publishing House, 1984), especially chapters 5 and 6.

15. Stanley Hoffmann, *Duties beyond Borders* (Syracuse, N.Y.: Syracuse University Press, 1981), chapter 2.

16. Ibid., 50-52.

17. But see James Turner Johnson, *Just War Tradition and the Restraint of War* (Princeton, N.J. and Guildford, Surrey, U.K.: Princeton University Press, 1981), and *Can Modern War Be Just?* (New Haven and London: Yale University Press, 1984).

18. James F. Childress, *Moral Responsibility in Conflicts* (Baton Rouge and London: Louisiana State University Press, 1982), chapter 3.

19. Hoffmann, 55.

20. Ibid., 59-61.

21. Michael Walzer, *Just and Unjust Wars* (New York: Basic Books, 1977), xiv.

22. Johnson, *Just War Tradition*, 20-30.

23. See further Johnson, *Ideology, Reason, and the Limitation of War* (Princeton and London: Princeton University Press), chapter 4.

24. Ibid., 259-74.

25. See further Anthony Hartle (Col., USA), "A Military Ethic in an Age of Terror." *Parameters* 17.2 (Summer 1987): 68-75.

26. Caspar W. Weinberger, *Report of Secretary of Defense Caspar W. Weinberger to the Congress*, 5 February 1986.

27. George P. Shultz, "The Ethics of Power" (Address at the Convocation of Yeshiva University, New York, 9 December 1984).

28. See notes 17 and 23 above.

29. Johnson, *Just War Tradition*, 330-38.

30. George Weigel, *Tranquillitas Ordinis* (Oxford and New York: Oxford University Press, 1987).

31. William V. O'Brien, *The Conduct of Just and Limited War* (New York: Praeger Publishers, 1981).

32. Stanley Hauerwas, *Against the Nations* (Minneapolis, Chicago, and New York: Winston Press, 1985).

33. National Conference of Catholic Bishops, *The Challenge of Peace* (Washington, D.C.: United States Catholic Conference, 1983).

34. Paul Ramsey, *War and the Christian Conscience* (Durham, N.C.: Duke University Press, 1961).

35. Childress, chapter 3.

36. James Brown Scott, *The Spanish Origin of International Law* (Oxford: Clarendon Press; London: Humphrey Milford, 1934.)

37. National Conference of Catholic Bishops, 47, paragraph 150.

38. Ibid., 67-69, paragraphs 215-19.

39. Ibid., 60, paragraph 190, and 58, paragraph 184.

40. Ibid., 68, paragraph 216.

41. Emerich de Vattel, *The Law of Nations or the Principles of Natural Law* (Washington, D.C.: Carnegie Institution, 1916), book 3, section 158.

42. National Conference of Catholic Bishops, "A Report on 'The Challenge of Peace' and Policy Developments 1983-1988." *Origins* 18.9 (July 21): 133-47.

43. Ibid., 144-45.

44. Here I am abstracting from the analysis in James Turner Johnson, *The Quest for Peace: Three Moral Traditions in Western Cultural History* (Princeton, N.J. and Guildford, Surrey, U.K.: Princeton University Press, 1987).

45. See Weigel, *Tranquillitas Ordinis*, and his essay in the present volume.

# THE CONVERSATION

Harry Summers began the discussion by observing that the just war tradition is alive and well in its substance, in the laws of land warfare, in the Hague and Geneva Conventions, and in the U.S. Uniform Code of Military Justice. Summers also suggested that the just war tradition reinforces three principles central to the American foreign policy debate: idealism, isolationism, and pragmatism. The tradition's insistence on moral imperatives in the conduct of war appeals to our idealism and our self-understanding as a people with a moral consciousness. The tradition's notion that there are certain wars we should not fight, regardless of their intrinsic justice, because they are beyond our means to win, appeals to that variant of isolationism which reminds us of the dangers of dissipating American power in a recalcitrant, chaotic world. Finally, the tradition's emphasis on moral reasoning coheres with our pragmatic strain and our skepticism toward ideological fanaticism.

That the principles embodied in the tradition are part of the American psyche was well demonstrated in the Vietnam War, where we did our utmost to abide by certain restraints in spite of an enemy unwilling to reciprocate. The revulsion felt by the American people toward the My Lai massacre, and the swiftness with which its perpetrators were brought to justice, illustrated Americans' instinctive regard for those principles which are the core elements of the just war tradition. In the past, the public has promptly rebuffed any military or political leader who has flouted the tradition.

Alberto Coll noted with appreciation James Turner Johnson's description of the just war tradition, not as a set of inflexible norms, but as a framework for moral reasoning that embraces natural law, prudential calculation, an ethic of motivation, the accumulated experience of statecraft, reflection on the rights of persons, and religious insight. The just war tradition forces decision makers to ask difficult questions and to lay bare their own implicit normative assumptions.

Coll disagreed with Robert Tucker's argument that the classical just war tradition is inimical to American culture, given the United States' supposed tendency to transform its wars into outpourings of limitless violence. According to Coll, the United States has not shown, at any point in its history, greater willingness to discard limits to warfare than its contemporaries. We did not wage the Revolutionary War, the Civil War, the two World Wars, or the Korean and Vietnam Wars any more viciously than our adversaries or friends. Tucker's use of the Eisenhower administration's strategy of "massive retaliation" as one of his illustrations was unpersuasive because such a strategy was part of a politically and economically conservative policy on the part of the United States, aimed at containing the Soviet Union without resort to general war or endless Third World interventions. While actual resort to massive retaliation would have been a case of unlimited violence, the employment of massive retaliation as a strategy of deterrence was a highly calculated bluff designed to keep the peace through moderate means.

Returning to the specifics of Johnson's paper, Coll underlined the close relationship between the just war tradition and the early development of international law, especially in their common recognition of the legitimacy of the use of force for purposes of self-defense against aggression, the apprehension and punishment of barbaric criminals, and the upholding of basic human rights against particularly vicious forms of tyranny. Unfortunately, continued Coll, the only one of these three useful links to the just war tradition that modern international law has retained is the notion that self-defense justifies the use of force. And even in this area, contemporary international law defines self-defense much more narrowly than moral reasoning would do; an example is the 1986 ruling by the International Court of Justice that Nicaragua's shipments of arms to the Salvadoran guerrillas did not constitute aggression against El Salvador and therefore could not justify the American use of force against Nicaragua.

International law would substantially enhance its credibility by returning to its roots in just war theory and prudential reasoning. This would enable it to broaden its definition of aggression to include unconventional forms of violence such as terrorism and guerrilla war. Similarly, it would allow international law to recognize the appropriate use of discriminate and limited force for the purpose of capturing and punishing the modern equivalent of seventeenth century pirates—terrorists. Finally, such a renovation of its early roots would permit international law to admit that force, when carried out with certain restraints, may be lawful in order to return the right of self-determination to peoples oppressed by unusually severe despotisms, such as Uganda under Idi Amin, Cambodia under Pol Pot, or Grenada under Bernard Coard.

Coll suggested that efforts to apply the just war tradition to national security policy, such as the criteria for the use of force enunciated by Secretary of Defense Weinberger in 1984, ought to be constructed more imaginatively than Weinberger had done. First, force is appropriate not only in response to clear-cut conventional aggression, but also to low-intensity forms of violence. Second, the United States should be prepared to use force not only in support of vital interests and allies as underlined by the secretary of defense, but also for the sake of upholding the global balance of power. It was important not to allow our adversaries to chip at the edges of Western power by gradually expanding their influence and reducing ours in various parts of the Third World. Third, the traditional just war notion that force is justified only when there is a reasonable prospect of success should not be interpreted too rigidly. Even if the prospects for success of the anticommunist guerrillas in Nicaragua, Angola, and Afghanistan were small, the United States was not morally compelled to turn down aid requests from such groups. By helping to sustain the resistance movements, American aid caused the Soviet Union to spend disproportionately larger sums of money in response, thereby leaving the USSR with fewer resources to devote to aggressive purposes and increasing the economic pressures on it to liquidate its Third World imperial holdings.

David Hollenbach agreed that the just war tradition is primarily oriented toward the pursuit of peace, and that it starts from the premise that the use of force is unlawful except in certain defined circumstances. Most of the scholars who have explored the tradition in recent years, including William O'Brien, John Langan, and James Childress, would also agree. But many religious activists and church leaders see the tradition as simply an instrument for legitimating violence, and they have functionally discarded it as unsuitable for our times.

Harry Summers perceived a similar dissonance within American society between the public's view of just war and the American military's. The U.S. Army clings tenaciously to the view that war can be fought for just purposes and with just means, and therefore prosecuted Lt. Calley and his accomplices in the My Lai massacre so as to maintain the integrity of those just war principles underlying the U.S. Uniform Code of Military Justice. The public's view, however, was different. Both the right and the left argued that Calley was a poor scapegoat, the right implying that such atrocities as he committed were a normal part of war and should not be prosecuted, and the left suggesting that war by its very nature is barbaric and the only way to civilize it is not to engage in it at all. Summers was worried that large segments of the American public seemed to posit an absolute antinomy between "war" and "justice."

John Ahearne remarked that most peace activists do not take the just war tradition seriously because, from their perspective, the tradition has rarely if ever been an effective brake on state violence. As illustrations, the peace activists cite the numerous "moral justifications" offered for Sherman's march to the sea, for strategic bombing in World War II and the atomic bombing of Japan, and for the launching of the Grenada invasion. It would be difficult, Ahearne argued, to find a case in which the just war tradition shaped national security policy by barring a particular course of action or prescribing a truly moral alternative. At this point, Summers indicated that the Vietnam war was an example of the just war tradition serving as an effective brake on military strategy. The North Vietnamese, argued Summers, knew that the United States could annihilate their country but would not do so because of domestic political and moral constraints. In Summers's view, the constraints perceived by Hanoi sprang directly from the living presence of the just war tradition in the American national psyche.

James Childress seconded Ahearne's point about the skepticism of religious activists, but thought that it was primarily directed against the application of just war criteria to morally ambiguous situations such as Vietnam or Grenada, rather than against the criteria themselves. If the United States became involved in an undisputably "clean" war, many activists would endorse the application of just war analysis to that war. Childress thought that the principles embodied in the just war tradition were less controversial, and more widely accepted, than their application to recent U.S. wars.

John Donahue added that many nonleftist, politically moderate Roman Catholics were uncomfortable with the just war tradition, in part because of reservations about natural law approaches to moral reasoning, but also because the post-Vatican II revolution in Catholic theology and spirituality had led them to rediscover the biblical tradition, which they interpreted as giving a near absolute character to Jesus' ethic of "love thy neighbor"—an ethic they deem incompatible with just war reasoning. For these Roman Catholics, biblical theology and ethics are a more authoritative guide than the natural law principles contained in the just war tradition.

James Turner Johnson thought that the U.S. Catholic bishops had missed a golden opportunity in their 1983 pastoral letter on nuclear weapons to introduce the laity and clergy to the intellectual riches of the just war tradition. The just war tradition has always recognized the importance of peace as a moral and political goal. But it defines peace, not as the mere absence of conflict, but as "rightly ordered peace": a situation in which persons are free to secure their liberty, dignity, and essential rights. This notion of "rightly ordered peace" has distinguished Catholic thought on peace from common variants of pacifism or "peace at any price." The bishops should have used their pastoral letter to educate the public about this vital distinction, and more broadly, about the complex relationship of national power and military force to international peace, justice, and order.

Robert Gessert detected in American culture a deep aversion to thinking about war in a philosophically or morally serious way. Agreeing with Robert Tucker, he argued that the Eisenhower strategy of "massive retaliation" was essentially an escapist strategy, a way to buy defense "on the cheap" without having to engage in the complex calculus of determining proportionality or discrimination. John Kennedy's pledge to unleash "the full retaliatory power of the United States" in response to the firing of a single missile from Cuba, and Robert McNamara's enshrinement of "Mutual Assured Destruction" as our key strategic doctrine, were other examples of the American tendency to eschew the kinds of complex, nuanced moral calculations implicit in just war doctrine. While the just war tradition is ultimately concerned with justice, the American public is mostly concerned with avoiding a costly military conflict.

David Wessels thought that contemporary just war theorists should devote greater attention to the classic criterion that a just war must be carried out by the "proper authority." In today's world it is necessary to rethink the definition of proper authority and to take into consideration norms of legitimacy prescribed and articulated by the United Nations Charter, the UN Security Council, the International Court of Justice, the Geneva Conventions, and the 1928 Kellogg-Briand Treaty outlawing war as an instrument of national policy. Given the mutual vulnerability of states to each other's military and economic policies, the mere fact that the legally constituted government of a nation-state decides on a particular policy does not make that policy the instrument of a "proper authority." That was true, for example, with regard to the U.S. mining of Nicaraguan harbors, which the International Court of Justice determined to be unlawful. In a case like this, it is appropriate to raise the question whether the U.S. government acted as a "proper authority" in following a policy that was internationally recognized as illegitimate.

Wessels also argued that greater attention should be paid to the ambiguity of the phrase "military necessity" in American military doctrine. Without careful qualification, the concept of necessity can eviscerate the substance of just war doctrine. Johnson agreed that there is an ambiguity, and that, historically, necessity has meant one of two different things: "everything that is necessary to win the war is lawful" or "you can do everything that is lawful." Only the second formulation is compatible with just war doctrine, while the first tends to nullify it. Wessels noted that, under the pressures of war, many officers and most common soldiers will disregard justice in the name of necessity and will interpret necessity in Johnson's first sense.

Harry Summers strongly disagreed. In his thirty-five years of military service he had found very few soldiers of the type described by Wessels. In fact, most American servicemen know that they are obligated to obey only lawful orders. Officers who attempt to cajole their men into violating the laws of war find that their troops will not obey them; they may fire at the target, for example, but will "miss." The principles of the just war tradition are deeply ingrained in most American soldiers, insisted Summers.

For James Woolsey, the *jus in bello* component of just war theory was not problematical. Not only do the American military understand its basic lineaments; it is also a set of principles with which the nation can live without endangering its security or vital interests. The real problem with just war theory is the *jus ad bellum*, which in a democracy comes to be interpreted so restrictively as to be a recipe for passivity. The Weinberger criteria for the use of force illustrated this, Woolsey thought. They failed to provide policy makers with the intellectual framework for responding to Soviet probings in less than vital areas of the globe such as Central America. By focusing on present threats, the *jus ad bellum* is also an inadequate source of guidance in a drawn-out contest with an adversary like the USSR that thinks several strategic moves ahead.

James Turner Johnson responded that contemporary just war theorists had spent too much time arguing with pacifists, and thus had concentrated on the *jus in bello* dimension of the tradition. It was time to take up Coll's challenge to examine the *jus ad bellum*'s application to contemporary forms of unconventional violence such as guerrilla warfare and terrorism. With reference to Woolsey's second point, Johnson observed that the just war tradition does not rule out preemption. One of the challenges faced by contemporary just war theorists is to develop the criteria under which preemption may be justified in order to check an expanding threat in its early stages.

David Hollenbach thought that the lines of just war development recommended by Coll and Woolsey would make it almost indistinguishable from *raison d'état*. In a world of nuclear weapons and unprecedented mutual vulnerability, the tradition can maintain its moral and intellectual integrity only by prescribing some radical restraints on the use of armed force, along the lines of the Weinberger criteria.

Coll demurred, arguing that, while there is always a danger of the tradition collapsing into *raison d'état*, there is the equally serious danger of just war theory not coming to grips with the moral implications of a collapse of the *pax occidentalis* as a result of Western passivity. In the highly interdependent world of the late twentieth century, the fairly civilized and humane international order upheld by Western power since 1945 faces indirect threats and unconventional forms of aggression which, unless addressed effectively, can undermine its strength over a period of time, resulting in eventual political defeat for the West.

Wrapping up the discussion, James Turner Johnson noted that the issues facing just war theorists were twofold. First, what was the place of the tradition in American culture? Was it deeply rooted in the American psyche, as Summers suggested, or was it in contradiction with basic American values, as Tucker and others argued? Second, how should just war thinking redefine the problem of peace in the modern world? How should the tradition sketch the meaning of a "rightly ordered peace" today? To what extent do various forms of unconventional violence, in combination with the power of authoritarian states, threaten such peace, and what criteria should the *jus ad bellum* develop for addressing these and other low-intensity threats to human freedom and order?

JAMES F. CHILDRESS

# Contemporary Pacifism: Its Major Types and Possible Contributions to Discourse about War

My intention is to offer an analytical framework for interpreting and assessing the contributions of pacifists to contemporary debates about war. Although much of what I present will be sketchy, it may offer a starting point for a discussion of various presuppositions and implications of pacifist positions. I will proceed by first trying to determine what is distinctive about pacifism relative to other positions—particularly just war theories—on the spectrum of modes of resistance to evil. While seeking what is distinctive, I will also note that both pacifists and just warriors appeal to some similar arguments for their suspicion of infringements of the moral limits they stress. Then I will present a typology of pacifist positions according to their mode of moral reasoning, while also adumbrating their approaches to grounds of justification, agents of pacifist action, and stringency and range of pacifist principles. Finally, I will consider ways in which pacifists may contribute to or confuse the contemporary debate about war.

## I. THE NATURE OF PACIFISM

Often supporters and critics alike assume that they know what pacifism is, but many different positions march under the banner of pacifism. It is thus important to begin to clarify the nature of pacifism, rather than simply asserting that we know it, just as we know pornography, when we see it. Any assessment of pacifism's contributions—or, more accurately, the contributions of pacifist positions—to contemporary discourse about war must attend to the variety of pacifist positions, as well as to what they share.

The term "pacifism" is a relatively recent addition to our vocabulary. The earliest use of the term recorded in the Supplement to the *Oxford English Dictionary* (1982) is 1902, when a Frenchman at an international peace congress used and perhaps even coined the word "pacifism" to mean "anti-war-ism."[1] As "making peace," pacifism may be defined by any particular proponent (or opponent) to include various *positive* attitudes and actions. Nevertheless, for our purposes, a first effort to identify the common element in pacifist positions should focus on their *negative* stance: opposition to war and/or to participation in war. I have defended this definition elsewhere,[2] but I am not totally satisfied with it, largely because, as I will argue, even just war theories could qualify as pacifist under a loose interpretation of "opposition" because of their presumption against the use of armed force. I now think that the best term for this opposition is "disavowal," as suggested by Reinhold Niebuhr, who once defined pacifism as an expression of a "critical attitude toward the use of force by *disavowing* it completely in at least one important situation."[3] During one period, Niebuhr himself disavowed the use of force in international conflicts and thus was appropriately considered a pacifist.[4] More recently, Stanley Hauerwas, a Christian pacifist, has construed pacifism as "any position that involves the disavowal of violence as a means to secure otherwise legitimate ends."[5]

Such a disavowal does not necessarily entail the denial of the use of armed force—and I will concentrate on *armed* force—in intranational affairs or even in self-defense. However, the criterion of universalizability does require the pacifist to identify the relevant similarities and differences between international conflicts where armed force is disavowed and other conflicts where it is accepted. While a pacifist may disavow either a nation-state's use of armed force in international conflicts or his/her own participation in such armed force, many pacifists disavow both. Nevertheless, as we will see later, this distinction is important, because some sectarian pacifists disavow participation in war, perhaps disassociating themselves from evil by refusing to serve in the military, to pay taxes, etc., without trying to alter the government's military policies or even proposing a political alternative to them.

Where does pacifism fall among the various modes of resistance to evil, including injustice? Christians and others have vigorously disputed where they should draw lines and set limits in individual and social responses to evil. Following is a spectrum of positions:[6]

(i)   Nonresistance
(ii)  Nonviolent resistance

(iii)   Limited violent resistance (discrimination and proportionality)
(iv)   Limited violent resistance (proportionality only)
(v)   Unlimited violent resistance

Even though there is some debate about how passive pacifism must be, there is general agreement that both (i) nonresistance, represented by traditional Mennonites, and (ii) nonviolent resistance, represented by Gandhi, King, and the Quakers, may fit under the pacifist rubric (though, again, pacifism itself involves disavowal of war). The doctrine of nonresistance, based on the New Testament admonition, usually permits responses to evil that merely attempt to persuade or convert the evil-doer; but some proponents interpret it to rule out ballots as well as bullets. Nonviolent resistance may encompass various acts, such as economic boycotts, as long as they do not involve violence. (Of course, there is considerable debate about the boundaries between nonviolence and violence.)

There is also general agreement that (iii) violent resistance involving war limited by the principle of discrimination (in addition to the principle of proportionality) qualifies as a just war theory. This position is affirmed by the Roman Catholic tradition, by such Protestant theologians as Paul Ramsey, and by such secular political theorists as Michael Walzer.[7] Some would deny that just war theory encompasses a position (iv) that limits violent resistance (including war) *only* by the principle of proportionality, while neglecting the principle of discrimination, or treating it only as a rule of thumb, or allowing it to be easily overridden by proportionality. However, it can be argued that Reinhold Niebuhr, who held such a position, was a just war theorist, though obviously not a traditional one.[8] The main difference between (iii) and (iv), then, is whether they limit violence by the principle of discrimination—noncombatant immunity from direct attack—and proportionality, or only by the principle of proportionality.

The 1944 responses by John C. Ford, S. J. and Niebuhr to Allied "area" or "obliteration" bombing are instructive. Although both Ford and Niebuhr argued against such bombing, their arguments reflect the differences between positions (iii) and (iv). Ford contended that "it is impossible to adopt this strategy [of obliteration bombing] without having the direct intent of violating the rights of innocent civilians. This intent is, of course, gravely immoral."[9] But even if this intent had not been present and the destruction had been indirect, it would still have been wrong because it lacked a proportionately grave cause. By contrast, Niebuhr was willing to assess the indiscriminate means according to their probable consequences, contending that as long as there were other alternatives, the obliteration bombing was not warranted and was even counterproductive. His negative judgment was based on proportionality.[10]

Position (v) unlimited violent resistance, represented by a crusade or holy war, recognizes no moral limits—whether nonviolence, or discrimination, or proportionality—in the effort to eliminate by armed force what is viewed as evil or unjust, perhaps because the evil or injustice that is opposed simply overwhelms any moral constraints on means.

It is important to note on the above spectrum that the first four positions *disavow* some means of resistance, i.e., those means affirmed by the *next* position on the spectrum. Moving from left to right, from (i) to (v), each position also rejects or modifies the *preceding* position on the spectrum by holding that it would allow terrible consequences to occur in its strict adherence to certain limits on means. Thus, proponents of (ii) nonviolent resistance contend that (i) nonresistance involves capitulation to evil, while proponents of (iii) insist that reliance upon nonviolent resistance alone in some circumstances would allow evil to triumph. The same points hold for (iv) in relation to (iii), and (v) in relation to (iv). These arguments have some rhetorical force because both pacifist and just war theories assert moral limits in the realization of justice in the world, even though they obviously disagree about the location of those limits.

Although positions (i)-(iv) draw lines in different places, their fundamental arguments for adhering to those limits, even in the face of bad consequences, are often very similar and sometimes even identical. The fundamental theological-ethical argument is one of *limited human responsibility*—both causal responsibility and liability—for outcomes: Human beings are not responsible for every evil or injustice that occurs, if the only effective means of resistance would cross the line or transgress the limit set on resistance, because God is ultimately in control of history. This theological conviction may undergird respect for limits even when the probable historical consequences appear to justify their violation. As we move across the spectrum, from left to right, each position guards against the next one in part by appealing to limits on human responsibility set by God's creation, providential order, and redemption. For example, the pacifist John Howard Yoder contends that the Christian is not responsible for using armed force to make history come out right because God is ultimately in control, whereas the just warrior Paul Ramsey invokes God's responsibility for history to argue against the violation of such moral rules as the prohibition of direct attacks on civilians.[11] Finally, Reinhold Niebuhr, who tended to focus less on God's actions in history than on God's will and order beyond history, rejected position (v) because it considered only one end—the eradication of evil or injustice—which is a transhistorical goal that cannot be achieved in history but can only be realized by God beyond history.[12]

Some related arguments support this primary argument about limited human responsibility and, especially in secular contexts, may even be primary: imperfect information—the limited human capacity to predict outcomes—and ethical fallibility—the limited human capacity to assess outcomes—especially in transgressing moral limits.[13] These arguments do not rule out discriminating moral judgments in history; they only caution us against justifying infringements of moral limits for the sake of predicted, desirable outcomes, especially in situations of multiple actors. For example, while supporting position (iv) in the war against Hitler, Reinhold Niebuhr rejected the widespread temptation to view the war as a holy war (v) to eradicate evil without regard for proportionality. He insisted on distinguishing the "proximate goals of justice" sought in the war from the holiness represented by God. He also held that the cause was not "holy" in the sense of being "unqualifiedly good"; the achievements of its defenders were "ambiguous," particularly because they had contributed to the rise of Hitler, and their weapons were "terrible" rather than holy.[14]

Niebuhr defended position (iv) against (v), but defenses of other positions on the spectrum have also appealed to imperfect information and ethical fallibility. For example, thinkers as diverse as Leo Tolstoy, Mohandas K. Gandhi, and Hannah Arendt have defended their reluctance to depart from nonresistance (i) or nonviolence (ii) on such grounds. Tolstoy emphasized both ethical fallibility and imperfect information in maintaining the law of nonresistance. In discussing the stock example of a criminal about to kill or molest a child, Tolstoy tried to show that for both the Christian and the non-Christian there is "no reasonable foundation" for the common justification of an act of violence against the criminal. Tolstoy first stressed imperfect information: "By killing the [criminal] he kills for certain; whereas he cannot know positively whether the criminal would have killed the child or not." Then Tolstoy turned to ethical fallibility: "Who shall say whether the child's life was more needed, was better, than the other's life?"[15]

Emphasizing ethical fallibility, Gandhi argued that *Satyagraha*, one's firm and steadfast adherence to one's own conception of Truth until convinced that it is mistaken, can never become so certain that the agent supposes that violence is justified on its behalf. Truth "excludes the use of violence because man is not capable of knowing the absolute truth and therefore is not competent to punish." There can only be "experiments with truth." "Ahimsa (nonharm) is the farthest limit of humility." "We have always control over the means but not over the end."[16]

Concentrating on imperfect information, Arendt raises serious questions about when violence is rational: "since we can never know with any certainty the eventual consequences of what we are doing, violence can remain rational only if it pursues short-term goals." The end of human action can never be reliably predicted, because its consequences persist

throughout time. While inaction is not warranted by imperfect information, the means of action take on special significance, for the odds are
better in betting on the act than on its consequences. For example, the
most probable result of violence is a more violent world because the act
of violence itself adds to violence, whatever its consequences might be.[17]

Despite their different philosophical and theological contexts, Arendt,
Gandhi, and Tolstoy invoke ethical fallibility and/or imperfect information to provide strong reasons for varying degrees of suspicion about
engaging in violence, but similar arguments are offered by proponents of
(iii) or (iv) against consequentialist pleas to break their set limits in order
to produce better outcomes in the world. In most positions of nonresistance (i) or nonviolent resistance (ii), appeals to ethical fallibility and
imperfect information, as well as to limited human responsibility, only
deepen the reluctance to engage in violence, just as they only deepen the
reluctance on the part of just war theorists to breach rules of discrimination and/or proportionality. These appeals do not themselves ground
any of the positions (i-iv); the grounds are found elsewhere, in other
ethical, theological, and anthropological convictions. I will explore some
grounds for pacifist positions as I develop a typology of those positions.

## II.   TYPES OF PACIFISM

It is not necessary to identify as many varieties of pacifism as Yoder
does in order to appreciate the diversity of pacifism and the large number
of targets opponents of pacifism must attack.[18] This variety is important
because evaluations of pacifism may depend on the type(s) of pacifism
being considered, and positive or negative judgments about some types of
pacifism may not extend to all pacifist positions.[19] The following typology
distinguishes four main types of pacifism according to their mode of
reasoning; i.e., whether the reasoning is deontological, consequentialist,
or a mixture. In addition, I will discuss whether the ground of the position
is alleged to be particularistic (e.g., based on revelation) or universalistic
(e.g., based on natural law or reason), and thus whether it is held to apply
to particular individuals or groups who can apprehend the fundamental
principles or to all individuals and groups, including nation-states,
because the fundamental principles are universal and human beings have
the natural capacity to grasp and apply them even in statecraft. The
ground of each position will also include various theological, metaphysical, and anthropological arguments. And it will determine in part who may
and should be agents of pacifism—individuals, the church, or the state.
Questions of ground and agency obviously involve issues of ecclesiology
such as those raised by Ernst Troeltsch in his distinction between

"church-type" and "sect-type."[20] It is also important to consider both the range and the stringency of the pacifist position: How strong is its disavowal of armed force in war—i.e., is it absolute, prima facie, or relative? What is its range—i.e., does it apply to all wars, only to modern wars, or only to certain kinds of modern wars? Such ideal types, in Max Weber's sense,[21] can help us see what is at stake in the debate between pacifists and just warriors, but they must be used with caution in full awareness that they necessarily oversimplify real positions. And in the final section of this essay I will suggest some ways in which pacifists have modified the traditional categories and classifications in recent years.

## 1. Legalistic-expressive pacifism

This type of pacifism may view Scripture as law and hold that the commandment of neighbor-love and the "hard sayings" obligate the Christian to refrain from violence. Or, in a somewhat different version, it may hold that Christians ought to express or witness to reality (e.g., Christ, God's sovereignty, or the Kingdom to come) or fundamental values (e.g., life) or norms (e.g., love). For example, John Howard Yoder holds that "nonresistance is right, in the deepest sense, not because it works, but because it anticipates the triumph of the Lamb that was slain."[22] And Thomas Merton insisted that "Nonviolence is not for power but for truth. It is not aimed at immediate political results, but at the manifestation of fundamental and crucially important truth."[23]

While the first version of this type of pacifism uses legal-like language of law and obedience, the second version uses aesthetic language of expressive or symbolic conduct, often set in the context of the Christian story or narrative. The second version may also focus on the virtues that Christian agents should embody and display (for several of these themes, see Stanley Hauerwas's various writings).[24] Whether this first type of pacifism focuses on Scripture as revealing a law that must be followed or as disclosing a reality that must be affirmed, expressed, or symbolized, its ethical theory is nonconsequentialist, because it holds that some features of acts other than their ends and consequences make them right or wrong; those features are fidelity to law or witness to reality.[25] Even though the mode of moral reasoning of this type of pacifism is most often deontological, it is better characterized as virtue-based when it determines the rightness and wrongness of acts according to what they display about the agent.

Max Weber's distinction between *Gesinnungsethik* and *Verantwortungsethik* and Ernst Troeltsch's distinction between church and sect are both relevant for considering the agents and the stringency of this type of pacifism.[26] In distinguishing major perspectives on the moral life in politics, Weber viewed a *Gesinnungsethik*—variously translated as ethics of intention or ethics of absolute values—as requiring adherence to or expression of a value regardless of the consequences, "even if the heavens should fall." An "ethic of responsibility," by contrast, recognizes the average deficiencies of human beings (in theological terms, original sin), human responsibility for the consequences of their actions (including what happens when others act in ways that could have been avoided if we had acted in certain ways), and a willingness to use "evil" means to bring about good states of affairs. A legalistic-expressive type of pacifism clearly is a *Gesinnungsethik* because it cannot justify the use of lethal force by nations against other nations even to avoid terrible consequences. More accurately, it can accommodate appeals to consequences only within the moral limits set by pacifist doctrine. (The theological-ethical argument about limited human responsibility presented in part I is often invoked by pacifists at this juncture—just as it is also invoked by just war theorists—to maintain their limits.)

Historically, legalistic-expressive pacifism has tended to be sectarian in the sense that it is cut off from and stands in opposition to the society's moral framework of just war criteria. James Johnson has argued that absolute pacifism, the total rejection of violence and war, has usually stemmed from world-rejection, rather than being an independent position: "Sectarianism rejects the ways of society first of all, and violence and war only as included in that larger rejection. Violence and war are thus not the central evil here; they are but expressions of it."[27] However, Christian pacifists may not view the "world" or "society" as monolithic, may oppose some parts of the "world" or "society" but affirm others, and may view the use of violence as paradigmatic of the world's fallenness. Thus, their condemnation of "Constantinianism" may focus primarily on the religious legitimation of armed force, rather than being directed at the society as a whole.

In any event, this position cannot easily offer directions for the policies of nation-states because of its own particularistic ground in revelation. It thus functions largely in a prophetic mode, even when it affirms that Christ's demands are addressed to all people.[28] If it does offer directions for policies, it will probably have to find a broader epistemological basis than revelation—e.g., natural law—or use for purposes of public ethics the society's dominant moral framework of just war criteria—e.g., pacifist appeals to just war criteria to condemn the war in Vietnam or to reject nuclear deterrence. Ad hoc appeals to the society's dominant moral framework to direct policies do not preclude criticism of that framework. That criticism is often external—ultimately, according to pacifists, the just war framework should be rejected because it is wrong even if it has penultimate value in limiting wars. Sometimes, however, the criticism is internal—pacifists argue that the supporters of just war theories must show that their criteria can yield negative answers.[29] Even if they make provisional appeals to the just war framework for purposes of moral discourse with the larger society, legalistic-expressive pacifists tend to level both external and internal criticisms against just war theories. Nevertheless, it is usually unclear how they ground their alternative policies, if they offer any, for nation-states.

Some proponents of legalistic-expressive pacifism—e.g., some Mennonites—have tended to be opposed to participation in war, and have often expressed their opposition through conscientious objection or refusal; they disassociate themselves from evil without necessarily defending their pacifism as an alternative for the larger society. This dualism has often been set up in terms of church *against* the world, but other versions have also appeared *within* the church—e.g., the affirmation of pacifism as a special vocation or higher way of life.

This dualistic interpretation of legalistic-expressive pacifism has been greatly modified in recent years, as more and more proponents have argued for its political relevance. As we will see later, this frequently depends on a broader definition of politics, often within a broader temporal perspective. Furthermore, even those who agree with Hauerwas that the church is a social ethic, rather than having a social ethic, are not precluded from seeking and even hoping for positive indirect social effects.[30] However, their justification of pacifism for individuals or the Christian community does not rest on those predicted consequences. Indeed, they usually expect pacifist individuals and communities to suffer within history. By contrast, the next type of pacifism does intend to offer an alternative for national policies, based largely on claims about the consequences of pacifism.

## 2. Consequentialist pragmatic-utilitarian pacifism

This type of pacifism holds that if individuals, groups, and even nations would adopt pacifism as their policy, their actions would on the whole produce a net balance of good over bad effects. Even though it is directed at national policies, this type of pacifism is not merely a political position, because it is based on a moral imperative to do the greatest good for the greatest number. Obviously, its predictions about the consequences of a nation's adoption of a pacifist stance will depend on some convictions about human nature and the world that will be widely debated—e.g., how can pacifists suppose that nonviolence will be effective, especially in confrontation with regimes pursuing evil? If the convictions that warrant claims about effectiveness and proportionality are theologically grounded, this type of pacifism will usually be subsumed under the third type, to be developed below.

This second type of pacifism might be alleged to be nonpacifist on the ground that it is subject to change in view of an altered prediction of consequences. However, this charge can be handled through the distinction between act consequentialism and rule consequentialism.[31] If a moral theory evaluates each act in terms of its consequences, then pacifism could be no more than a maxim or rule of thumb without binding power on particular actions. We would rightly hesitate to use the label "pacifism" for such a position, even though it might reject a particular war. If, however, a moral theory evaluates rules rather than acts in terms of their consequences and then evaluates acts by their relation to the rules (rule consequentialism), then pacifism could be viewed as a stable position within this framework. Even so, it would be difficult to defend an absolutist pacifism within a consequentialist perspective; at most, nonviolence would appear to be prima facie binding. And the fundamental problem remains: the justification of claims about the positive long-term effects of pacifist policies in the face of immediate consequences that appear to be terrible and perhaps even irreversible if pacifism is followed.

Of course, it is relevant to note that wars do not always achieve their ends and are almost always unsuccessful for one side and often unsuccessful for both. Furthermore, theorists of effective nonviolence answer the charge of irrationality by pointing to the interdependence of means and ends and also to comparative costs of nonviolent and military efforts. For example, Gandhi conceded that the costs of nonviolent resistance are high and that a nonviolent defense of India against Japan in the 1940s would risk the loss of several million lives, but he claimed that the cost would be no greater than the cost of military action and that the ends brought about by different means would be quite different.[32] Such proponents of nonviolence as Gordon Zahn hold that the problem is not that nonviolence is ineffective but that insufficient effort has been devoted to making it work, particularly in comparison with the support for violent solutions: "Nonviolent alternatives to war are the answer, but until now we have devoted far too little effort to discovering ways to make them effective."[33] However, in the end, larger theological-metaphysical-anthropological claims become central and will be addressed below.

Some versions of consequentialist pacifism are negative rather than positive. For example, when Reinhold Niebuhr was a pacifist, his argument was less that pacifism would work than that international violence would be "worthless" and "suicidal."[34] Pacifist policies would thus produce the least evil. In its modern form, this negative pacifism often blends with technological pacifism (to be discussed below), because of its emphasis on the terrible destructiveness of modern war.

### 3. Redemptive witness pacifism

This third type of pacifism combines features of the first two. Whereas the first type holds that pacifism is right even if it is ineffective, and the second type holds that pacifism is right because it is effective, the third type holds that pacifism is both right and effective. Or, put differently, it holds that pacifism is right on two scores: Pacifism is faithful to a revealed code or disclosed reality, and it also produces good consequences.

In this version of pacifism, by renouncing the use of lethal force, individuals, groups, or nations express their trustworthiness (i.e., that they will not harm others) and their trust in others. Their actions can thus evoke the trust and trustworthiness of others.[35] Nonviolent actions are therapeutic and even redemptive. Even if nonviolent agents are attacked, their attackers will fail in the larger public forum in which they have to justify their actions. In combining elements of the first two positions, this third type of pacifism is subject to objections about both the obligatoriness and the effectiveness of pacifist actions. In particular, the claims about effectiveness often appeal to general views of human nature and metaphysical or theological perspectives, such as the Quaker conviction that it is possible to reach what is of God in every person; Gandhi's contention that "the law of suffering will work, just as the law of gravitation will work, whether we accept it or not"; Martin Luther King, Jr.'s belief that there is "some creative force that works for universal wholeness" and that "unmerited suffering is always redemptive"; or James Douglass's affirmation of "the power of voluntary suffering."[36] Against their realist critics, such as Reinhold Niebuhr, some recent pacifists, such as Duane Friesen, have tried to develop "a realist pacifist perspective," which takes account of the reality of human sinfulness as expressed in "the egoistic self-interest and exploitation of political and economic systems."[37]

### 4. Technological, especially nuclear, pacifism

The fourth type of pacifism is very different, because it accepts the validity of just war criteria but holds that they require negative judgments about modern, especially nuclear, wars because the technologies employed violate the *jus in bello* standards of discrimination and/or proportionality or the *jus ad bellum* standards of reasonable chance of success and proportionality. All of these standards may be invoked by the nuclear pacifist, such as David Hollenbach, to reject all use of nuclear weapons.[38] The U.S. Catholic bishops express "profound skepticism about the moral acceptability of any use of nuclear weapons" and try to "draw a moral line against nuclear war." Their "no" to the idea of nuclear war appeals to the standards of discrimination and proportionality of *jus in bello*, but their argument against even limited nuclear war, involving the retaliatory use of nuclear weapons in a limited exchange, rests primarily on the criterion of "a reasonable hope of success in bringing about justice and peace": "We must ask whether such a reasonable hope can exist once nuclear weapons have been exchanged. The burden of proof remains on those who assert that meaningful limitation is possible."[39]

While the U.S. Catholic bishops oppose nuclear war, others may extend their opposition to modern conventional wars on the grounds that such wars may escalate into nuclear conflicts. There is an ambiguity: "Nuclear pacifism" may mean (a) disavowal of all modern wars because of the moral evil of nuclear war and the danger that nonnuclear wars will lead to nuclear wars, or (b) disavowal of only nuclear wars. If, however, only nuclear wars are opposed, on the basis of just war criteria, while other wars are accepted, then there is reason to doubt that the position should be called a form of pacifism at all. If all modern wars are opposed, the opposition may be considered pacifist, even though the grounds are that conventional wars may lead to nuclear warfare. Of course, the peculiarity of this position is that it is shaped by the available technology of warfare, that it applies only to the present age, and that its criteria are drawn from the just war tradition. Its "no" to modern (especially nuclear) warfare is what attracts the label "pacifist," but its logic of reasoning is clearly distinctive vis-à-vis the other types.

Even though its proponents may use absolutistic language, nuclear pacifism is still a contingent position that could change as weapons and defenses develop. Because it is based on just war criteria, nuclear pacifism is addressed to nation-states as well as to individuals and to religious communities. However, it may not offer clear policy directions even about nuclear deterrence; for example, it may accept nuclear deterrence at least under strict conditions, as the U.S. Catholic bishops did. It is not clear that nuclear pacifists, to be considered such, must disavow possession, as well as use.

## III. PACIFISTS' CONTRIBUTIONS TO
## DISCOURSE ABOUT WAR

A decade ago, I made the following claim in the conclusion of an essay on just war criteria:

> Pacifists and just-war theorists are actually closer to and more dependent on each other than they often suppose. They share a common starting point, which just-war theorists sometimes overlook: non-violence has moral priority over violence, and violent acts always stand in need of justification because they violate the prima facie duty not to injure or kill others whereas only some nonviolent acts need justification (e.g., when they violate laws). While pacifists can remind just-war theorists of this presumption against violence, pacifists also need just-war theorists. In a world in which war appears to be a permanent institution, debates about particular wars require a framework and structure, which can be provided by the criteria of the just-war tradition, properly reconstructed. In addition, there are degrees of justice and humanity within violence and warfare, and the just-war theorists can emphasize these moral constraints which the pacifist view of war as hell or murder (shared by some realists) tends to obscure. Even the pacifist has a stake in the integrity of just-war criteria as the coin of the political realm. The pacifist finally cannot be satisfied with that coin, just as the just-war theorist finally cannot be satisfied with the weight pacifism gives to the duty not to injure or kill that both recognize. What they share, however, can be neglected only at great peril to all of us.[40]

I still affirm those points, but more needs to be said. I would now emphasize even more strongly what is shared. As an outgrowth of the shared commitment to the presumption against violence as the starting point, both pacifist and just war traditions require that we seek alternatives to violence and thus to war. Pacifists are right that our society has not taken seriously enough this responsibility to seek effective alternatives to armed force, a responsibility that is recognized in both traditions. Pacifists and just warriors together have a stake in making sure that the state satisfies just war criteria in preparing for, undertaking, and waging war; they should call the state to integrity; i.e., to actions in accord with these public criteria.[41] When just war criteria are actually and seriously applied, pacifists and just warriors will agree in many cases that a particular war is unjust and unjustified, even though their ultimate reasons may differ. In addition, I would note that nonviolent protests often depend on a societal affirmation of and respect for just war criteria. For example, nonviolent protesters often presuppose their opponents' and observers' commitment to such principles as discrimination (noncombatant immunity from direct attack); that commitment may reduce the likelihood that nonviolent protesters will be met with violence and may increase the likelihood of negative public opinion if they are met with violence.[42]

I would also emphasize the shared theological-anthropological arguments pacifists and just warriors offer to increase individual and societal reluctance to depart from their norms; these include the arguments about limited human responsibility, ethical fallibility, and imperfect information, which I discussed in part I. Of course, there are numerous important differences between these two traditions. One matter they share, their focus on war—pacifism disavowing war, and just war theories justifying war under some circumstances—is perhaps a liability. As Richard Miller suggests, this focus on war may put what could be called a "limit situation" too much in the center of our moral reflections.[43] However, both pacifist and just war traditions imply that peace—though not by itself—should be central in our vision. I also agree with David Hollenbach that "*both* the pacifist commitment to nonviolence and self-sacrifice as the way to justice and the just war tradition's commitment to justice as the way to peace and mutual love are essential if the full content of Christian hope is to be made visible in history" and that each is *incomplete* by itself.[44] The hard questions are how to relate them and how to choose between them when choice is inevitable.

Regarding the relation of the two traditions (or subtraditions) of pacifism and just war, the metaphors of overlap and convergence are the most plausible, because they are consistent with significant differences between the traditions. In general, metaphors of combination of the two traditions into a whole—in contrast to overlap and convergence—may not be satisfactory and may distort actual and possible relations between the traditions.[45] Indeed, strands of either the pacifist or the just war tradition may not be compatible with other strands in the same tradition and may be so divergent as to raise questions about the appropriateness of the labels "pacifist tradition" or "just war tradition." Nevertheless, some combinations of pacifist and just war theories are possible—for example, the traditional Roman Catholic affirmation of vocational pacifism within the context of just war theory, or Reinhold Niebuhr's location of pacifism (nonresistance) as the unrealizable but relevant ideal within just war theory. Thus, questions of relation obviously depend in part on the ways the traditions are conceived (and I will return to conceptions of traditions below). Because Reinhold Niebuhr's conceptualization, classification, and negative judgments about pacifism have been so influential in setting the terms of the debate, it may be useful to sketch its main lineaments.

In terms of my typology of pacifist positions, Niebuhr had a genuine appreciation for absolute legalistic-expressive pacifism that concentrated mainly on the question of participation in violence and did not attempt to offer a political alternative. He viewed this type of pacifism as part of a general religious withdrawal from the world in an effort to attain perfection. According to Niebuhr, this pacifism rightly presents a stringent interpretation of the norm of love expressed in the teaching of Jesus and the Cross, and does not offer this nonresistance as a political alternative, but rather specifically "disavows" political responsibility.[46] As such, this type of pacifism is "a valuable asset for the Christian faith," for it reminds the Christian community of the distinction between what is normative or ideal and what is normal or real, and thus helps to keep alive an uneasy conscience about participation in war. However, in the final analysis, for Niebuhr, this pacifism is still politically irrelevant and irresponsible. The second and third types of pacifism, which claim to offer effective political alternatives, are, from Niebuhr's perspective, confused and even heretical in their interpretation of the New Testament as endorsing nonviolent resistance rather than nonresistance and in their acceptance of the humanistic faith in the goodness of human beings to respond to nonviolent resistance. For Niebuhr, "a responsible relationship to the political order . . . makes an unqualified disavowal of violence impossible."[47] (There is debate about whether Niebuhr himself accepted a version of the fourth type—nuclear pacifism—but that need not occupy our attention here.)[48]

Imaginative and exciting developments have occurred in the pacifist tradition in recent years. Pacifists such as Yoder, Hauerwas, Friesen, and Sider, among others, have developed positions that challenge the powerful realist conceptualization, classification, and critique offered by Niebuhr and more recently affirmed (without Niebuhr's rigor and subtlety) by Guenter Lewy.[49] I want to make several general points without discussing these pacifist contributions in detail, without supposing that some of their positions are finally adequate, and without attending to their structural or organizational base.

First, even though many of these pacifists operate from a legalistic or expressive perspective, they often refuse to accept Niebuhr's consignment to political irrelevance. They are not interested only in avoiding participation in evil; they are also interested in politics and refuse to be classified as nonpolitical or as apolitical. They often reject the "mainstream" realist and just war definition of politics in terms of the use of armed force, arguing instead that the "political" has "to do with the *polis*, the common life of men" or that "genuine politics" involves the "conversation necessary for a people for discover the goods they have in common."[50] This definitional shift is very important, because the interpretation and application of just war criteria to armed force take place in a sociocultural context, where various institutional and cultural forces shape interpretations of situations as well as interpretations of the criteria. For example, if the sociocultural context is one of militarism, it will shape the resort to armed force. Hence, pacifists can participate in the debate about war and peace on a political level, by addressing questions of the sociocultural context of judgments about the justification of armed force. Furthermore, because of the moral priority of nonviolence and the moral necessity of seeking nonviolent alternatives before resorting to armed force—even within the just war tradition— pacifists can participate with just warriors in developing institutions and policies to try and test those alternatives.

Part of the debate concerns the specificity as well as the content of appropriate pacifist participation in politics. Lewy contends that "pacifism is a personal philosophy of non-violence rather than a prescription for public policy," and "there is no such thing as a political position that is truly pacifist."[51] However, his claim really rests on the problematic Niebuhrian limitation of pacifism, or true pacifism, to its legalistic- expressive versions, limited to the individual rather than being extended to the society. In contrast to Lewy, pacifists are not necessarily being inconsistent in offering policy recommendations. And they may even make their recommendations, without inconsistency, by invoking public just war criteria. In contrast to Lewy, pacifists are not relegated to silence on such matters.[52]

Second, realists such as Niebuhr have been inclined to dismiss pacifist proposals as unrealistic and even idealistic, but recent pacifists have offered several responses. One response, already adumbrated, is that realism offers an impoverished view of political reality, particularly by concentrating so much on (armed) force. Another response is that realists who accept the legitimacy of armed force often have a closed view of reality and thus cannot see various nonviolent options, even though just war theories require that they seek nonviolent alternatives before resorting to force.[53] After all, even though Niebuhr argues that the differences between nonviolence and violence are only pragmatic, the logic of his own position is very different.[54] His position is that violence is a necessary evil and an *ultima ratio*, a matter of last resort. It is hard to make sense of that claim without assigning moral priority to nonviolent alternatives. By contrast, pacifists concentrate on those nonviolent alternatives and argue that society needs to devote resources, effort, planning, and the like, to try and test them to see if they might be effective.[55] And in developing those alternatives, they are not necessarily blinded to self-interest and the will to power because of an optimistic vision of human nature, so properly criticized by the realists.

Still another pacifist response to the realist charge that pacifism is idealistic notes that just war theories, especially (iii) but perhaps also (iv) on the spectrum of resistance—though the latter is usually viewed as realistic—are themselves idealistic in that they try to support moral norms over against self-interest and the will to power.[56] Niebuhr defined realism in moral and social theory as "the disposition to take all factors in a social and political situation, which offer resistance to established norms, into account, particularly the factors of self-interest and power."[57] Those factors of self-interest and power offer resistance to the application of just war criteria too, and, on their own terms, just warriors may be excessively idealistic in asserting their norms over against uncontrollable political realities. Without more attention to this problem than just warriors usually provide, pacifists rightly wonder whether just war criteria simply yield to or legitimate national self-interest and will-to-power.

Even though, as I have emphasized, pacifists help to keep alive the primacy of nonviolence over violence and the moral necessity of seeking nonviolent alternatives—both points are central to the just war tradition but are too often overlooked or downplayed—they may actually diminish the significance of the criteria of *jus in bello*. Conceptually and normatively, pacifists so emphasize the boundary between nonviolence and violence, between peace and war, that they have little to say about right conduct within war. Historically, they have even been blamed for contributing to the erosion of the constraints of the *jus in bello*—especially the principle of discrimination—between World War I and World War II.[58] They share with some realists the conviction that war is hell or even murder and the only moral question is whether or not to enter it. Those who start war are to be blamed; the only moral goal is to restore peace as quickly as possible. In short, even though pacifists may help to maintain a lively sense of the *jus ad bellum*, they may obscure the importance of the *jus in bello* if war does erupt. However, pacifists could (and, I believe, should) distinguish penultimate from ultimate judgments and recognize, on a penultimate level, that there is a morality, represented by the requirements of *jus in bello*, in what they construe as a situation of evil.

Many critics neglect pacifists' inadequate attention to the *jus in bello* because they concentrate on pacifists' standards of justice regarding the ends of any violent or nonviolent conflict. Indeed, it seems that Lewy's major criticism of pacifists is not their alleged logical and moral inconsistencies but rather their standards of justice for judging the ends of conflict. These standards of justice identify the injustice, or evil, that should be opposed, by either nonviolent or violent means. Lewy's fundamental charge seems to be that contemporary pacifists tend to apply egalitarian standards of justice and thus criticize communism less severely than many just warriors. As a result, these pacifists have often been more critical of U.S. governmental policies than Lewy finds acceptable. Thus, the call for the reformation of pacifism, issued so fervently by Lewy and others, is largely a call for a different standard of justice.[59]

Both pacifist and just war theories require some standards of justice to judge causes that merit support or opposition. Pacifists and just warriors can defend any kind of social, political or economic order, depending on their theory of justice. The real issue between pacifists and just warriors is one of *means* to whatever end of justice is sought. Even if pacifists and just warriors sometimes or even often disagree about the *ends*, similar kinds of dispute may erupt within either tradition of reflection. But such disputes have little to do with the pacifist and just war traditions as such, for both are compatible with various theories of justice regarding the ends of violent or nonviolent conflict.

Disputes about standards of justice often surface when just warriors charge contemporary pacifists with inconsistencies. First, just warriors charge that pacifists inconsistently favor one side over another in armed conflicts. Lewy contends that a "pacifist's principles preclude his having favorite wars or revolutions."[60] However, neither logical nor moral inconsistency is evident when pacifists, using only nonviolent means, favor one side over another in armed conflict. Standards of justice affirmed by pacifists may lead them to identify the ends or cause of one side as ethically superior to the other even in a violent conflict. A second and related charge is that pacifists are inconsistent in criticizing U.S. policies more than the policies of other countries in situations of conflict. But pacifists are not inconsistent if their criticism (and nonviolent resistance) is directed at U.S. policies, or at the policies of some other regime, because of their operative standards of justice. If just warriors are opposed to the standards of justice that many pacifists use, they should attack those standards directly rather than accuse pacifists of inconsistently choosing sides or of inconsistently arguing for particular policies in the political arena.

Both pacifists and just warriors must recognize each other's shared commitments to justice and peace. For just war theorists, a just peace is the end of a just war waged justly. For pacifists, a just peace is also the end sought through nonviolent means. Neither should gainsay the other's commitment to both justice and peace, however much they may disagree in their interpretations of those social-moral goals. Disputes about the meaning and also about the weight of justice and peace do not suggest that either is unimportant for either group.

In conclusion, both the just war and the pacifist traditions are living and developing. Such developments are essential if each tradition is to survive and flourish.[61] Each tradition can help the other develop, as well as remain faithful to its fundamental and essential principles. Of course, if "tradition" is made a primary category, there are still important questions about boundaries, about what is essential and what is peripheral, and about the conflict and overlap or convergence of moral traditions such as pacifism and just war. Alasdair MacIntyre defines a tradition as "an argument extended through time in which certain fundamental agreements are defined and redefined in terms of two kinds of conflict: those with critics and enemies external to the tradition who reject all or at least key parts of those fundamental agreements, and those internal, interpretative debates through which the meaning and rationale of the fundamental agreements come to be expressed and by whose progress a tradition is constituted."[62]

It is possible to construe the modern debate about war as a debate between (at least) two moral traditions with various roots, or, within Christianity, as a debate between two subtraditions within the larger tradition of Christian thought and practice. These different construals will certainly make a difference in the way the debate is conducted, particularly regarding shared authorities, principles, and modes of reasoning. However the lines are drawn, it is possible to consider the encounter of traditions or subtraditions, loosely labeled just war and pacifism, so that each, in the process of understanding and debating the other, can also call the other to integrity, i.e., to faithfulness to its own authorities, principles, and modes of reasoning. The call to integrity is not reducible to the call for consistency, however close they may be at times and however prominent the charge of inconsistency is (for example, as we have seen, in recent critiques of pacifism). Integrity is both more and less than consistency, because it involves fidelity to fundamental authorities, principles, and modes of reasoning.[63] Pacifists may help just warriors avoid ideology, rationalization, and bad faith in their application of just war criteria, particularly by proposing nonviolent alternatives that should be tried—and prepared in advance—before resort to war can be justified (that is, justified on just warriors' own terms). On the other hand, just warriors may remind pacifists that sometimes if nonviolence fails, justice may be lost without resort to armed force (even though armed force may not be sufficient to protect justice) and that the conduct of war needs to be subjected to the moral standards of discrimination and proportionality.

## Notes

1. Jenny Teichman, *Pacifism and the Just War* (Oxford: Basil Blackwell, 1986), 1-2.

2. See James F. Childress, "Moral Discourse about War in the Early Church," *Journal of Religious Ethics* 12 (Spring 1984): 2-18.

3. Reinhold Niebuhr, "Pacifism and the Use of Force" (1928), in *Love and Justice*, ed. D. B. Robertson (Cleveland: World Publishing Co., Meridian Books, 1967), 248.

4. For a discussion of Niebuhr's pacifism and critique of pacifism, see James F. Childress, "Reinhold Niebuhr's Realistic Critique of Pacifism," *Moral Responsibility in Conflicts* (Baton Rouge: Louisiana State University Press, 1982), 29-61, and "Niebhur's Realistic-Pragmatic Approach to War and 'the Nuclear Dilemma,'" in *Reinhold Niebuhr and the Issues of Our Time*, ed. Richard Harries (Grand Rapids, Mich.: William B. Eerdmans Publishing Co., 1986), 122-56. See also Richard Harries, "Niebuhr's Critique of Pacifism and His Pacifist Critics," in *Reinhold Niebuhr and the Issues of Our Time*, 105-21.

5. See Stanley Hauerwas, *Against the Nations: War and Survival in a Liberal Society* (Minneapolis: Winston Press, 1985), 134.

6. This spectrum is drawn from Childress, "Niebuhr's Realistic-Pragmatic Approach to War and 'the Nuclear Dilemma,'" 127ff.

7. See Joseph C. McKenna, S. J., "Ethics and War: A Catholic View," *American Political Science Review* 54 (1960); National Conference of Catholic Bishops, *The Challenge of Peace: God's Promise and Our Response* (Washington, D.C.: U.S. Catholic Conference, 1983); Paul Ramsey, *The Just War: Force and Political Responsibility* (New York: Charles Scribner's Sons, 1968); and Michael Walzer, *Just and Unjust Wars* (New York: Basic Books, 1977).

8. James Turner Johnson, *Just War Tradition and the Restraint of War* (Princeton: Princeton University Press, 1981).

9. John C. Ford, S. J., "The Morality of Obliteration Bombing," *Theological Studies* 5 (1944): 261-309, reprinted in *War and Morality*, ed. Richard Wasserstrom (Belmont, Calif.: Wadsworth Publishing Co., 1970).

10. Reinhold Niebuhr, "Is the Bombing Necessary?" *Christianity and Crisis* 4 (3 April 1944): 1-2.

11. John Howard Yoder, *The Original Revolution: Essays on Christian Pacifism* (Scottdale, Pa.: Herald Press, 1971), 132-47; and Paul Ramsey, *Deeds and Rules in Christian Ethics* (New York: Charles Scribner's Sons, 1967), 108-9, and *The Just War*.

12. Reinhold Niebuhr, "Just or Holy?" *Christianity and Crisis* 1 (3 November 1941): 1.

13. See Childress, *Moral Responsibility in Conflicts*, 57-61.

14. Niebuhr, "Just or Holy?", 1.

15. Leo Tolstoy, *Tolstoy's Writings on Civil Disobedience and Non-violence* (New York: New American Library, 1968), 181-90.

16. For many of Gandhi's major statements on nonviolence, see *Non-Violent Resistance*, ed. Bharatan Kumarappa (New York: Schocken Books, 1961). See also Raghavan Iyer, *The Moral and Political Thought of Mahatma Gandhi* (New York: Oxford University Press, 1973).

17. Hannah Arendt, *On Violence* (New York: Harcourt, Brace, and World, 1970), 4 and 79.

18. John Howard Yoder, *Nevertheless: A Meditation on the Varieties and Shortcomings of Religious Pacifism* (Scottdale, Pa: Herald Press, 1971). See also the excellent studies by Peter Brock, including *Twentieth-Century Pacifism* (New York: Van Nostrand Reinhold Co., 1970).

19. My formulations have been influenced by some lectures by Carroll Feagins of Guilford College.

20. See Ernst Troeltsch, *The Social Teaching of the Christian Church* (Chicago: University of Chicago Press, Midway Reprint, 1976), vol. 1, 331-49.

21. See E. A. Shils and H. A. Finch, eds., *Max Weber on the Methodology of the Social Sciences* (Glencoe, Ill.: The Free Press, 1949).

22. John Howard Yoder, *The Original Revolution*, 64.

23. Nevertheless, Merton also insisted that nonviolent resistance is "per se and ideally, the only really effective resistance to injustice and evil." And this combination of themes would locate him more in the third position to be identified below. See Merton, *Faith and Violence* (Notre Dame, Ind.: University of Notre Dame Press, 1968), and Gordon C. Zahn, ed., *Thomas Merton on Peace* (New York: McCall Publishing Co., 1971).

24. See Stanley Hauerwas, *The Peaceable Kingdom: A Primer in Christian Ethics* (Notre Dame, Ind.: University of Notre Dame Press, 1983). See also *Against the Nations*, and Hauerwas's commentary on "In Defense of Creation," in Paul Ramsey, *Speak Up for Just War or Pacifism* (University Park: Pennsylvania State University Press, 1988).

25. For the distinction between revealing a law and disclosing a reality, see James M. Gustafson, "The Place of Scripture in Christian Ethics: A Methodological Study," *Theology and Christian Ethics* (Philadelphia: Pilgrim Press, 1974), chap. 6.

26. Max Weber, "Politics as a Vocation," in *From Max Weber: Essays in the Sociology of Religion*, ed. H. H. Gerth and C. Wright Mills (New York: Oxford University Press, 1958), 77-128.

27. James Turner Johnson, *The Quest for Peace: Three Moral Traditions in Western Cultural History* (Princeton: Princeton University Press, 1987), xx.

28. Yoder, *The Original Revolution*.

29. Yoder, *When War Is Unjust: Being Honest in Just-War Thinking* (Minneapolis: Augsburg Press, 1984).

30. Hauerwas, *The Peaceable Kingdom*, chap. 6.

31. See Tom L. Beauchamp and James F. Childress, *Principles of Biomedical Ethics*, 3d ed. (New York: Oxford University Press, 1989), chap. 2.

32. M. K. Gandhi, *Non-violent Resistance* (New York: Schocken Books, 1961), 377, 153.

33. Gordon Zahn, "Afterword," *War or Peace? The Search for New Answers*, ed. Thomas A. Shannon (Maryknoll, N.Y.: Orbis, 1980), 242.

34. Niebuhr, "Pacifism and the Use of Force," *Love and Justice*, 248.

35. See Childress, *Moral Responsibility in Conflicts*, chap. 1.

36. Gandhi, *Non-Violent Resistance*, 384; see also 58, 88, and 387; Martin Luther King, Jr., *Stride toward Freedom* (New York: Harper and Row, 1964), 84; and James Douglass, *The Non Violent Cross: A Theology of Revolution and Peace* (New York: Macmillan Co., 1969), 71.

37. Duane K. Friesen, *Christian Peacemaking & International Conflict: A Realist Pacifist Perspective* (Scottdale, Pa.: Herald Press, 1986). See also David A. Hoekema, "A Practical Christian Pacifism," *The Christian Century* (22 October 1986): 917-19.

38. David Hollenbach, *Nuclear Ethics: A Christian Moral Argument* (Ramsey, N.J.: Paulist Press, 1983).

39. *The Challenge of Peace*. See also the nuclear pacifism expressed by the Methodist Bishops in *In Defense of Creation: The Nuclear Crisis and a Just Peace*

(Nashville, Tenn.: Graded Press, 1986) and the critique of that document by Paul Ramsey from a just war perspective and Stanley Hauerwas from a pacifist perspective in Ramsey, *Speak Up for Just War or Pacifism.*

40. Childress, "Just-War Criteria," in *War or Peace? The Search for New Answers*, 40-58.

41. Yoder, *When War Is Unjust.* For a rich discussion of institutional integrity, see Ronald Dworkin, *Law's Empire* (Cambridge, Mass.: Harvard University Press, The Belknap Press, 1986), esp. chap. 6.

42. Walzer, *Just and Unjust Wars.*

43. Richard Miller, "Christian Pacifism and Just-War Tenets: How Do They Diverge?" *Theological Studies* 47 (1986): 448-72.

44. Hollenbach, *Nuclear Ethics*, 31.

45. See James Finn, "Pacifism, Just War, and the Bishops' Muddle," *This World* 7 (Winter 1984), 31-42.

46. Niebuhr, *Christianity and Power Politics* (New York: Charles Scribner's Sons, 1940), chap. 1.

47. Niebuhr, *An Interpretation of Christian Ethics* (New York: Meridian Books, 1954), 170.

48. James Johnson, *Just War Tradition and the Restraint of War*; Childress, "Reinhold Niebuhr's Realistic Critique of Pacifism" and "Niebuhr's Realistic-Pragmatic Approach to War and 'the Nuclear Dilemma.'"

49. Guenter Lewy, *Peace and Revolution: The Moral Crisis of American Pacifism* (Grand Rapids, Mich.: William B. Eerdmans Publishing Co., 1988). For important critical responses, see Michael Cromartie, ed., *Peace Betrayed? Essays on Pacifism and Politics* (Washington: Ethics and Public Policy Center, 1990). Several of these critical responses make clear the extent to which Lewy's book suffers from inadequate categories and tendentious historical analysis, perhaps because of its strong ideology. For a similar but more rigorous and nuanced critique of pacifism, see George Weigel, *Tranquillitas Ordinis* (New York: Oxford University Press, 1987), and Weigel, "Five Theses for a Pacifist Reformation," in *Peace Betrayed?*

50. Yoder, *The Original Revolution*; Hauerwas, "Epilogue: A Pacifist Response to the Bishops," in Ramsey, *Speak Up For Just War or Pacifism*, 171.

51. Lewy, *Peace and Revolution*, 241; Lewy, "Pacifists in a Democratic Society," in *Peace Betrayed?*

52. Lewy writes: "When the pacifist's conscience does not allow him to support policies that utilize force or the threat of force, the proper course for him is to remain silent." *Peace and Revolution*, 248. In response to some criticisms by David Little ("The Logic of Pacifism," in *Peace Betrayed?*), and others, Lewy qualifies his statement: "When the pacifist encounters what he sees as an insoluble conflict between desirable ends and unacceptable means—that is, when he agrees that certain policies are necessary to prevent worse ones but those necessary policies utilize force or the threat of force—in these situations, and only in these situations, the proper course for him is to remain silent, to refrain from taking a position." *Peace Betrayed?*

53. Yoder, "'What Would You Do If . . . ?' An Exercise in Situation Ethics," *Journal of Religious Ethics* 2 (1974): 81-105. See also Yoder, *What Would You Do?* (Scottdale, Pa.: Herald Press, 1983).

54. See Childress, "Reinhold Niebuhr's Realistic Critique of Pacifism."

55. Yoder, *When War Is Unjust*, 81-82.

56. Hauerwas, "Epilogue: A Pacifist Response to the Bishops," 152.

57. Niebuhr, "Augustine's Political Realism," in *Christian Realism and Political Problems* (New York: Charles Scribner's Sons, 1953).

58. See, for example, G. E. M. Anscombe, "War and Murder," *The Collected Philosophical Papers of G. E. M. Anscombe* (Minneapolis: University of Minnesota Press, 1981), vol. 3, chap. 6.

59. See Lewy, *Peace and Revolution*; Weigel, *Tranquillitas Ordinis* (New York: Oxford University Press, 1987); Weigel, "Five Theses for a Pacifist Reformation," in *Peace Betrayed?*

60. Lewy, *Peace and Revolution*, 240.

61. For example, in "Just-War Criteria" and *Moral Responsibility in Conflicts*, I have tried to "reconstruct" just war criteria in terms of the logic of prima facie duties and specifically the prima facie duty of nonmaleficence. An earlier version appeared as "Just-War Theories: The Bases, Interrelations, Priorities and Functions of Their Criteria," *Theological Studies* 39 (September 1978): 427-45.

62. Alasdair MacIntyre, *Whose Justice? Which Rationality?* (Notre Dame, Ind.: University of Notre Dame Press, 1988), 12.

63. For the distinction and relation between integrity and consistency, see Dworkin, *Law's Empire*, chap. 6.

# THE CONVERSATION

James Finn began his critique of James Childress's paper by noting that pacifism has acquired a new prominence and a higher degree of legitimacy in the public debate over war and peace as a result of two trends: increasing anxiety about nuclear weapons, and the ongoing "discovery" of the Gospel message as a source of moral guidance on issues of war and peace. On the whole, Finn argued, Childress went too far in deemphasizing important disjunctions between the pacifist and just war traditions. Pacifism pushes its adherents toward an absolutist position that never allows the use of force; just war thinking entails the balancing of multiple moral principles in determining those situations where the use of force may be appropriate. The kind of moral reasoning involved in just war thinking is pluralistic in the sense of resorting to several norms; pacifism is monistic or centered around a single norm.

Moreover, Finn suggested, just war thinking contains a full-blown theory of statecraft; thus emphasis on war is off the mark. Within the framework of just war thinking, war is one among several instruments of policy that may or may not be morally justified, depending on the circumstances. Other instruments embraced by the statecraft implicit in just war thinking include such alternatives to war as nonmilitary instruments of coercion, diplomacy, and recourse to international law.

Childress responded that each of the traditions contains elements of deontological and consequentialist modes of reasoning. The form of moral reasoning in each tradition is not as distinct as Finn argues. Pacifism, for example, grounds itself not only in a normative prohibition of violence but also in a practical concern about the destructiveness and futility of war. The just war tradition, on the other hand, includes both prudential considerations about safeguarding national security in a turbulent world and deontological norms about the value of preserving justice and freedom and the obligation to act with right intentions. Contemporary nuclear pacifism, by justifying its position on the basis of traditional just war theory, verifies the links between the traditions.

George Weigel thought that there were two key issues to address. First, what is the place in American culture of the "new pacifism" to which both Childress and Finn refer? Where is the tradition alive? Second, how new is the "new pacifism"? To what extent is the "new pacifism" simply a replay of the utopian tendencies of the 1930s against which Reinhold Niebuhr and other Christian realists inveighed?

David Wessels argued that one of the key trends in American society over the last century has been its steady militarization. Pacifism, therefore, is not only an intellectual current fed by moral and religious yearnings for nonviolence, but also a social movement that seeks to reverse American militarism and set in motion something akin to a process of "pacification." This assertion was vigorously contested by John Cooper, who pointed out that neither in terms of the percentage of its gross national product devoted to military spending, nor in the attitudes inculcated in its youth by its educational system, can the United States be described as a militaristic society.

John Langan thought that Childress needed to examine more closely the relationship between pacifism and citizenship. There is an interesting tension between these two paradigmatic figures—the pacifist and the citizen—and their respective obligations, and even a degree of mutual dependence. The pacifist raises a useful moral warning flag to the rest of society about the moral dangers of resorting to military force, but in order to state his case he needs the freedom of conscience and the political sanctuary made possible by the willingness of nonpacifists to bear arms in defense of a free society.

Childress agreed that there is a tension between the pacifist and the citizen, but argued that it would be inaccurate to describe pacifism as inherently apolitical or incompatible with the duties of citizenship. Like his just war counterpart, the pacifist sees political processes and institutions as means for affecting the behavior of others, but he tries to make sure that nonviolent forms of exercising power are fully explored and exhausted. In doing so, the pacifist is exercising his political obligations in a uniquely constructive manner.

James Turner Johnson agreed with Finn that Roman Catholics have kept the just war and pacifist traditions distinct; they are different modes of the Christian life, and Childress's attempt to mix the two is ahistorical. Peter Steinfels then suggested that the strict separation of the two traditions is not philosophically necessary. At most, it is a historical accident, a reflection of the medieval church's dualism between the spheres of the perfect and the imperfect life. The modern church is veering away from dualistic modes of thinking and emphasizing the responsibilities common to our life in this world and our heavenly calling, the duties enjoined by our joint membership in the City of God and the City of Man. It is thus understandable why the Catholic bishops in their pastoral letter on nuclear weapons attempted a synthesis of pacifism and the just war tradition. They recognized that neither pacifism nor just war theory provides by itself a complete account of the Christian's obligations regarding the use of force. In David Hollenbach's words, the pacifist and the just war traditions are complementary because neither one embodies the full implications for the church of the Christian eschatological vision.

John Langan noted that the pacifist has a special burden of proof because he denies the validity of a widely accepted social norm; he is, by necessity, a dissenter. Hollenbach responded that it is precisely the prevailing social acceptability of violence that the new pacifists, such as John Howard Yoder and Stanley Hauerwas, challenge. These pacifist theorists argue that the burden of proof ought to be on the "just warriors," on those who believe that under certain conditions force is morally acceptable. Langan agreed that the burden can indeed be shifted from the pacifist to the "just warrior," especially if the discussion remains at the theological level and one takes Scripture as the starting point. The question remains, however, whether shifting the burden of proof away from the pacifist is ultimately a good thing either morally or politically.

James Finn worried that many new pacifists are becoming less pacific and more inclined to approve of revolution, even violent ones, to replace supposedly unjust political structures. He alluded to Guenther Lewy's book, *Peace and Revolution: The Moral Crises of American Pacifism* (1988), which documents such a shift within four prominent American pacifist organizations over the last three decades.

In response to Weigel's earlier query, George Stephanopoulos replied that pacifism is liveliest today in those places like the Philippines, South Korea, and Poland where it is the only alternative open to groups that want to move society in the direction of justice, freedom, and human dignity. It serves as a morally and politically unassailable foundation from which to challenge an unjust regime.

Weigel replied that pacifism should not be confused with a preference for nonviolence. Corazon Aquino is not a pacifist. Unlike pacifism, the preference for nonviolent options is incumbent on all moral individuals. Indeed, the just war tradition has a built-in preference for nonviolence, and it is prepared to justify the use of force in certain circumstances only if nonviolent alternatives are unavailable or ineffective.

Disagreeing with Childress, William O'Brien questioned whether the just war tradition shares with pacifism a presumption against war. Just war principles help a decision maker arrive at a point where war is not only justified as an unfortunate necessity, but positively enjoined as a prudential act. This is radically different from the pacifist's fundamental disavowal of violence.

O'Brien also expressed his discomfort with the participation of pacifists in debates over national security issues. As someone who takes an absolute stand against the use of violence, a pacifist lacks credibility when he engages in arguments against particular kinds of weapons, be they the Strategic Defense Initiative or the MX. Since the pacifist is against the use of any and all weapons, how can he pretend to be of help when we argue the relative moral merits or drawbacks of specific weapons? Such kinds of moral balancing are appropriate only for people who, on principle, are prepared to use some weapons in certain circumstances, but not for those whose agenda is to abolish the use of force altogether. In Finn's words, pacifists ultimately reject the validity of just war criteria; hence, they cannot be expected to abide by such criteria in their reasoning or policies, and we should not trust them when they claim to do so.

Agreeing with O'Brien and Finn, James Woolsey suggested that an apt analogy would be an atheist's participation in Catholic theological debates. Having decided in advance that God does not exist, how can an atheist credibly immerse himself in arguments that assume the existence of God? John Cooper added that, beneath the arguments they make against particular weapons systems or military policies, pacifists have a more radical hidden agenda when they enter national security debates, and that is the abolition of all military power. This hidden agenda undercuts the intellectual legitimacy and sincerity of the pacifist's involvement in such debate.

Peter Steinfels vigorously dissented. A person's reasons are as good as his reasons. Pacifists are not the only people who bring hidden agendas or philosophical presuppositions to policy debates. If we try to probe the hidden philosophical or psychological springs of every person's arguments, we will end up dismissing much of what they are saying instead of looking at the substantive merits of the arguments themselves. A pacifist's critique of SDI is no more illegitimate on its face than a defense of SDI by a just war theorist whose reasoning may be unduly clouded by different sorts of philosophical or political inclinations. Agreeing with Steinfels, Jerry Powers remarked that if we exclude pacifists from national security policy debates because they do not share just war assumptions, we also would have to exclude many exponents of realpolitik who have no use for the just war tradition.

David Hollenbach said that beyond the question of whether it was legitimate for pacifists to use arguments derived from just war theory, there was the equally important question of whether pacifists might have a valuable contribution to make in helping us to understand how the just war tradition itself ought to be interpreted. The just war tradition has too often succumbed to the pressures of political realism and military necessity; it has accepted war as part of the natural order too readily, and it has frequently become an elegant moral rationalization for whatever military policies those in power choose to follow. By challenging nonpacifists and calling the church back to the principles of the Gospel, by reminding us of the uncomfortable implications of Christian eschatology, pacifism helps the just war theory to remain faithful to its highest normative aspirations and keeps it from caving in under the enormous pressures which the relentless logic of politics and war places upon it.

George Weigel thought that there was common room, and even common ground, in the policy debate for both pacifists and just war theorists at the level of practical reasoning. If the issue is not warmaking, but peacemaking—the construction of political and economic structures within domestic societies and in international relations that will facilitate a rightly ordered peace—then it is possible for pacifists and just war theorists to work together fruitfully. There is no need for the pacifist-just war dialogue to focus only on warmaking and weapons systems.

Weigel, Langan, and Finn thought that the Catholic bishops had been mistaken in their 1983 pastoral letter by trying to merge the pacifist and just war traditions so as to arrive at a consensus acceptable to all. They did this by claiming to ground their analysis of the nuclear dilemma and their policy prescriptions on the just war tradition, while also stating that pacifism is an acceptable option at the individual level. The costs of this effort, however, were a blurring of the key distinctions between the two traditions and a great deal of intellectual confusion. It would have been much better to have produced two documents, a majority report based on just war reasoning and a minority report articulating the pacifist position.

As the discussion drew to a close, James Turner Johnson reminded the group that pacifism is not monolithic, and that there are significant differences in the quality of discourse one can have with various pacifists. It is possible for a just war theorist to argue with Childress's "consequentialist-pragmatic pacifist" or his "technological pacifist." It is impossible, however, to carry out a meaningful dialogue with "legalistic-expressive" pacifists such as John Howard Yoder, because their frame of reference is not politics as it exists in the real world but a divinely revealed command interpreted in absolute terms.

# J. BRYAN HEHIR

# Intervention and International Affairs:
# A Normative and Empirical Assessment

In his introduction to a series of essays on intervention and world politics, Hedley Bull asks: "Is the gap between the rule of non-intervention and facts of intervention now so vast that the former has become a mockery with which it would be better to dispense altogether, or does the proscription of intervention remain a vital part of the normative structure on which international order depends?"[1] Other authors in the Bull volume note, in different ways, the disparity between the pervasive reality of intervention and the difficulty of analyzing it politically or normatively.

The reason for this disjunction between the universal acknowledgment of the reality of intervention and plurality of views about its significance or legitimacy is found, in my view, in three factors. First, the normative tradition on intervention is itself divided in its assessment of intervention. Second, the empirical reality of the contemporary international system is more complex than either side of the normative debate can account for. Third, the gap between the factual reality of intervention and the assessment which the normative tradition makes of intervention means that evaluation of specific cases of intervention demands an effort of political-moral analysis, reshaping the traditional ethic in light of the actual conditions of international politics today. The normative tradition is usable but not simply ready for application.

The structure of this paper flows directly from the preceding assessment. The first section examines the foundations of the normative tradition of intervention. The second section assesses the role of intervention in the contemporary system, focusing upon the pattern of intervention during the Cold War era, and the likelihood of intervention in a post-Cold War system.

## I. THE NORMATIVE TRADITION:
## THE MORAL AND THE LEGAL

The ethical analysis of intervention has historically been part of the wider argument about the use of force. While the contemporary phenomenon of intervention is broader than military intervention, there is analytical value in examining how military intervention has been evaluated. The more complicated task of assessing other modes of intervention can be based upon the detailed casuistry which has been used for military intervention. Limiting the investigation to military intervention also illustrates the basic division found in the normative doctrine.[2]

To state the difference sharply: the moral tradition—based on the just war ethic—has predicated a duty of intervention and then set limits on the duty; the legal tradition—based on international law—has predicated a rule of nonintervention and then developed a list of exceptions to the rule. The stark difference of these two judgments is rooted in the different premises on which the moral-legal arguments are based. I will summarize and exemplify the differences in terms of (a) the concept of political community used; (b) the ethic of force employed; and (c) the conclusions drawn about intervention.

### A. The moral tradition:
### The just war doctrine and intervention

The moral doctrine on intervention flourished in the High Middle Ages. The political concept which sustained that tradition envisioned European society as the *Respublica Christiana*; within this Christian commonwealth the prevailing ethic of war was the just war doctrine. These two ideas produced a normative case which made intervention a moral duty for political authorities. Here it will be possible only to summarize the content of the political and strategic premises, then to exemplify the medieval tradition in the work of Aquinas and Grotius.

**1. The political concept: *Respublica Christiana*.** The political system known as the *Respublica Christiana* took shape in the High Middle Ages. Its roots lay in the Carolingian period and the remnants of its structure endured until the sixteenth century. The distinguishing note of the *Respublica* was that it was both a political community and a religious entity; it was both church and state. Political loyalties were understood in terms of religious beliefs, and faith was a prerequisite for full participation and membership in the society.[3] The unity of society was confirmed and consecrated by a shared perspective of faith visibly embodied in the role the church fulfilled.

Gierke has described this concept of society as the organic model in which the individual understood his/her place in light of the total social framework and in which the common good was the directive political idea.[4] Both the role of law in society and the structure of authority combined to highlight the idea of a single organic community. The unity of the society was reflected in its legal system. The source of all law was the *lex aeterna* or divine plan for history. The *lex aeterna* was grasped through the medium of natural law, whose fundamental principles and deduced premises constituted the "higher law" against which all positive law was tested. The unified legal system in turn was reflected in the structure of political authority in the *Respublica*.

The problem of political authority was cast in terms of the spiritual and temporal power of church and state.[5] The key to understanding these terms, however, is that these two powers or institutions were presumed to have existence only in the one society which was Christendom. The unity of society was the presumption upon which all discussions of church and state were based.

The convergence of these themes produced an ethical mindset in the *Respublica* which is best described as an ethic of solidarity. The substance of this ethic described societal relations in familial terms; this in turn imposed upon the members of society a duty of responsibility for others. This philosophical bond of duty in turn was then reinforced by the Christian ethic of love. The ethic of solidarity was not simply a theory in the *Respublica*. There existed a visible organizational structure through which the relations of responsibility were coordinated and exercised. The organizational structure was the church.

The pope as principal power in the *Respublica* assumed the role of guardian of the rights of states, guarantor of treaties and architect of the principles governing the laws of neutrality and the rights of neutrals. The papal role was to insure that the community stayed unified in fact, and that the moral bonds of solidarity, explicated in terms of the rights and duties of natural law teaching, were observed by all, rulers and subjects alike.

**2. The ethic of war: Just war doctrine.** The executive power of the papal office included the right to use coercive measures. The instruments of coercion included the *ultima ratio*, the use of military force. Supporting the right to use force was the rationale of the just war doctrine. LeRoy Walters has argued convincingly that it is imprecise to speak of a doctrine: it is more accurate to describe "various just-war theories within an ongoing just war tradition."[6] Preeminent among these theories in the *Respublica* was that of Thomas Aquinas (1124-1274).

, When faced with the dilemma of reconciling the use of lethal force with the Gospel ethic, Aquinas, the preeminent theorist of *Respublica* doctrine, sought to legitimize the use of force as necessary to protect the unique needs of the political community for security, order, and defense. The right of the state to use force is based upon the responsibility of the state for the public order of society. The content of this public responsibility has two dimensions for Aquinas. First, there is the police function of maintaining order within society. Second, closely patterned on the police model, but distinct from it, is the power to make war against those threatening the commonwealth from outside. Since the state by its very nature has this obligation, it also has the right to those means necessary to fulfill the obligation, specifically the right to use force.

It is important to note that the ethical argument is cast in terms of a police power model. War is not a right of the state or the sovereign to be used at will, for any and all purposes; it is a specifically delineated power to be utilized in well-defined circumstances.[7] These circumstances are elaborated under the rubric of just cause, which includes the response to a criminal act that should be punished, and some actions in defense of the commonwealth, its members, or their goods. The description of war as a penal action presupposed a certain organization of the medieval international system. The connecting link between the moral doctrine of the just war and the maintenance of political order in the medieval international system was the executive role of the papacy. The effective execution of this office depended upon two factors which were validated in the medieval system: the acceptance of an explicitly articulated moral norm (natural law) and the acknowledgment throughout the system of the pope as the authoritative interpreter of the moral norm.

The shared morality established a unified world of discourse for evaluating and justifying the use of force in the political community. Commonly recognized moral categories provided the means for designating specific forms of behavior as a threat to the community and for galvanizing other forces in the community to restrain, repel, and/or punish the culpable party. The just war doctrine made it possible for states both to identify categories of action as substantial threats to the commonwealth and to legitimize the use of military force as a defensive or punitive measure. The final determination of which empirical situations called for the use of force was entrusted to the pope as head of the Christian commonwealth.

The legal order of the Middle Ages was sustained not only by moral doctrine and respect for the papal office, but also by political convictions about the *Respublica Christiana*. To be part of this community implied a sense of responsibility for its defense, for the condition of justice within it, and for the shared values which bound the community together. When some in the community violated those values and disrupted its order, the other members of the community, especially those who had been directly injured, possessed the right and the responsibility to pass judgment and to execute sentence. In the High Middle Ages, this process was carried out under the leadership of the pope. Later, the princes of the commonwealth assumed responsibility on their own. In both instances, however, the political and ethical problem included specific decisions about intervention. This can be seen in the responses of two of the leading writers on this topic: Aquinas and Grotius.

3. Intervention in the *Respublica Christiana.* An exposition of the ethics of intervention based on the medieval model of *Respublica Christiana* can be divided into two distinct phases of development. The first phase is represented by Aquinas, the second by Hugo Grotius (1583-1645). The basis of the distinction between Aquinas and Grotius is the emergence of the modern state.

*Aquinas on Intervention:* Aquinas never explicitly addressed specific cases of intervention. Lacking explicit texts, it is necessary to resort to inference. Some of the commentators on Aquinas have attributed to him a sweeping interventionist position.[8] I find his position interventionist, but also carefully limited in scope.

• Aquinas does justify the use of force as a power inherent in the state for the purpose of protecting the political community. In this view, the limits on using force are set by the boundaries of the political community in question. The key question in understanding Aquinas's view of intervention is how broadly he defines the political community: is it a local unit? does it extend to all of Christendom? does it extend to the welfare of those beyond Christendom?

To answer these questions, it is necessary to take account of two distinct themes in Aquinas's political writings which are held in tension and never explicitly resolved by him. On the one hand, the political and social thought of St. Thomas can be regarded as an ideal type of the medieval political world. Ernst Troeltsch, who uses Aquinas as the epitome of the medieval mind, argues that the central aspect of his thought was that he assumed the existence of a Christian society, a fundamental harmony between the church and the social system. The logic of these ideas moved toward an interventionist position of universal scope: the bond of solidarity was the basis of the obligation, the note of universalism defined the scope of responsibility in terms of the known Christian world, and the doctrine of the just war as interpreted by the pope specified the conditions under which the bond of solidarity became operative. The conclusion of this position was that every prince was somehow responsible for the welfare of the total *Respublica* as well as for his own specifically defined territory. Consequently, he might be called upon to resist aggression, unjust treatment of subjects, etc., any place in the *Respublica Christiana*. In these cases, intervention became a duty fulfilled in the name of the wider community.

The thrust of this dimension of Aquinas's thought, however, cannot be analyzed in isolation from another less explicit but countervailing set of ideas. If the previous theme casts Aquinas in the mold of a citizen of the *Respublica Christiana*, the second theme indicates that he was not unaware of the political forces which were to supplant the medieval form of polity. His sensitivity to these secular trends led him to conceive the meaning of political community in terms described by Thomas Gilby, O.P., as: "The *civitas*, the *regnum*, the *provincia*, a self-governing, self-contained community possessing the attributes of the Greek city described by Aristotle, but enlarged to territories much larger than those of Athens or Sparta."[9]

Because he assumed the existence of a unified Christian civilization, it seems inconceivable to think of Aquinas adopting anything resembling the later positivist position of nonintervention which would isolate the *regnum* from the *Respublica*. On the other hand, Aquinas clearly did not identify himself with the prevailing canonist doctrine of his day which amounted to a papal monarchy, attributing to the pope the right to command and issue binding decrees to all nations, and to intervene extensively, using the military forces of designated Christian princes in the affairs of territories, kingdoms, and regions, even beyond the frontiers of Christendom.

Somewhere between these polar types of the positivist and canonist positions, it is legitimate to infer that Aquinas held an interventionist position, tempered and limited by his sense of the rising demands of national sovereignty. The shape of this limited interventionist position admits reconstruction in general but not specific terms. The primary referent for the use of force is the self-contained, independent political community which resorts to force as a measure of self-preservation. It is by analogy and extension of this line of reasoning that one can reasonably conclude that Aquinas would legitimate, and even command at times, an interventionary course of action beyond the *regnum* in the service of the *Respublica*. The themes of solidarity, responsibility, and universalism would at least support the position of an obligation of the *regnum* to offer some support to what Aquinas defined in one place as the commonweal of the faithful. In addition, LeRoy Walters has shown that Aquinas proposed a specific set of reasons to justify religious wars. These wars often involved a form of intervention outside the frontiers of Christendom, yet

Aquinas found no difficulty in simply extending his basic line of reasoning about just cause to include the suitable causes of religious war.

In summary, therefore, this analysis points toward the conclusion that the elements for an interventionist position are inherent in the political ethic proposed by Aquinas. The approval of intervention in principle does not appear to be a problematical issue for him. On the other hand, Aquinas had a fundamental respect for the rights of sovereigns. What we do not find in Aquinas is how this balance between an affirmation of the substance of the right of intervention and a limitation of its scope would work out in specific cases. Save for the instances he offered as justifiable causes for religious war, he proposed no casuistry to fill out an explicit doctrine of intervention.

*Grotius on Intervention:* Hugo Grotius (1583-1645) is regarded as the founding father of modern international law; Grotius is classified here, however, as a representative of the medieval rather than the modern period of international ethics.[10] The reason for this choice can be understood only if we distinguish the political views of Grotius from his ethical vision.

Politically, Grotius is very much a man of the modern period of interstate relations; he was confronted with the finished product of the process which Aquinas had intuitively sensed, the development of the sovereign state. Grotius predicated his political concept of international society upon the existence of the sovereign state as he saw it incorporated in England, France, Spain, and his own land. Ethically, however, Grotius was more an heir of the medieval tradition than the forerunner of the modern era. He recognized that the political structure which had supported the medieval ethic was incompatible with the fully developed doctrine of sovereignty, but he sought to rescue the substance of the medieval ethic by providing it with a new structure. His doctrine of intervention is rooted in his desire to preserve the medieval moral vision.

The most substantial difference between the world of Aquinas and that of Grotius was in the political order: the *Respublica Christiana* had passed into history. By the time Grotius wrote *De Jure Belli ac Pacis* (1625), the international system was not an interdependent community in which states had some independent existence, it was a group of independent states in search of some minimal form of community to halt the escalating violence engulfing seventeenth century Europe.

This transformation of political life was in part the result of the demise of the church as an acknowledged center of authority in the life of states. The religious and ecclesiastical context in which the natural law and just war ethic had held sway had been severely eroded by the combined influences of political change (sovereignty), religious strike (the Reformation), and cultural transformation (the Renaissance).

In his effort to salvage the medieval ethic for the modern period, Grotius made a frontal attack on two problems. Epistemologically, he sought to ground the natural law ethic in secular soil. In doing so, he sought to save the moral and legal order from the demise which religious authority experienced after the Reformation.[11]

Organizationally, Grotius sought to create a surrogate for the religious community which had been the foundation of political community in the medieval period. Grotius recognized a bond of solidarity among Christians, but the source of that bond was not the church; it was a legal bond, the law of nature, which created a universal legal community among men. This idea of a legal community of humanity ruled by the law of nature was analogous to the concept of *Respublica Christiana*, but the distinctive difference in Grotius is that there is no central authority to interpret or enforce the dictates of natural law. The new problem was that of demonstrating the existence of a legal order among states—an order of international law.

The fundamental purpose behind this elaborate intellectual exercise of preserving the medieval substance while accepting the modern structure of international life was to keep alive in the minds of people and the actions of states the principles of solidarity, responsibility, interdependence, and charity which Grotius believed were the enduring legacy of the *Respublica Christiana*. If these principles were to be preserved, the concept of intervention as a moral as well as a political reality also had to be preserved. Recognizing this fact, Grotius set forth his doctrine of the laws and limits of intervention in the international arena.

Grotius asserted a basic responsibility for intervention, then rendered judgment on specific cases of intervention. The principal justification for intervention was elaborated in terms of the right to punish wrongdoing. The extension of the right to punish into the right to intervene was made in Grotius's general discussion of punishment found in Book II of *De Jure Belli ac Pacis*:

> It is also proper to observe that kings and those who are possessed of sovereign power have a right to exact punishment not only for injuries affecting immediately themselves or their own subjects, but for gross violations of the law of nature and of nations, done to other states and subjects.[12]

The *substance* of Grotius's interventionist position resides in this broad grant of executive power, enabling any sovereign to act in the name of the human community. As Grotius defined their role, kings, "besides the care of their own immediate states and subjects, may be regarded as protectors of the human race."[13] The *scope* of the right to intervene in the Grotian doctrine extended to every part of the human community.

This formulation of the right of intervention flowed from Grotius's conception of the international order forming a single legal community with explicit bonds of responsibility existing among the members. In a paradoxical fashion, Grotius, the last of the medieval expositors, set forth the most fully developed articulation of the medieval model of interventionist policy. The universal right of intervention which Grotius accorded to every sovereign was the logical consequence of the bond of solidarity affirmed in the medieval ethic.

Between Aquinas and Grotius stood Francisco de Vitoria, who had taken Aquinas's teaching on war and drawn specific conclusions about intervention.[14] Grotius, in turn built up and expanded the work of Vitoria. Grotius's justifying causes for intervention included religious reasons (to prevent harassment of Christians and to suppress idolatry); [15] commercial reasons (to guarantee the right of innocent passage and freedom of the seas);[16] diplomatic reasons (to punish treaty violations);[17] and military reasons (to assist the just cause of an ally).[18]

In summary, we can say of just war teaching on intervention that the political premises of the medieval polity, most visibly embodied in the *Respublica Christiana* of the eleventh to the thirteenth centuries, sustained the political and ethical vision of Grotius long after the polity had disappeared.

## B. The legal tradition: International law and intervention

The post-Grotian tradition of international law moved decisively away from Grotius's teaching on intervention. In the development of modern international law, the central political concept was state sovereignty. The normative doctrine of warfare gave way to a concept of the sovereign state's *compétence de guerre*. International society was conceived as a world of sovereign states, whose defining characteristic was their right and capability to resort to war in the diplomatic moment of truth. In this context, nonintervention was affirmed as the duty of all states; the medieval normative doctrine had been reversed.

1. **The political concept: State sovereignty.** The movement from the medieval commonwealth to the modern state system involved the interplay of three major forces: political structures, philosophical ideas, and religious institutions. The political dimension was the appearance and consolidation of the territorial state; the philosophical dimension was the development of a theory of sovereignty; the religious dimension was the division of Christendom by the Reformation. These three themes

shaped the modern international system, which was given visible form in the Peace of Westphalia (1648) and continues in modified form today. The principle of nonintervention, which expresses "the ethic of intervention" of the modern state system, is a corollary of the doctrine of sovereignty.

Ernest Barker described the period from the thirteenth to the eighteenth century in Europe as the movement from kingdom to state.[19] The kingdoms recognized by Aquinas as distinct political entities rested securely within the *Respublica*. The exact relationship of the *regnum* to the *Respublica* was always less than clear, but the unity of the commonwealth was not seriously questioned. By the eighteenth century, when the kingdoms had become states, in fact and in law, the unity of the medieval world was destroyed.

The key element in the transition from kingdom to state was the emergence of the doctrine of sovereignty exemplified most notably in Bodin's *Six Livres de la République* (1576). Bodin articulated a doctrine of internal sovereignty, locating supreme authority within the nation. Although it was left to others, like Hobbes, to develop a clear doctrine of external sovereignty, the germ of the idea was already contained in Bodin's idea of sovereignty as "the absolute and perpetual power of a republic."[20] The consequence of this view for international relations was that the sovereign state accepted no higher political authority than itself.

Faced with this new factual and theoretical reality, each of the normative theorists from Grotius to Vattel sought to salvage the role of natural law in the community of nations. As each author attempted to reconstruct a *jus gentium* in the next context, they moved progressively away from previously accepted concepts of international political community. Pufendorf (1632-1694) substituted the state for the role of moral authority previously played by the church, while Wolff (1679-1754) left the formulation of positive law to scholars, since no universally accepted authority any longer existed.[21]

Each of the sovereign states possessed the attributes of independence, equality, and the right of self-preservation which formed the basis of the principle of nonintervention. The third attribute, declaring each state free to preserve its independence and sovereignty in ways it saw fit, provided the foundation of the new ethic of war: *compétence de guerre*.

**2. The ethic of war: *Compétence de guerre*.** The right of self-preservation constituted the basis of the state's right to make war. Neither concept coincided with the ethic of the just war.

The shift in normative doctrine from *bellum justum* to *bellum legale* was effected by the authors whom James T. Johnson calls the "secularizers" of just war doctrine, principally Pufendorf, Wolff, and Vattel.[22] The substance of the shift can be grasped by contrasting the views of Aquinas and Vattel (1714-1767). In Aquinas, the use of force is a police action which only those with proper authority can initiate in the name of the political community and in response to an act which is both objectively wrong and subjectively culpable.

Vattel's conception departed completely from this penal model. The right to make war belonged to each sovereign ruler, who could resort to force whenever he judged it to be in the interest of his state. This is the substance of *compétence de guerre*, which Johnson defines as the right and authority of each sovereign to decide when just cause for war existed.[23] By the eighteenth century, war was a policy measure and an act of self-help, not an instrument of vindictive justice.

The development of the *compétence de guerre* doctrine fundamentally changed the relationship between war and the political community. The changing conception of war and politics is reflected in the normative writings after Grotius. The old concepts are used but they are filled with the new content. Lacking both a sense of international community and a substantive ethic of force, the post-Grotian authors shaped an ethic of intervention which was the antithesis of the traditional view. For Pufendorf, the only justification for intervention was an act of self-help to enforce a state's own rights. Both Pufendorf and Wolff rejected any intervention based on a penal model of community enforcement as an unwarranted intrusion on the equality and liberty of each state. In the name of protecting the independence and liberty of states, the post-Grotian lawyers affirmed a norm of nonintervention.

**3. Nonintervention as the norm.** Emmerich Vattel and the positivist school inherited and used the doctrines of state sovereignty and *compétence de guerre* in their normative evaluation of intervention. The positions of Vattel and the positivist authors of the nineteenth century were not identical but they were substantively related. Vattel established the framework regarding sovereignty, war, and intervention from which the later positivist position developed.

The way in which Vattel defined natural law manifested points of difference with and dependency upon Grotius. The decisive difference is that the political community of which Vattel writes is a community of states, not the *societas humana* of which Grotius continued to speak even when the political structure of the medieval model had collapsed. The weight given to the independence or liberty of each state highlights the qualitative difference between Vattel and any of the authors writing in the tradition of the *Respublica Christiana*. Rather than a conception of international community within which members have a place and a degree of freedom shaped by responsibilities toward others in the society, Vattel's conception assumes a situation of independent states whose responsibilities toward each other and relationships with each other are determined principally by the standard of preserving the maximum amount of liberty for each.

For Vattel, liberty was the concept which joined the idea of state sovereignty and the duty of nonintervention. To be sovereign is to be independent; since states equally possess this right of independence, the norm of nonintervention must govern their relationships so that each may enjoy liberty and preserve sovereignty. Vattel's evaluation of intervention involved two steps: affirming a rule of nonintervention, then specifying two exceptions to the rule.

He introduced his discussion of nonintervention with a brief statement of the reasons which justify resort to force among states: in fulfillment of the duty of self-preservation, a state could use force for the three traditional reasons of defense, punishment, and the redress of grievances. It was in terms of these categories that Grotius and Vitoria had cast the right of intervention. Vattel proceeds immediately, however, to exclude intervention from the three legitimating reasons for using force:

> It clearly follows from the liberty and independence of Nations that each has the right to govern itself as it thinks proper, and that no one of them has the least right to interfere in the government of another. Of all the rights possessed by a Nation that of sovereignty is doubtless the most important, and the one which others should most carefully respect if they are desirous not to give cause for offense.[24]

Vitoria and Grotius defended both secular and religious reasons for intervention. Vattel rejected in principle both sets of reasons as infringements on the liberty of the sovereign state. The authors who stood in the medieval tradition would probably have adopted as their commentary on Vattel's work the observation of Albert de Lapradelle:

> His work, permeated with the spirit of liberty, is not sufficiently imbued with the spirit of solidarity.[25]

Yet, even as Vattel laid the basic principles for the doctrine of nonintervention which prevailed in the next two centuries of international law, he acknowledged two exceptions to the principle. The exceptions illustrate how Vattel stands as a bridge between the natural law tradition and the positivist school of international law. In one exception he reflected, almost in spite of the rest of his writing, a dependence on Grotius. The justifying cause in this instance was intervention on behalf of cities rebelling against tyrannical rule. Vattel makes clear that this is an exceptional case. The injustice on behalf of the sovereign must be an "insupportable tyranny"; the citizens themselves must revolt and request or accept outside aid; and Vattel adds the final caution that "this principle should not be made use of so as to authorize criminal designs against the peace of Nations."[26]

The second exception to the nonintervention principle acknowledged by Vattel was intervention to preserve the balance of power. In recognizing this exception, Vattel was building upon Westphalia, which established the basis of the balance of power system, and he was anticipating the writings of the positivists who adapted the principle of nonintervention to succeeding forms of the balance of power system.

Nonintervention seemed to belong to the balance of power system.[27] Yet, even though this principle stood out as the basis of state relations, many of the positivists did not hold to an absolute rule of nonintervention. In the view of T. E. Lawrence, author of a standard text of international law in the positivist period, an absolute adherence to nonintervention is unworkable in a community of states. Intervention should be used sparingly, but it needs to be used effectively at times.[28] The determination of when intervention should and could justifiably be used in a legal sense engaged all the major authors of the period. The structure of their normative response was patterned on Vattel's approach, but they significantly expanded the number of exceptions to the nonintervention principle.

Although it is possible to extract from the literature the definition of an interventionary action as coercive interference directed at the domestic structure or independence of another state, there is no standardized classification of the exceptions to the rule of nonintervention. The principal categories of exceptions were: humanitarian intervention, counter-intervention or intervention to preserve the balance of power, intervention to enforce treaty rights, and intervention in the name of self-preservation.

Entering the twentieth century, the rule of nonintervention was in possession; it was part of a whole systemic perspective on international affairs. World War I called that perspective into question and inaugurated a series of proposals, particularly the League of Nations, designed to shape a different conception of sovereignty, the use of force, and the meaning of international community. The premises upon which the principle of nonintervention had rested were called into question. The principle today remains part of the contemporary international order, but it has been placed in a new context.

## II.   INTERVENTION AND THE SYSTEM: ASSESSING CHANGE AND CONTINUITY

To move from the normative history of intervention to an empirical assessment of the place and role of intervention in world politics today is to encounter the gap between the view of the world which sustained either version of the normative doctrine and the shape of the contemporary system. It is simple enough to recognize the radical disparity between the *Respublica* and the system of our day. Neither the religious presuppositions of the medieval system nor its feudal political structure nor its widely acknowledged (if often violated) ethic of solidarity fits our conception of world politics.

A less frequently acknowledged but more significant disparity also exists between the premises of the Westphalia system and the facts of international politics. The premises of the Westphalia system still undergird much of the analysis of international politics and the strategy of foreign policy. Westphalia stands as the "standard model" of international affairs. The model incorporates three ideas: (1) the sovereign state is the basic unit and principal actor in world affairs, qualitatively different in its importance from all other actors; (2) states relate to each other and can be compared with each other in terms of two elements: military power and political influence; and (3) a basic distinction is made between domestic affairs and foreign policy; a function of the sovereign state is to insulate the domestic polity from external forces. These formal propositions continue to hold a secure position in political and legal analysis of international politics. Their persistence is due to the truth they convey. The propositions reflect reality, but they cannot account for the daily fabric of international affairs today. The propositions stand in need of amendment, and the changes hold implications for intervention.

The fundamental principle, the role of the sovereign state, has survived several declarations of its demise. The state remains the basic fact of world politics, but its endurance should not divert attention from the new context in which the state functions. The sovereign state is challenged today by three distinct forces: transnational actors, transnational problems, and international law.

Transnational actors are not a new phenomenon in international politics, but the scope and size of their activities have given them a new status. Transnational actors are typically based in one place, active in several, and are in possession of a trained corps of personnel, a single guiding philosophy, and a sophisticated communications system. Since the late 1960s, the number and variety of transnational actors have attracted the attention of analysts. In a 1973 *World Politics* article, Professor

Samuel Huntington argued that a "transnational revolution" had taken place since World War II.[29] In fields as diverse as economic and energy policy, human rights and religious practice, the impact of transnational actors places constraints on classical conceptions of sovereignty.

This challenge is complemented by transnational problems which also reshape the context for the exercise of sovereignty. Transnational problems test the idea of sovereign control of events implied by the Westphalia model, and they force a revision of the idea that interstate relations are totally encompassed by political-strategic issues. Transnational problems are the foundation of what is today called "complex interdependence," the network of issues ranging from trade and monetary problems to population policy and environmental policy.[30] The nature of these diverse issues— some more central to world politics than others, but none dispensable—includes two characteristics. First, the issues are by nature beyond the capacity of any single state to resolve; even the most powerful states require cooperative engagement by others to find workable solutions to complex interdependence. Second, the logic of relationships required to address these problems differs fundamentally from the political-strategic agenda. The logic of military competition—save for the unique case of nuclear deterrence—fits the model of a zero-sum game; the competition at a certain point produces clear winners and losers. The logic of complex interdependence is that of a mixed-interest game. To press one state's interest to its logical fulfillment can involve a threat to the framework (e.g. the monetary system) which makes the competition possible. Both the nature and the logic of transnational problems demand some revision of the Westphalia model of statecraft. To press a zero-sum conception of strategy across the spectrum of foreign policy today can be counterproductive for the state trying it and catastrophic for the system on which all states depend.

The third challenge to the sovereign state derives from international law, long considered sovereignty's principal ally. Much of international law still fulfills this function, but one important dimension has shifted, the law on human rights. Developing conceptions of international law on human rights have cracked the shell of sovereignty by going beyond the rights of states to the rights of persons. This shift in the law points to a broader theme which transforms the context for the sovereign state: the near collapse of the distinction between domestic polity and foreign policy. The causes of this change vary throughout the system. Among developing countries, it is the weakness of the state or deep divisions within society which generate calls for outside help. In the industrialized nations, the degree of state involvement in the economy and the close ties among these economies are the sources of "linkage" of domestic and foreign policies. In the North-South relationship, immigration policy and the debt crisis illustrate the linkages between states of quite different capacities.

Each of the modifications of the "standard model" discussed thus far— the limits on the state, the expansion of "high politics" beyond strategic issues, and the linkage of domestic and foreign issues—has a bearing upon the role of intervention in world politics. To use a judgment of Professor Karl Kaiser, the concept of intervention "stemming from the conceptual universe of the early nation-state system has become too narrow to encompass the phenomena of interference which are a structural characteristic of the contemporary international system."[31]

The increase in interventionary activity derives from the nature of the contemporary system. It is hardly the organic unit of Christendom, but it is surely not the clinically neat system of discrete units envisioned by Vattel. Describing intervention today requires that it be situated in a post-Westphalia conception of politics. Before proceeding with that description, it is necessary to state the prevailing normative position on intervention.

## A. Intervention and the United Nations Charter

The prevailing normative doctrine on intervention is not identical to either of the positions we have examined earlier. The doctrine in possession today is the evaluation of intervention in the United Nations Charter. If one examines the Charter, however, it is clear that it draws selectively from the two traditions we have examined.

If we compare the Charter's principles on the use of force with the two normative models of just war doctrine and international law, it can be argued that the Charter incorporates elements of both models without identifying with either of them. The Charter's premise on sovereignty and force sets it off from the presumptions of unrestricted independence and *compétence de guerre* which characterized the positivist doctrine. At the same time, the UN system is qualitatively less integrated and less restrictive of members' sovereign rights than the medieval normative doctrine. The limits on sovereignty in the Charter are significantly more restrictive than Vattel or the positivists would allow, but substantially less constraining than the *Respublica* of Aquinas or the *societas humana* of Grotius. The restrictions on recourse to force in the Charter contradict *compétence de guerre*, but the model of collective use of force is much less ambitious than the penal model of Aquinas or Grotius.[32]

Finally, the ethic of intervention manifests the same reflection of the two traditions, respecting sovereignty but restricting its scope. The clearest example of this is the way the themes of intervention and human rights are related in the Charter system.

The ethic of intervention is set by two controlling texts which join the principle of nonintervention to other principles in the UN system. The two texts are article 2(7) and the declaration of nonintervention contained in the General Assembly resolution 2125 (24 October 1970). The two principles are directed toward two distinct sets of relationships within the international system: the UN and individual states; then our state vis-à-vis others.

Article 2(7) controls the relationship of the UN as an organization toward its member states through the concept of domestic jurisdiction. The article reads:

> Nothing contained in the present Charter shall authorize the United Nations to intervene in matters which are essentially within the domestic jurisdiction of any state or shall require the Members to submit such matters to settlement under the present Charter; but this principle shall not prejudice the application of enforcement measures under Chapter VII.

Without surveying the intricate debate about what "domestic jurisdiction" encompasses, it is possible to indicate the normative function of the article. In American political parlance, it would be defined as a "states rights" article; the presumption of political authority rests with the sovereign state's right to control its affairs; the burden of proof in this article rests with the UN to show cause for intervention.

In analyzing the domestic jurisdiction clause, it is possible to find again in the UN Charter reflections of the medieval and modern ethics. The medieval system, universalist in principle and procedure, accorded the presumption of law to the central authority; in the medieval relationship of *regnum* and *Respublica*, it was the *regnum* which was subordinate; the Charter reverses this dynamic. At the same time the Charter does place the domestic jurisdiction principle within a setting of law, responsibility, and obligation which the nineteenth-century understanding of sovereignty would not acknowledge.

The limits placed on the United Nations become clear in the question of human rights. The effect of UN declarations has established the protection and promotion of human rights as a responsibility of the international community. While this responsibility is acknowledged in the UN system, the prohibition on intervention in fact severely limits the action which can be taken by a UN agency, unless the violation of human rights can be classified as a threat to peace and the enforcement procedures of chapter VII of the UN Charter can be invoked.

What of individual states? Here the profound ambivalence about intervention is made clear. In a sense, both the League of Nations and the UN Charter were designed to remedy the Westphalia system. The rule of nonintervention, cast in absolute terms, was part of the system to be remedied. The post-World War II legal protection of human rights was an expression of the effort to build a more cohesive international regime. But the disparity of power in the contemporary system, combined with the multiple opportunities which interdependence offers for intervention, led the small and new states in the system to set severe restraints on intervention. The 1970 declaration on "Principles of International Law concerning Friendly Relations and Cooperation among States" affirmed nonintervention in more explicit terms than the Charter had ever used.

The normative doctrine, the product of two earlier distinct traditions, is now suspended between two perspectives on its role. One asserts the need to "adjust" the nonintervention principles to the realities of the contemporary system; the other feels the unity of the system and the immense power disparities within it require strict adherence to nonintervention in spite of interdependence and transnational linkages.

## B. The pattern of intervention: The Cold War legacy

What would it mean "to readjust" the nonintervention rule? All agree that it does not correspond to the actual dynamics of world politics today. Most agree that some recasting of the rule would close the gap between theory and practice. But the question remains whether "readjust" is simply another way of saying the normative barriers to intervention should be lowered. Can the rule be refashioned without eroding its limited but significant role in the international system? To respond to that question requires a review of the pattern of intervention in the Cold War competition, and an assessment of likely possibilities in a post-Cold War world.

Stanley Hoffmann described the Cold War system as one of "generalized" intervention.[33] The root causes for the expansion of intervention were the degree of ideological conflict in the system, the abundance of targets of opportunity, and the displacement of the superpower competition from direct engagement to a struggle over who governs and how in strategically important areas of the system. These three proximate causes of intervention have been reflective of more fundamental characteristics of the contemporary international system. Historically, both bipolar and balance of power systems generated intervention, but in diverse ways. Today the system is strategically a bipolar world, but economically multipolar and increasingly interdependent; this combination of characteristics yields the interventionary results of both prior models in the same system. The ideological conflict inherent in bipolarity generates one kind of intervention; the density of interdependent relations invites manipulation as a standard policy tool.

One way to sketch the pattern of intervention in the Cold War is to limit the analysis to the superpower competition. While not an exhaustive survey, it does follow the truth of Hedley Bull's comment that "The great intervening powers of modern history, although by no means the only ones, have been the great powers, and a great power is, among other things, a power that cannot be intervened against. . . ."[34] In the past forty-five years, three areas of superpower intervention which can be identified are: direct intervention in the central strategic relationship, intervention within each side's defined sphere of influence, and intervention in the "open spaces" of the system.

In contrast to previous bipolar systems, direct superpower intervention against one's adversary has not characterized the Cold War competition. Save for the Berlin and Cuban crises, the caution of the superpowers has been notable. It is also understandable: the moderating mechanism has been the fear of nuclear conflict and anything which might catalyze such an encounter. One consequence of this caution, however, is that both superpowers have been free to intervene within their own self-defined sphere of influence without fear of counterintervention. The Soviet invasions of Hungary and Czechoslovakia went uncontested, and the Polish declaration of martial law was opposed within very well-defined limits. The U.S. invasion of the Dominican Republic, Grenada, and Panama met no Soviet resistance, and the U.S. role in Chile in 1973 encountered a less vigorous response than the Soviets (or the Poles) experienced in 1982. Superpower restraint in their direct competition has left countries within their immediate ambit in a highly vulnerable position.

The third case—competition in the open spaces of the international system—amounts to intervention in developing countries. Here the rules have never been codified, and the developing world has been the laboratory for superpower intervention. Because no consensus existed comparable to the first two cases, two consequences ensued.

First, in a continuation of the Melian dialogue, small or divided nations remained quite vulnerable either as stakes or pawns in the superpower competition. This remains a fact even if it is also true that many of the developing countries have learned how to manipulate the larger powers within some well-defined limits. Second, the failure to find any procedural or substantive consensus for superpower behavior in the "open spaces" has frustrated the policies of three quite different U.S. administrations.

The Kissinger version of détente faltered not on nuclear weapons or the European theatre, but on the Soviet refusal to agree to U.S. conceptions of stability and legitimacy in the developing world. The Carter administration, using a different vision and different tactics (in line with the 1976 Notre Dame speech), found its attempts to reshape the rules of the game labeled vacillation and weakness from the Horn of Africa to Iran to Central America. The Reagan administration, disdaining both Kissinger and Carter, was never able to build a domestic consensus for the Reagan Doctrine (Afghanistan notwithstanding), nor was its policy any advance over the two previous attempts to regulate superpower competition in the open space of the developing world.

As both Hedley Bull's collection and R. J. Vincent's *Nonintervention and International Order*[35] attest, the most vociferous and consistent support for the rule of nonintervention is found in the states of the developing world. This is due not only to their experience of and vulnerability to classical military forms of intervention, but also because the other non-military forms of intervention arising from interdependence also threaten them. Collective intervention by international institutions in the strategic realm remains a theoretical proposal, but an analogue exists in the area of political economy. The role of the IMF austerity plans and World Bank structural adjustment loans, even when negotiated with governments, as they must be, take on the aura of intervention for many developing countries.

## C. Possibility of intervention: The post-Cold War era

Stanley Hoffmann concludes his assessment of the problem of intervention with the judgment that the only nonutopian solution to intervention is to shape an international system where states are strong enough to resist outside pressure and the main competitors are ideologically disarmed.[36] At the outset of the 1990s, neither of these conditions has been met, but a substantial shift has occurred between the main competitors in the world which may at least approximate a systemic change. The developments within the Soviet Union in the late 1980s, the collapse of Soviet rule in Eastern Europe in 1989, and consequences of both of these events for U.S.-Soviet relations will inevitably influence the question of intervention.

A post-Cold War world is not a guarantee that intervention will disappear as a fact of life, but the pattern and problems of intervention will be changed. In the last forty years, direct intervention by either superpower in the internal affairs of the other was simply too dangerous; the ultimate danger—of nuclear confrontation—still exists and it is now complemented by a political climate which has "normalized" the superpower relationship. Both caution and cooperation support the nonintervention principle at the highest level of international politics.

The stringent stability of Cold War politics should be more civil but no less stable regarding intervention in the 1990s.

The issues become more complex and less reassuring in the cases of intervention within the superpowers' sphere of influence. The most volatile arena of the Cold War, Soviet intervention in Eastern Europe, has been decisively altered. While one should seldom say "never" in world politics, it seems almost impossible to conceive of the Soviet Union—in its present political and economic condition—repeating a 1956 or 1968 in the newly liberated states of Central and Eastern Europe. Here again, the movement beyond the Cold War reinforces nonintervention.

But the very conditions within the Soviet Union which make foreign intervention unlikely, raise the possibility of widespread use of Soviet forces in the republics of the Soviet Union and/or in the Baltic states. Timothy Garton Ash's ominous judgment is a sobering reminder of how frequent Russian "interventions" within the Soviet Union might become: "Of course a peaceful harmonious transition of the USSR to a democratic federation, confederation, or merely commonwealth would be preferable to a conflict-ridden, halting, sometimes violent disintegration. But the latter is more probable."[37]

If Ash is correct, "generalized intervention" may become a pattern *within* the Soviet Union. Effective responses from the West would be limited to the use of economic leverage in a style resembling the pressure applied to U.S. allies in the 1970s and 1980s in the name of human rights.

Within the U.S. sphere of influence, the Grenada and Panama interventions illustrate the untrammeled freedom still available to a superpower. For the United States restraint will have to be a product of internal forces—principles of policy, convictions about international law, and public opinion. None of these were highly visible in the Grenada and Panama debates. The interventions found support within the two countries and in the United States, but there was little normative assessment of the policy choices. Partly as a result of these "successful interventions" and partly due to the legacy of the Reagan doctrine debates, there remains in the United States a certain constituency which espouses an interventionary posture in the name of fostering democracy.

Precisely because of declining Soviet capabilities to function on a global basis, the fate and future of the principle of nonintervention rests heavily on the content of the U.S. policy debate. The background for the debate about intervention will be framed by two realities—one empirical, the other normative.

The empirical change is the new possibility which exists to address intervention in the "open space" of the developing world. This has been the most enticing arena for superpower intervention and the most difficult to regulate. Since the opportunities for intervention arise often from local and regional conflicts with indigenous roots, there is little hope that the *possibilities* for intervention will decline. The changing content of superpower relations, however, does provide the foundation for shaping rules of restraint for outside actors. This would be less ambitious than Hoffmann's process of "ideological disarmament," but it could serve to keep local conflicts local, depriving them of the increased firepower and ideological intensity which accompany the engagement of either big power in a local or regional dispute. In the outcome of the Iran-Iraq war and in Namibia, there were some signs that the superpowers could find ways to limit conflict and even to facilitate peace. The domestic needs of both and the change in their political relationship provide both super-powers with reasons to support the nonintervention principle.

This possibility in the practical order should be pursued in light of the broader normative issues raised by Hedley Bull's opening question—how close the gap between the actual dynamics of international affairs and the ethics of intervention? The twin characteristics of a highly interdependent international system with enormous disparities of state power require a strong reaffirmation of the nonintervention principle. Here the words and deeds of the superpowers can be critical. Precisely because their changing relationship allows for a decrease in interventionary activity (a purely empirical reality), they can valuably contribute to the norm and the practice of nonintervention.

To reaffirm nonintervention by states is to leave unattended the criticism that such a rule fails in the vision of solidarity and responsibility which animated the moral doctrine on intervention. Three reasons which are frequently proposed in the theoretical literature as justifications for intervention are humanitarian intervention, intervention in support of self-determination, and intervention on behalf of human rights.[38] While all three provide "just cause" arguments for intervention, the just means, intentionality, and hope of success criteria raise formidable doubts about the possibilities of keeping such interventions contained and disinterested. In all three cases the preferred mode of execution would be some form of collective intervention.

Acknowledging the marginal possibilities for mounting collective action, I would find the humanitarian case—preventing genocide or other *massive* violations of human rights—the most compelling reason to justify military action by a state. The self-determination and human rights cases provide a "just cause," but should not be understood as justifying reasons for *military* intervention. Rather, the just means test—especially the proportionality test—requires that action by states to assist self-determination or to prevent human rights violations be restricted to the normal instruments of foreign policy short of force. These restraints apply also, in my view, to intervention on behalf of democracy. While an entirely worthy and necessary objective of U.S. policy, the pursuit of it ought to be effected through methods and means of "daily diplomacy," not through the use of force.

Nonintervention is not an invigorating moral style; but the principle embodies a certain wisdom in a world of states. The wisdom should be reaffirmed and respected even as its limits are acknowledged. Exceptions to the principle can be justified, but in this case, the fewer the better.

## Notes

1. H. Bull, ed., *Intervention in World Politics* (Oxford: Clarendon Press, 1984), 6.
2. The normative sections of this chapter are drawn from Hehir, "The Ethics of Intervention: Two Normative Traditions," in P. G. Brown and D. MacLean, eds., *Human Rights and U.S. Foreign Policy: Principles and Applications* (Lexington, Mass.: Lexington Books, D. C. Heath and Co., 1979), 121-40.
3. For an exposition of the premises and philosophical position which sustained the *Respublica*, cf. A-H Chroust, "The Corporate Idea and the Body Politic in the Middle Ages," *Review of Politics* 9 (1947): 423-52; M. Wilks, *The Problem of Sovereignty in the Late Middle Ages* (Cambridge: University Press, 1963); G. Ladner, "Aspects of Medieval Thought on Church and State," *Review of Politics* 9 (1947): 403-20.
4. O. Gierke, *Political Theories of the Middle Ages*, trans. F. W. Maitland (Cambridge: University Press, 1938), 7-8.
5. For an analysis of the church-state issue as it was perceived in the Middle Ages, cf. Y. Congar, *Catholicisme, hier, aujourd'hui, demain*, vol. 3, s.v. "Eglise et etat," 1430-41 (1952); J. C. Murray, *We Hold These Truths: Catholic Reflections on the American Proposition* (New York: Sheed and Ward, 1960), 197-211.
6. I. B. Walters, Jr., *Five Classic Just-War Theories: A Study in the Thought of Thomas Aquinas, Vitoria, Suarez, Gentili and Grotius.* Unpublished Ph.D. dissertation, Yale University, 1971, 420. The analysis of Aquinas, Vitoria, and Grotius in this essay draws extensively from Walters' superbly constructed work.
7. The just war theory appears in Aquinas in a very sparsely delineated form. For an analysis of the multiple criteria which have been used in just war theory and are accepted today as defining the circumstance legitimating the use of force, cf. R. Potter, *The Moral Logic of War* (Philadelphia: Department of Church and Society, United Presbyterian Church, n.d.); J. Johnson, "Just War Theory: What's The Use?," *Worldview* 19 (1976): 41-47. For Aquinas, cf: II-IIae, q. 40; q. 64.
8. For commentators who find a broad conception of intervention, cf. R. Regout, *La Doctrine de la guerre juste de Saint Augustin à nos jours d'après les théologiens et les canonistes Catholiques* (Paris: A. Pedone, 1934); D. Beaufort, *La Guerre comme instrument de secours on de punition* (The Hague: Martinus Nijhoff, 1933). While both authors assert that Aquinas would hold for the right of a state to intervene anywhere on behalf of those in need, neither author indicates how,

on the basis of texts from Thomas, they would justify intervention which was
not carried out to defend or vindicate the state executing the intervention.

9. T. Gilby, *Between Community and Society* (London: Longmans, Green &
Co., 1953), 58.

10. Grotius's two major works were *De Jure Praedae Commentarius*, trans. G.
L. Williams and W. H. Zeydel, *Classics of International Law*, 2 vols. (Oxford:
Clarendon Press, 1950); *De Jure Belli ac Pacis*, trans. A. C. Campbell (Washing-
ton, D.C.: M. W. Dunne, 1901). Future references to *De Jure Belli* (hereafter
*JBP)* will be cited with book number, paragraph number, and page number from
the Campbell edition.

11. Grotius's strategy is embodied in the following famous quotation: "What
we have been saying would have a degree of validity even if we should concede
that which cannot be conceded without the utmost wickedness that there is no
God, or that the affairs of men are of no concern to him." *JBP*, Prolegomenon II,
cited in J. Tooke, *The Just War from Aquinas to Grotius* (London: S.P.C.K., 1965),
197. For an extended discussion of the relationship of the religious and
philosophical elements in the Grotian doctrine, cf. Tooke, 195ff.

12. *JBP* II, 20, p. 247.

13. *JBP* II, 20, p. 249.

14. For a comparison of Vitoria and Grotius, cf. Walters, cited, 339-41, 343-
50. The key texts for Vitoria include J. B. Pate, trans., *Francisco de Vitoria, De
Indis et de Jure Belli Relectiones* (Washington, D.C.: Carnegie Institute, 1917).

15. *JBP* III, 20, pp. 393-400; II, 18, p. 202; p. 212 and *JBP* II, 20, p. 247.

16. *JBP* III, 1, pp. 293-94.

17. *JBP* III, 17, pp. 377-78.

18. *JBP* II, 25, pp. 285-88.

19. E. Barker, *Church, State and Society: Essays* (London: Methuen & Co.
Ltd., 1930), 67.

20. Quoted in F. Hinsley, *Sovereignty* (New York: Basic Books, 1966), 158.

21. For a discussion of Pufendorf and Wolff, cf. W. Schiffer, *The Legal
Community of Mankind: A Critical Analysis of the Modern Concept of World Organization* (New York: Columbia University Press, 1954), chap. 3.

22. J. T. Johnson, *Ideology, Reason and the Limitation of War* (Princeton:
Princeton University Press, 1975), 16. Cf. also J. Kunz, "Bellum Justum and
Bellum Legale," *American Journal of International Law* 45 (1951): 528-34.

23. Johnson, cited, 16.

24. E. Vattel, *The Law of Nations or the Principles of Natural Law* (1758); ed.
and trans. C. G. Fenwick (Washington, D.C.: Carnegie Institute, 1916), II, 54, p.
131.

25. A. de Lapradelle, "Introduction" to *The Law of Nations*, cited, p. liv.

26. *The Law of Nations*, II, 56, p. 131.

27. Cf. Schiffer, cited, 93.

28. T. E. Lawrence, *The Principles of International Law* (Boston: D. C.
Heath and Co., 1911), 135.

29. S. Huntington, "Transnational Organizations in World Politics," *World
Politics* 25 (1973): 333-68.

30. For an analysis of this theme, cf. R. O. Keohane and J. S. Nye, *Power
and Interdependence* , 2d edition (Boston: Little Brown, 1989).

31. K. Kaiser, "The Political Aspects of Intervention (I)," in L. G. M.
Jaquet, ed., *Intervention in International Politics* (The Hague: Netherlands
Institute of International Relations, 1971), 76.

32.  The controlling texts in the Charter governing the use of force are Article 2(4) and Article 51. The first prohibits the use or threat of force against the territorial integrity or political independence of any state; the second reserves to states the right of individual or collective defense. Both texts are complemented by chapter 7, which provides for the authorization of collective defense through a competent organ of the United Nations.

33.  S. Hoffmann, "The Problem of Intervention," in H. Bull, cited, 19.

34.  Bull, cited, 1, 2.

35.  R. J. Vincent, *Nonintervention and International Order* (Princeton: Princeton University Press, 1974), 237ff.

36.  Hoffmann, cited, 28.

37.  T. G. Ash, "Ten Thoughts on the New Europe," *The New York Review* (June 14, 1990): 20.

38.  M. Walzer, *Just and Unjust Wars: A Moral Argument with Historical Illustrations* (New York: Basic Books, Inc., 1977), 86-108; M. Smith, "Ethics and Intervention," *Ethics and International Affairs* 3 (1989): 1-26; S. Hoffmann, cited.

# THE CONVERSATION

Charles Krauthammer opened the discussion by noting that his chief difficulty with Bryan Hehir's paper was its failure to distinguish sufficiently between theory and practice: between the theorist's view of "norms," on the one hand, and the norms reflected in actual state practice. In discussing norms, one must distinguish between the *declaratory* norms enunciated by theorists and scholars, and the operative norms reflected in the conduct of states in international relations.

Krauthammer thought that Hehir's omission of Machiavelli in his survey of pre-eighteenth century writers was particularly notable. For Machiavelli was not so much advancing a radical normative conception of statecraft as he was describing the reality of international politics among the Italian city-states as he saw it. One cannot look at pre-eighteenth century conceptions of "intervention" in terms of the declarative norms enunciated by Aquinas and others, while ignoring the operative norms that emerge from a study of actual state practice at that time and the views of thinkers like Machiavelli who claimed to be describing things as they really were instead of as they ought to be.

A similar problem distorted Hehir's discussion of the contemporary norm of nonintervention, according to Krauthammer. Hehir locates the contemporary norm in the tension between the UN Charter, which has some interventionist overtones, and more recent resolutions of the UN General Assembly that have an absolute anti-interventionist cast. But this misses the key point, viz., that international declarations (in the Charter or by the General Assembly) have little to do with the norms that actually guide states as they decide whether or not to intervene in a particular situation. Considerations of international law play only a very secondary role in this decision-making process. True, states will justify their interventions in terms of international law, as the United States did when it characterized the invasion of Grenada as a "rescue mission." But these are "nonserious" arguments that obscure the real norms shaping a state's conduct. One ought not confuse the norms to which states pay lip service with those that truly motivate a state's intervention in a particular situation. What Hehir calls "the norms of intervention" are not the norms that actually shape intervention.

Further, while Hehir argues that *interdependence* has forced states to return to a norm of intervention, it is actually *the bipolarity of the international system* that prevents nonintervention from being an operative norm. The postwar world has been divided between two superpowers and their allies: each with diametrically opposed value systems, each competing for the "open spaces" between them. So it is virtually impossible to speak of a common norm governing intervention, as if a world community speaking with a single, normative voice existed. At best, there are a variety of norms in today's international system.

Krauthammer also objected to Hehir's description of the Reagan Doctrine as "an exception to the norm of nonintervention" in the modern world. As the chief author of the Reagan Doctrine, Krauthammer thought he could say with some confidence that the Reagan Doctrine was not, in fact, original, but was the analogue and counter to the doctrine of "national liberation" proclaimed by the Soviet Union in the 1950s. For decades, the Soviet Union has pursued a policy of national liberation in contravention to formal notions of national sovereignty; the USSR also has stated, repeatedly, that the goals of "peace," "social justice," and world revolution supersede the norms of nonintervention and national sovereignty. Far from being a unified community, the world in which the Reagan Doctrine was enunciated is one in which one of the major powers denied the norm of nonintervention for many years both by its rhetoric and its deeds.

Even at the United Nations, Krauthammer continued, nonintervention is practiced only "on Mondays and Tuesdays," that is, selectively. When the General Assembly intervenes against Israel or South Africa, it preserves its fictional commitment to "nonintervention" by arguing that these states are not legitimate sovereign entities to which the norm would apply. So there is an obvious gap between the UN's declaratory norm and its operative norm (intervention).

Concluding his critique, Krauthammer argued that the U.S. approach to the issue of intervention ought to be clear and simple. We would prefer a world in which nonintervention is the norm. If we were dealing only with states that shared our values, an operative norm of nonintervention could guide our policies. But we live in a radically different world, in which a powerful rival system of states does not share our values or perspective. In the "state of nature" that characterizes contemporary international relations, and in the absence of reciprocity from our rivals, a unilaterally declared norm of nonintervention is a prescription for retreat and ultimately disaster: the functional equivalent of unilateral disarmament. So long as the USSR remains interventionist, the West cannot adopt nonintervention as a controlling norm.

A general discussion then ensued, with William O'Brien pointing out that virtually every state in the world—including those Third World states that proclaim "nonintervention" most loudly at the United Nations—has its own doctrine of "just intervention," i.e., a list of causes or issues on behalf of which it thinks it permissible to intervene in the affairs of others. O'Brien added that the "nonintervention principle" is not central to the United Nations Charter. The Charter does not mention such a principle, and its only reference to intervention is in the context of authorizing UN intervention in certain cases under article 2(7). General Assembly resolutions may deplore intervention, but such resolutions are not legally binding under international law.

David Newsom suggested that much of the contemporary emphasis against intervention reflects the experience of African and Asian states under colonialism and the desire of these states that the great powers not meddle in their affairs. Newsom also argued that Krauthammer mistakenly downplayed the importance of UN resolutions. In Newsom's experience, UN resolutions sometimes had been the foundation for significant diplomatic initiatives, like the Camp David accords. Moreover, our European allies pay close attention to UN resolutions as indicative of the degree of international consensus on various issues.

Joseph Nye had reservations about both Hehir's paper and Krauthammer's critique. Both approached the problem as if the key moral and political issues could be framed in terms of "intervention versus nonintervention." In fact, though, we live in a world of continual intervention. So states must make distinctions between the kinds of intervention that are legitimate and those that are not. Moreover, Nye argued, there has always been a tension between declarative norms and operative norms (called by Krauthammer "empirical"). This was true even at the height of the nineteenth-century Concert of Europe, which both Hehir and Krauthammer incorrectly characterized as a period of uniform consensus on the validity of nonintervention. The width of the gap between declarative and operative norms does vary, depending on the circumstances of the international system; it was narrower in the middle of the nineteenth century than at the height of the Cold War. But there has always been a gap or tension here. As Krauthammer himself recognized, nations try to justify their behavior in accordance with the declarative norms. We can call this process "the tribute that vice pays to virtue," but it also means that the declarative norms exist, that they embody a moral value, and that their violation carries a price. By assuming that the post-1945 world is radically different from previous periods, Krauthammer concludes that the United States must imitate Soviet behavior and implement its own doctrine of "national liberation movements." This is not, however, the right way to approach the problem. We should simply ask ourselves what norms we should follow, and what our goals are; there is no need to act like the Soviets.

Nye also argued that Krauthammer's emphasis on the moral gulf separating the United States and the USSR, and his radical differentiation of the post-1945 period from previous centuries, led him to obscure two key points. First, differences in values are a relative matter; the United States has more in common with Mikhail Gorbachev than with Ayatollah Khomeini. Second, shared norms sometimes don't make much of a difference in the conduct of states. A common outlook among Europe's Christian rulers in the eighteenth century did not prevent them from going to war against each other repeatedly, nor did it bar them from partitioning among themselves the Christian kingdom of Poland.

Hehir also gives us an incomplete picture, according to Nye, by framing the problem in terms of "intervention versus nonintervention," when the real issue is to develop the just war criteria by which we can distinguish among different kinds of intervention and measure the moral appropriateness of a particular intervention. Among the questions here are the following: (1) Are there situations in which agreement is possible on the existence of a *just cause*? (2) How does one evaluate the *prospects for success*? (3) How does one think of *proportionality*? (4) What limiting role does the principle of *discrimination* play (for example, in a situation where the first three criteria may justify an intervention, but discrimination may prohibit terrorizing or destroying innocent targets)? In other words, we need to hear more about the application of just war principles in a world where we constantly have to make choices, not about whether to intervene or not, but about how far and in what ways we ought to intervene.

Charles Krauthammer quickly pointed out that he did not want to imply that there was no gap between theory and practice prior to 1945 or 1917. Rather, a world divided between two ideologically irreconcilable systems had important implications that could not be ignored. In the pre-1917 world, one could imagine a slow and painful process leading to the development of a genuine international order with a common morality, including a common norm of nonintervention. But such a process is difficult to imagine today. Given this, we cannot act as if there were a common international morality; nor should we refrain from doing to the Soviets what, in effect, they had been doing to us for years.

In response to Nye and Krauthammer, Hehir agreed that there has always been a gap between declaratory and operative norms in international relations, just as in personal morality. International law helps us to narrow that gap by solidifying some of the larger moral principles into customary or treaty law, and thereby increasing their political weight in international affairs. But since the sphere of morality is much larger than that of law, international law is only a useful, preliminary guide on questions of intervention; it cannot always tell us whether a particular intervention is justified or not. To answer that question, we must have recourse to moral reasoning and to the kind of just war criteria suggested by Nye. Hehir also argued that, while there is no unified world community, there are certain characteristics of the contemporary international system, including various forms of interdependence, which on strictly empirical grounds force us to act as if our world were more of a unified community than it actually is.

Alberto Coll argued that there was no reason why "nonintervention" should be accorded such a high priority in international morality's hierarchy of values. Only self-defense should rank as a compelling or "primary" norm of international morality. Nonintervention should be seen, like justice or human rights, as a "secondary" norm or moral principle claiming no greater weight for itself than other valuable secondary norms against which it should be balanced.

John Ahearne drew the group's attention to the high degree of intervention all states practice, not only militarily, but also politically and economically. The United States, for example, puts various forms of pressure on other countries to promote its interests. We try to keep certain countries from acquiring nuclear weapons; we cajole some into buying our weapons systems; we put pressure on others to admit more of our goods into their markets. In doing so, we are intervening quite pervasively in other countries' affairs, just as they do in ours. To focus on military intervention as something distinctly significant is likely to lead us to miss the much more fundamental forms of intervention in which states routinely engage.

Carl Gershman returned to the problem of the United Nations by remarking on the moral incongruity at the root of the UN system: the inclusion within the United Nations, at its very founding, of Eastern European and Soviet states whose sovereignty was nominal only. This foundational corruption has led to an Orwellian process in which various norms have been redefined to mean precisely the opposite of what they ought to mean. Thus, "sovereignty" became a cover under which the USSR set up numerous puppet states. "Self-determination" was defined, not as the freedom of human beings to determine the kind of regime under which they wish to live, but as the freedom of a particular regime to rule the state in opposition both to its native population and to former colonial powers, such that it can do to its people whatever it wishes so long as it is "antiracist" and "anti-imperialist." Even "law" became defined, not as the UN Charter, but as the dynamics of the class struggle against the "imperialist" powers.

Still, there are some more hopeful prospects for the emergence of a common international morality through the peaceful spread of liberal democratic ideology. We live in a world which, if not interdependent, is much more interactive than ever before. Not just in the "open spaces," but in Eastern Europe and the USSR itself, people are aware of the decrepitude of Communist ideology and eager to move on to a post-totalitarian future. We should encourage this process, quietly and peacefully; such assistance would not be an immoral form of intervention because the peoples most closely affected want it. The end result of this form of intervention would be the peaceful dismantlement of the totalitarian system and an international order truly suffused with shared values.

Harold Saunders suggested that there were at least five or six major philosophical systems in the world, not just two as Krauthammer and Gershman argued. But this philosophical diversity must be viewed in the context of a world that now has the capacity to destroy itself through nuclear weapons. The sovereign state no longer has the independence it once thought it had. Common global problems are already bringing about some international cooperation. "Regulated relationships" focused on a specific issue emerge; the parties work out tentative solutions and specify the limits of what they are prepared to tolerate from the opposite side in regard to that issue. Through this gradual interaction, states gain a better understanding of those forms of intervention that are acceptable to other parties and those that are not. Thus, in spite of philosophical diversity, pragmatic processes can develop through which states work out tentative definitions of their mutual expectations on significant issues. Normative consensus is not necessary for this to happen.

Charles Krauthammer emphasized again that the critical problem was the derivation of international norms in a secular age. Such norms, as Michael Walzer suggests, can be determined by observing both what people do and what they say. It would be a mistake for the United States to guide its foreign policy on the basis of what countries at the United Nations say, while ignoring what those countries actually do. Our decision-making process should begin with the norm that emerges from the conduct of states in international relations. We can look at what the USSR does, and conclude that similar behavior on our part in the form of the Reagan Doctrine would be permissible. But this is not the end of the argument. Not everything that is permissible is appropriate. For instance, it may be permissible to assist anti-Communist national liberation movements in general, but this does not mean that we should intervene in the Kampuchea civil war, where our assistance to the insurgents may have the consequence of facilitating Pol Pot's return to power. The norms derived from actual state conduct define the outer limits of what we *can* do, but they do not specify what we *should* do. For guidance on this, we ought to turn, not to the declarations of the United Nations, but to our own Western normative tradition.

In response to John Ahearne's earlier criticism, Bryan Hehir admitted that the military model of intervention offered specificity at the price of sacrificing complexity. What we need is a typology of interventions accompanied by reflection on the norms appropriate to each type. The source of those norms could be a religious tradition, international law, the activities of international actors, or a combination of these.

Disagreeing with Harold Saunders's earlier comments, Bruce Weinrod remarked that the sharp differences in values between the United States and the USSR limited the possibilities for diplomatic agreements between them. It may be in our interest to sign verifiable accords with the Soviets on certain specific, narrow issues. But the absence of a common moral framework makes it difficult and unwise for us to trust them or to engage in the kinds of far-reaching processes of diplomatic interaction and functional cooperation Saunders described.

The United States ought, rather, to follow a dual-track policy. Toward allies and other states that share our values or bear us no ill will, we can follow policies grounded on the norms of nonintervention and reciprocity. To the rest, we can send a different message: until you change, we will compete with you ideologically, economically, and politically, even while avoiding direct military conflict.

Weinrod also noted the role of American public opinion in shaping the norms that guide U.S. foreign policy. Every administration has to proclaim certain international norms and justify its policies in accordance with them even if, in a practical sense, it would have pursued those policies anyway and simply cited the norms as ex post facto support. No administration can afford to be perceived as acting lawlessly or immorally. So we should not allow ourselves to be boxed in by norms that will hamper the protection of our interests; the legal and moral norms we choose must give us the protection we need when we invoke them in justification of our policies.

James Woolsey wanted to qualify and develop Joseph Nye's earlier comment about the inability of shared values alone to guarantee orderly international behavior. In Woolsey's view, neither individuals nor states live up to their proclaimed values unless forced to do so as a consequence of their power being kept in check. As both Lord Acton and Reinhold Niebuhr reminded us, in a world of original sin the limitation of power is an indispensable foundation of ethical behavior. The strongest guarantee of widespread adherence to civilized norms of international conduct is a world in which the external power of states as well as the internal power of governments over their citizens are limited.

Thus, one of the justifications for intervention is helping to establish a society or regime in which power is limited. Through these kinds of interventions, we could move on to Carl Gershman's "post-totalitarian" age, a world in which the majority of states have governments with sharply limited powers. At *this* point, a consensus of values among states would have a meaningful impact on orderly international conduct because these governments, unlike their autocratic counterparts in the eighteenth century, would be restrained by domestic public opinion and political institutions from engaging in international conduct that violated the shared moral norms.

In conclusion, Charles Krauthammer suggested that two criteria should guide U.S. interventions: (1) Is it in our strategic interest? (2) Is it morally correct; i.e., does the intervention serve to promote human rights, democracy, and freedom? The second criterion means that we have to ask the question, "If I were a Nicaraguan or a Kampuchean, would I want this intervention?" Any intervention on our part must satisfy both criteria. In addition, after screening an intervention through these two *ends*-related tests, we also need to subject it to a *means* test: Are the means required to carry out the intervention so morally costly or outrageous as to throw into question its overall worth?

Bryan Hehir then reminded the group of three key themes in his paper. First, there is a repository of moral wisdom in the norms articulated by those who have thought and written on the question of intervention. Second, there are certain factual characteristics of the international system, such as interdependence, which place limits on state aggression and supply incentives for cooperation. Third, such cooperation can proceed even in the absence of ideological harmony, as practical norms of limitations emerge in the process of diplomatic interaction. In spite of the rivalries of its members, there is a functioning international system in which the superpowers can carry out an ongoing pragmatic discussion on issues of intervention.

ROBIN W. LOVIN

# Community, Morality, and Survival: Religious Dimensions of The Ethics of War and Peace

No one is surprised when religious leaders in the United States speak out on issues of war and peace. The connection between our religious traditions and the human longing for peace is so ancient, and the involvement of religion in the great issues of American public life is so well established that silence, not speech, is what would be remarkable.

This speech, however, raises questions which quickly take us beyond the policy issues of deterrence, arms control negotiations, and nuclear strategy. To understand the distinctive contributions of religious thought to the American search for peace, we need to know not only where religious leaders and communities stand, but how their ideas relate to basic convictions about the world and their place in it. We need to know, too, why their ideas should make a difference in a political system where many do not share these convictions. How does the commitment to peace embodied in a variety of religious traditions connect with specific issues of national security? When religious leaders speak, do they address all citizens concerned with the policy choices, or only the adherents to their own faiths? And whomever the leaders address, are there reasons why others involved in the public discussion might need to listen?

There are a variety of ways to approach these questions. In this volume, George Weigel traces the American debate about national interest and national purpose, showing the historical contribution of religious thought to that debate and, more importantly, demonstrating that John Courtney Murray's approach to social ethics offers an important solution to present questions at issue. John Langan turns to the more basic theoretical problem of how moral thinking about national security issues is possible at all. In this essay, I want to examine four types of moral thinking that indubitably do go on in religious communities (and other communities as well, perhaps), and to show that these different understandings make for important differences in the ways that religious leaders claim their place in the public discussion.

To begin, I will distinguish positions that build their cases primarily on the moral truths distinctive to their own traditions from those that hold that the basic moral ideas on which their commitments rest are available in common human experience. Each of these positions, which I will call *traditionalism* and *realism*, respectively, may hold an exclusive or an inclusive view of the moral claims put forward by those who work in other traditions, cultures, or methods of inquiry. That is, both traditionalists and realists may hold that their own moral claims are exclusively true in ways that render the claims of others false or inadequate, or inclusively true in ways that allow argument, mutual correction, and possibly moral consensus to occur across the boundaries between traditions, cultures, and methods of inquiry.

The four resultant categories—exclusive traditionalist, exclusive realist, inclusive traditionalist, and inclusive realist—provide a helpful typology for organizing religious approaches to public questions. Each type can be identified in contemporary discussions of peace, though the actual debate is not, of course, as neatly balanced as the typology. Those who hold the exclusive position in its traditionalist or realist forms, having little confidence in the ability of others to grasp the truths that are important to them, are apt to offer summary answers to public questions, or to withdraw from the public debate altogether; and the "exclusive realist" position, as we shall see, is in its most familiar contemporary form an argument *against* moral and religious approaches to policy questions. The positions of greatest interest for our purposes, then, are those of the "inclusive traditionalist" and the "inclusive realist." Both are eager to achieve a moral consensus on questions of peace and national security, but they differ over how they understand that consensus, and, accordingly, over how they expect it to develop and how far they expect it to reach.

On the basis of this typology, one might expect sharp differences between inclusive traditionalists and inclusive realists in the literature of religious reflection on peace. The actual debate is clouded, however, by a tendency among religious leaders and thinkers to take up inclusivism in *both* traditionalist and realist forms, often in the same document, if not in the same paragraph. While exclusive traditionalists and realists are usually quite clear where they stand and who is with them and who is not, the inclusive reach for moral consensus often leads to a kind of obscurity about what a moral position is claiming in the first place. I will argue, however, that the choice between traditionalist and realist understandings of moral inclusivism makes important substantive differences in how the sought-after moral consensus will be understood. While the purpose of this essay is primarily analytical, identifying and distinguishing different types of religious argument, the analysis will lead us toward a constructive case for inclusive realism as the most adequate basis for religious participation in public discussions of war and peace.

This initial formulation of the typology that will guide our inquiry has necessarily been rather abstract. Let us see if we can specify the details and identify some of the players.

## TRADITIONALISM VERSUS REALISM

How theologians approach a public discussion of policy questions depends in important ways on how they understand the truth of the normative ideas they apply to contemporary issues. The history of the Christian tradition exemplifies two quite different positions on this issue.

• On the one hand, the theologian may stress the distinctive character of the religious truths, which perhaps have parallels in other traditions and ways of life, but which are fully available only in the Christian community and its way of life. Augustine, reflecting on the disordered beliefs and desires that characterize fallen humanity, concluded that even the virtues of non-Christian society were but splendid vices, lacking the genuine love of God from which all true virtue proceeds.[1] In the twentieth century, Karl Barth has pronounced the philosophical search for the good by unaided reason as a failure, and insisted that we must turn instead to an ethics that begins with a divine command if our moral terminology is to retain any meaning at all.[2]

The most recent statements of this position are not so critical of non-Christian moral efforts. Rather, they stress the close connections between truth, meaning, and communities of discourse. Understanding what terms mean and learning how to use them are abilities gained by experience in communities. Religious communities teach, as George Lindbeck puts it, the "grammar" which determines the meaning of religious terms and the uses to which they may properly be put. Lindbeck does not intend by this "cultural-linguistic" account of doctrine to set religious discourse at a disadvantage compared to some more public, universal way of speaking, but rather to stress the role of tradition and community in sustaining *all* systems of meaning, especially those that have strong normative implications. The supposedly neutral, outside observer cannot claim to make an objective assessment of Lindbeck's Christian claims. He or she can only note their incommensurability with the religious, philosophical, or ideological system that shapes the observer's own use of language. The ethical relativity that this implies is a fact that everyone must learn to accept.[3]

⁘ It is this position which I have designated the *traditionalist* account of religious truth and meaning. By assigning that label to it, I do not imply that traditionalists are necessarily conservative on questions of theology and ethics. I refer only to the close connection this position builds between truth and particular traditions and, especially, to the incommensurability between different communities of discourse which this is often taken to imply.

⁌The second position, which I have called the *realist* account of religious truth and meaning, while not necessarily denying that some religious truths may be known only by revelation, emphasizes the large body of knowledge, especially knowledge about human nature and the moral life, that is available to reason and can be learned by reflection on ordinary human experience.[4] The search for the human good which seems to be common to all cultures and communities may be distorted by self-seeking and limited loyalties, but it is not utterly fruitless, and the commandments of God in the biblical revelation complete this search, rather than demolishing it. If the traditionalist stresses the idea of the Fall in its account of the limits of human insight, the realist stresses the doctrine of Creation, the one reality which is both an expression of the will of God and the matrix of experience in which all persons and cultures live.

For the theological realist, the norms by which people live are not simply the product of culture, although all significant thinking about norms takes place in some specific cultural context. The realist sees the diversity of cultures, but also a common effort in all of them to fit human aspirations to the constraints of human nature and the external world, and so to determine, not what we want to do, but what we must do to live the best lives we can. Moral norms are about what we must do to live as we would in a world that is as it is.[5] A theological realist sees this sort of reflection at work in the formation of the Christian tradition, and so is hardly surprised when that tradition converges at important points with other serious attempts to arrive at a moral understanding of the human situation.

The realist position I have outlined includes some key ideas from the Western traditions of natural law, but the realist account as I have formulated it encompasses a number of other positions as well.[6] John Courtney Murray's understanding of natural law as a discovery that is articulated in a cultural consensus, but not exhausted by it, belongs here.[7] So, too, does H. Richard Niebuhr's "radical monotheism," with its insistence that every individual affirmation of value refers, at least implicitly, to a shared center of value.[8] And most important for my argument in this essay, so does Reinhold Niebuhr. Despite Niebuhr's insistence that his Christian realism is a political idea,[9] it was his realism about the origins and authority of moral language that allowed him to engage in critical dialogue with political and religious traditions quite unlike his own. Paul Ramsey was right when he wrote some years ago that a comparison of Reinhold Niebuhr's position with the range of contemporary possibilities would show how much he is in fact dependent on the tradition and theory of natural law. "Or rather, it shows how his [Niebuhr's] judgments are grounded in the same facts of moral experience and truths grasped by reason (or by reason illuminated by revelation) which were enshrined, with more or less adequacy or inadequacy, in this ancient teaching."[10]

## INCLUSIVE VERSUS EXCLUSIVE

The two large bodies of thought I have here labeled "traditionalism" and "realism" broadly cover the ways that theologians have understood their own truth claims, but this simple, twofold classification hardly accounts for the variety of positions that actually appear in religious approaches to public discussion. Some of the actual diversity, no doubt, results from personal biases, disagreements about facts, or simple confusion—elements which defy easy formulation into classificatory schemes. Nevertheless, we can provide a more adequate, recognizable ordering of the possibilities if we also consider how theologians regard the claims made by other participants in the public discussion. As we suggested at the outset, traditionalist and realist positions both admit of at least two responses to the claims of others, an exclusive and an inclusive one. The classification that results directs our attention to four ideal types that illuminate important differences between religious leaders, theologians, and communities of faith as they relate to public issues.

### Exclusive traditionalist

From this perspective, the most important problem in relating theology to public questions is the high standard the biblical tradition sets for human conduct. The New Testament ethic requires a love of neighbor and an unqualified rejection of force that is far more rigorous than the ordinary standards of moral acceptability. Historically, this exclusive differentiation between Christian truth and other morals has prompted either a sectarian withdrawal from most social institutions, or a sharp distinction between the "two kingdoms" that allows the Christian to render obedience and perform services in the secular realm according to standards different from those that govern the Christian life.[11]

In contemporary religious social ethics, this exclusive traditionalism suggests less a sectarian withdrawal from public life than a stance of active witness to the ideal possibilities of the Christian alternative.[12] Witness, not argument, is required, because the values of love and nonresistance cannot be stated in secular discourse. Stanley Hauerwas argues, for example, that the obligation to cherish and protect helpless human life which lies behind the Christian rejection of abortion cannot be argued in ways that count in the courts and legislatures of a modern liberal democracy.[13] A similar point lies behind his insistence that what the churches have to say about nuclear war ought to be said primarily to themselves. It simply will not be understood elsewhere.

> [T]he church's social task is first of all its willingness to be a community formed by a language that the world does not share. I do not deny the importance for the church from time to time to speak to the world in statements and policies, but that is not the church's primary task. The widespread attention given to the Catholic Bishops' recent Pastoral on nuclear war can be misleading in this respect, since it looks as if they have had an impact on the public debate if not policy. Thus the churches are tempted to think they will serve the world well by drafting more and more radical statements. Yet the church's social ethic is not first of all to be found in the statements by which it tries to influence the ethos of those in power, but rather the church's social ethic is first and foremost found in its ability to sustain a people who are not at home in the liberal presuppositions of our civilization and society.[14]

The problem, as Hauerwas sees it, is not just that the demands of Christian action are too high for the realities of political life, but that the language that gives those actions their moral meaning is incommensurable with the values that guide choices outside of the tradition.

### Exclusive realist

Recall that the realist, in contrast to the traditionalist, supposes that a common experience of reality obviates the possibility of incommensurable systems of meaning between cultures and traditions that is a central problem for traditionalist accounts. The fact that all of our systems of meaning relate at least at some points to the world in which we all have to live means that we can arrive at understanding with even those whose ways of life are very different from our own.

Some versions of realism do not, however, extend this confidence to the full range of methods that persons have of investigating and speaking about the world. In the *exclusive* formulations of realism, the confidence in mutual understanding may be restricted to a single method of inquiry or to a rigorously literal language, stripped of metaphors, symbols, and expressive meanings.

The version of exclusive realism that is perhaps most relevant to our inquiry is what Morton White calls "reductive naturalism," an approach to ethics that attempts to ground normative claims in statements of scientific fact and to minimize any appeal to values or concepts that cannot be verified empirically.[15] Carl Sagan's approach to nuclear ethics exemplifies this reductive naturalism: We can demonstrate that the explosion of a certain number of nuclear devices would trigger a "nuclear winter" that would destroy most highly developed forms of life. The policy imperative which follows from this fact—a matter of "elementary planetary hygiene," as I once heard Sagan put it in a televised panel discussion—is to reduce the number of nuclear weapons in the world until it is below the number that could trigger the ecological catastrophe.[16] More speculative considerations about the stability of the geopolitical situation that would ensue, to say nothing of appeals to other values that might be sacrificed in the effort, are irrelevant.

Exclusive realism is more likely to be used to rule theology out of public discourse than as a way to introduce it, though there are theologies which begin with the premise that religious language is expressive, rather than cognitive, and attempt on that basis to obviate the moral differences that may arise out of differing religious commitments.[17] In the modern world, the language and methods of natural science, rather than theology, are most often used to stake out an exclusive claim to literal truth. We need, however, to note at least briefly the forms that this exclusive realism can take in public discussion, in order to fully appreciate the quite different approach suggested by an inclusive realism.

### Inclusive traditionalist

While traditionalism emphasizes the distinctive religious sources of its own moral claims, the traditionalist is by no means committed in advance to a position like Hauerwas's, which declares that theological ethics is incommensurable with public discourse about choices and values. Where Hauerwas sees insurmountable differences between Christianity and liberal democracy, another important contemporary perspective sees close connections.

Consider, for example, the important role that moral traditions play in Michael Walzer's *Just and Unjust Wars*. "The proper method of practical morality is casuistic in character," Walzer says at the outset,[18] and he proceeds to develop specific guidelines for modern warfare from the broad outlines of the just war tradition as received. Walzer's position, while it is not theological, is paradigmatically traditionalist. He makes no case that the values of the just war tradition are universal moral truths, or that they could be affirmed on rational grounds by all people. He would no doubt recognize that one important strand of the tradition makes such claims, but that is no part of *his* case. Indeed, questions about the "foundations" or justification of this morality are explicitly set aside. If we yield to the philosopher's fascination with foundations, we will never get to the practical guidance which we are seeking and which the experience summed up in "the war convention" is able to provide.[19]

Walzer's method of practical morality will prove useful through the remainder of this essay, because he provides an explicit statement of the inclusive traditionalism that appears, unself-consciously, in many recent efforts to make a theological contribution to the public discussion of war and peace. Walzer regards his practical orientation as an improvement on theological discussions of the just war. He has the impression that theologians move too quickly to provide ontological foundations for their moral principles, but it is not clear which theologians he may have in mind. In fact, a rather large part of the modern religious discussion of war, and rights, and international law has been resolutely traditionalist in just the way that Walzer tries to be, providing a detailed statement of obligations, and leaving the justifications to take care of themselves.[20]

Paul Ramsey, for example, reintroduced the tradition of just war thought into contemporary Protestant ethics as a way to provide more normative specificity than either public discussions of war and peace or Protestant theological ethics had been wont to do.[21] A just war casuistry governs his thinking on war and peace from his first treatment of nuclear deterrence, through his early defense of American involvement in Vietnam, down to his latest call for Protestants to make a clear and conscious choice between the inclusive and exclusive forms of this tradition.[22] On this subject, at least, the availability of a shared moral tradition allows him to participate in the public discussion without an awkward reconciliation of his underlying divine command theory of ethics with the forms of moral authority that are recognized in a secular society. As long as convergent normative traditions are available, the inclusive traditionalist can make a public statement by contributing to the casuistry within the traditions. There is no need to argue for the traditions themselves, since it is assumed that no one outside of them is listening to the discussion.

The use of traditionalist casuistry as a point of entry into public discussion appears also, I think, in the Roman Catholic bishops' pastoral letter on war and peace. Catholic moral theology has usually moved into public discussion more easily than divine command ethics, because it took that discussion to be a field of moral discourse in which bishops and theologians shared the same natural law premises as their rightly reasoning secular counterparts.[23] In *The Challenge of Peace*, the bishops move away from the strong claim made in earlier moral theology that this natural law doctrine "has no Roman Catholic presuppositions."[24] Though the pastoral letter strongly affirms the idea of natural law, it articulates the doctrine as the response of a particular tradition to a particular set of problems. It is in light of "the framework of Catholic teaching on the nature of peace, the avoidance of war, and the state's right of legitimate defense" that the bishops "spell out certain moral principles within the Catholic tradition which provide guidance for public policy and individual choice."[25] It is the overlapping moral consensus shared with the wider public, rather than the natural law idea itself, that provides the starting point for the argument about nuclear weapons.

The United Methodist bishops likewise appear to take a traditionalist view of the authority of the just war tradition. They turn to it as a compendium of historic wisdom on the moral uses and moral limits of force. In their case, however, the traditionalist interpretation of just war doctrine ends in a judgment that it is inadequate to the demands of the present situation, and they proceed to construct a more naturalistic theology of "just peace," based on an understanding of the requirements of the created order.[26]

From this inclusive perspective, the incommensurability that demarcates radically different traditions is not between the high standards of Christian faith and the rather weaker demands of public discourse, but between the world of Western democracy, with its Jewish and Christian roots, and other ways of understanding life that lie beyond its limits. While almost all religious statements deplore the ideological divisions that split the world between East and West, the inclusive traditionalist is nonetheless able to draw a rather sharp line between those who are in the moral discussion and those who stand outside of it, deaf to its arguments and unconstrained by its norms.[27]

### Inclusive realism

In contrast to the reductive naturalism of exclusive realism, theological realism usually rests its moral claims on a "nonreductive" or "liberal" naturalism.[28] That is, both exclusive and inclusive realism derive their moral claims from what can be known about the natural world, human nature, and human aims and aspirations. Inclusive realism, however, does not limit knowledge to empirical observations or to results obtained by scientific methods. Instead, inclusive realism assumes that all forms of discourse provide ways to communicate and reflect critically upon this human knowledge of reality. Science does this, but so do systems of law and theology, and religious rituals, and literary traditions—and also folk medicine, common sense, urban legends, and old wives' tales.[29] These discourses may be more or less adequate. Some are very good at incorporating new information, while others tend to perpetuate ineffective ways of acting. Some aim at a comprehensive explanation of human life and its destiny in a universal order, while others limit their attention to everyday aches and pains. What they have in common, nonetheless, is the aim of providing knowledge that can guide action within the constraints imposed by our natural environment and by our own inherent limitations.

This does not imply that all traditions must in the end be saying the same thing. Some or all of them may be wrong about one or many (but probably not all) of the features of this reality. Nor does it imply that it will be easy for persons steeped in one tradition to understand the claims of another tradition, or to make their own beliefs clear to those who do not share them. What it does imply is that the radical incommensurability posited by traditionalist accounts of meaning is not likely to occur among members of the human species on this planet. As Hilary Putnam puts it, "We share a huge fund of assumptions and beliefs about what is reasonable with even the most bizarre culture we can succeed in interpreting at all."[30] For practical purposes, we may assume that when traditions appear to be saying radically different things, this is not because they have different, incommensurable systems of meaning, but because they disagree about the way the world is.

That seemingly pugnacious way of putting the matter suggests, in fact, a possible resolution of conflicts, since parties who disagree can devise forms of argument to persuade one another, or forms of investigation to test and refine their claims, while those who have simply different ways of thinking can only reiterate their positions and circle the wagons to defend themselves against the dislocations that would occur if their culture were invaded by this meaningless babble from outside. The realist position, moreover, requires us to suppose that as long as those who disagree with us have languages in which that disagreement can be framed in the first place, they share with us the ultimate aim of getting it right.

The traditionalist, as Walzer suggests, proceeds to determinate moral conclusions by "casuistry," giving normative specificity to an accepted moral tradition. The realist, by contrast, assesses a moral position in terms of how it is defined and defended in relation to alternative positions. There is more genuine moral argument between competing positions than the traditionalist expects, and whatever clarifications take place happen as a result of the comparison between competing viable options.

The criteria that govern this assessment have seldom been spelled out in detail, but they can be inferred from an accepted example, such as Reinhold Niebuhr's defense of democracy in *The Children of Light and the Children of Darkness*.[31] A realistic moral position, like the traditionalist one, will attend to the lessons of history, but it will also nuance its stance in relation to the positions that others have taken. It will avoid an exaggerated estimate of its own virtues, assuming that the values it holds have meaning beyond its own community and are only partly represented by its own formulations of them. Most important, it will assess actions in light of human nature more generally considered, neither expecting superhuman virtue nor settling for a cynical reduction of all motives to short-term self-interest.

Just what conclusions this realism would lead to in contemporary debates about issues of peace, armaments, and national security is an open question, but the pattern of argument would surely be quite different from the just war casuistry suggested by Walzer. With regard to nuclear deterrence, for example, the realist would be largely unimpressed by assessments based on the casuistic application of just war principles. (Those arguments can, in any event, go either way.)[32] The forty-year record of restraint imposed by the balance of nuclear power would be a more impressive realistic argument for deterrence, though this would have to be tempered by the realization that the whole experiment would be accounted a disastrous failure if it were to become necessary to report instead that the nuclear peace lasted only, say, forty-seven years. An even more skeptical appraisal of deterrence might follow from the realist's attention to human nature, for justifications of possession and deployment of nuclear weapons based on the exigencies of Soviet threat might be discounted as exaggerations of our own virtue, while reassurances about the unlikelihood of accidental or unauthorized use of nuclear weapons would certainly be dismissed as exaggerations of human perfectibility. In any event, the realist would almost certainly insist that no assessment of the morality of nuclear weapons framed against the historical backdrop of superpower monopoly could be adequate to a world in which most medium-sized industrialized nations, several determined Third World dictators, and one or two disgruntled nationalist movements could also mount a credible nuclear threat.

If the emphasis on historical details and human limitations suggests connections between this inclusive realism and the main themes of political realism, the religious aspect of inclusive realism appears in an effort not only to be inclusive of various forms of knowledge, but also to be comprehensive in one's perspective on reality. Inclusive realism, after all, encompasses a spectrum of discourse that ranges from mushroom hunting to metaphysics. Religion concerns itself with the broader accounts of our situation. Indeed, H. Richard Niebuhr has suggested that the primary impact of religion on the public ethos is to provide an ability to understand life in its "ultimate context." Religion is the most inclusive account we can give of the realities that impinge upon us and establish the possibilities within which we must live and choose.[33] James Gustafson articulates a similar theme in his idea of "ethics from a theocentric perspective." The point of placing God at the center of our moral reflection is not that we are able thereby to assume a God's eye view of life, but rather that when we recognize God as God, we are able both to recognize the limits of our own perspective and to expand the scope of our concern to the widest extent possible.[34]

Religious ideas are therefore most important not as we assess technical questions about means, but as we try to formulate the ends of public policy. The argument of a realistic public theology will typically be that the aims of a proposed course of action are or are not compatible with a more comprehensive view of human goods and aspirations.[35] From the perspective of inclusive realism, religious participants turn public discussions toward a more comprehensive view of human circumstances and away from the purely technical reasoning in which the goals of policy are taken as given.

## PUBLIC THEOLOGIES OF PEACE

A thorough understanding of religion's contribution to the public discussion of peace, then, requires an assessment of how those who bring religious convictions to bear on that discussion understand their own theological language. Some differences between religious voices on these matters must be traced, not to proximate judgments about policy, but to more basic disagreements over how the ethics of the religious community relates to discussions of value and choice in the wider society. While it is beyond the scope of this paper to make a definitive argument for one or another of the four ideal types that have just been reviewed, it is possible to make some observations about the shape the public discussion takes if one or another of the theological positions becomes an important participant in it.

For the "exclusive" versions of both traditionalist and realist positions, the question of a distinctive religious contribution to the public discussion does not arise. Exclusive traditionalists, with their emphasis on the religious witness to an alternative system of values, are quite clear about this, though they differ among themselves as to how far this witness may extend into actual political participation. Exclusive realists who insist that all public arguments must be made in terms that fit their reductive naturalism, clearly would exclude appeal to religious ideas as grounds for public action. Religious thinkers who take the position that faith is a noncognitive orientation toward experience, rather than a claim about what is really the case, would presumably agree that religion cannot provide *arguments* for doing one thing or another.

Those who exclude religion from the public discussion thus are usually admirably clear about why it is excluded. Those who seek religious participation, by contrast, are often unclear about the grounds on which they enter the public discussion. In fact, despite the clarity with which we can distinguish "inclusive traditionalism" from "inclusive realism" as ideal types, it is often difficult to tell which of these types a particular religious thinker represents. Pastoral letters and theologians' essays appeal in one paragraph to the traditions of just war as a common human heritage and in another to the realistic constraints of human pride and fallibility. The more expansive treatments even reach for the exclusive appeals to divine commandment or the naturalistic arguments about nuclear winter. Some documents, like the United Methodist bishops' pastoral letter, *In Defense of Creation*,[36] appear at one point or another to hold every one of the four positions I have identified in this essay.

One might, therefore, ask whether there is any practical point to distinguishing inclusive traditionalists from inclusive realists. Both are committed to dialogue with a fairly wide range of nonreligious positions. Both seem as a matter of fact to have arrived at an appreciation of the just war criteria as important starting points in the religious search for peace.[37] Probably some of the participants have not thought enough about the differences between realism and traditionalism to know which position they do hold. Is it really important to make them decide?

The importance of the choice lies, I think, in some differences between traditionalism and realism that point to significant choices that must be made in the public discussion of war and peace. A decisive choice by the religious community between these positions could have an important effect on the outcome of the public discussion as a whole.

Consider, first, the approach to the public discussion of peace that emerges when theologians take an inclusive traditionalist position. We have seen that Michael Walzer's exemplary treatment of the norms of warfare proceeds in this casuistic vein, and that this inclusive traditionalism seems to be rather more prevalent in the theological discussion of nuclear weapons than Walzer himself thinks. Inclusive traditionalism coexists in some tension, however, with other theological methods, and its usefulness as a general approach to religious participation in public discussions requires some careful evaluation.

Where a developed tradition of moral reflection exists, as in the case of just war thinking, a traditionalist approach allows religious thinkers to join at once in the casuistry of public policy. They may need carefully chosen advisers on the technical questions, but as long as they show a competent mastery of the shared moral tradition, their right to speak will be challenged only by the most militant guardians of the separation of church and state. On the other hand, there may be few issues around which such a well-developed consensus exists, or for which the principles of the consensus have a degree of generality that easily permits further casuistic development. Certainly, few parallels to the just war tradition come to mind in a survey of Western thought. So the inclusive traditionalism that works fairly well on issues of war and peace may quickly prove an insufficient basis for a more general theological approach to public ethics.

A more important problem with inclusive traditionalism is the loss of critical perspective on the consensus itself. It is crucial to this traditionalism that one's problems with the consensus be construed either as disagreements over casuistic applications (which is what moral argument is about), or as explanations of how the consensus is to be justified, about the "substructure of the ethical world," to put it in Walzer's terms.[38] On the latter questions, any number of alternative explanations are apparently to be accepted, provided that they do not make particularistic claims that interfere with the serious work of casuistry. Any fundamental questioning of the consensus, however, perforce sets the questioner outside the parameters of moral discourse.

In fact, however, important questions about moral traditions do arise. There are questions about whether the consensus is adequate to provide guidance in new circumstances that are more complex technically or pose greater risks—even the risk of human extinction—than the conditions under which the consensus was formulated. There are also critical questions about the extent to which the consensus not only formulates moral judgments that are widely shared, but also incorporates particular interests in stability rather than in change, or legitimates systems of power which should, in fact, be distinguished from the moral values they purport to uphold. To raise these questions, one must at least temporarily move beyond the agreements that constitute the tradition, and so, from the traditionalist perspective, move the questions beyond the framework in which there are moral answers. This suspension of the moral discussion is not without consequences for action, as we shall see when we turn to a class of situations that Walzer calls "supreme emergency."

## THEOLOGY AND SURVIVAL

However the inclusive traditionalist may assess those outside the consensus, it is clear that moral argument can take place only within its boundaries. Why should that be a problem that would make us pause before adopting a theological version of inclusive traditionalism as the basis for a religious contribution to public discussions of war and peace?

The problem is not that traditionalists, limiting their moral discourse to their own community, may take that as license to treat others immorally. There is ample historic precedent for moral disregard of "infidels" and "heathens," but these abuses result from power and opportunity, rather than from moral argument. A consistent moral relativism recognizes that duties which are binding because one's own community accepts them do not lose their obligation just because some other community does not.[39] The problem that inclusive traditionalism poses is not chiefly a matter of confidence in ordinary moral relationships with those outside our own community. That is an issue that both traditionalism and realism must face, and a thoughtful traditionalist has ways available to deal with it.

The problem is rather that traditionalism has no way to bring a challenge to the tradition itself within the scope of moral argument. When the survival of the community that sustains the moral discussion is at risk, rules of conduct that have maintained our identity as a people and preserved our continuity with the tradition that has shaped us lose their point, and no casuistry can tell us how they should be applied. The tradition tells us that we should observe moral restraints, even when others violate them, and even at substantial cost to ourselves, because those constraints are essential parts of our own identity. But if a situation arises in which "we" may cease to be, not only as individuals, but as a people, then the rules lose their meaning, and may be set aside. What must be done is what we must do to survive.

This logic, it seems to me, is inherent in the traditionalist position, and it is worked out with admirable consistency by Michael Walzer in his concept of "supreme emergency."[40] Walzer rightly hesitates over the difficulties this exception to the binding rules of war implies. He knows that there will be a temptation to exaggerate crises in a cynical exploitation of this loophole in the "war convention," and there will be hysterical miscalculations that invoke the supreme emergency before it really exists. Walzer hedges his own definition of a supreme emergency with stringent qualifications. One may not override the rules of war to shorten the conflict, or reduce the damage, or even to avoid a defeat which, however costly, leaves the moral fabric of one's community sufficiently intact to carry on in continuity with one's past and to live decently in light of one's own values. To be a supreme emergency, the survival of our highest values must be at risk.

> We might say that it is possible to live in a world where individuals are sometimes murdered, but a world where entire peoples are enslaved or massacred is literally unbearable. For the survival and freedom of political communities—whose members share a way of life developed by their ancestors, to be passed on to their children—are the highest values of international society.[41]

Walzer is right, of course, about the horror of this annihilation. In a century of terrors, the Holocaust, the massacre of the Armenians, and the massive killings in Cambodia remain so dreadful that they still numb our minds. But it is not the magnitude of the human catastrophe that warrants the declaration of supreme emergency. It is the threat to a moral community.

> When Churchill said that a German victory in World War II "would be fatal, not only to ourselves, but to the independent life of every small country in Europe," he was speaking the exact truth. The danger was a general one. But suppose that it had existed for Britain alone. Can a supreme emergency be constituted by a particular threat—by a threat of enslavement or extermination directed against a single nation? Can soldiers and statesmen override the rights of innocent people for the sake of their own political community? I am inclined to answer this question affirmatively, though not without hesitation and worry.[42]

The judgment Walzer invokes against the threat of enslavement and extermination is not a *moral* judgment, such as the international community might make in conventions to prohibit genocide or in interventions across borders to protect human rights.[43] Walzer's point is rather that the actions a state takes to prevent the extinction of its own people fall outside the scope of moral praise or condemnation. That conclusion follows, despite his hesitation before it, because if the community which sustains moral meanings for a people ceases to exist, there is no more basis on which moral praise and blame might be awarded.

Despite the otherwise close parallels between Walzer's inclusive traditionalism and the way that many theologians and religious leaders have used the just war tradition in public discussions, there is no parallel to the "supreme emergency" in recent moral theology.[44] Indeed, when theologians have sought to identify what is distinctive in their approach to nuclear war, they have often singled out their disagreement with the "survivalist" values of their secular counterparts. The survival of

American, or Western, or Christian culture cannot count in Christian ethics as a decisive reason for or against the possession or use of nuclear weapons. Paul Ramsey's position is instructive in this connection, precisely because it is otherwise often so close to a traditionalist formulation in his theology of peace. On this point, however, he is insistent that even the survival of the human species as a whole is not a goal which would, of itself, justify a nuclear policy.[45]

This rejection of survival as an ultimate value in the ethics of war and peace appears, when explored in a more complete account of Christian ethics, to rest on a theological version of inclusive realism like that outlined earlier in this essay. Part of the comprehensive view of human beings and their relations that theological realism brings to public discussions is a confrontation with the limits, not only of individual lives, but of human communities and the human reality as a whole. H. Richard Niebuhr points out that when human beings confront these ultimate limits, their initial response is always "an ethos of defense" or "an ethics of survival" that seeks to identify the enemy that poses this threat, and to overwhelm it. It is just at this point that a theological account of our "ultimate context" must challenge the ethics of survival.

> The great religions in general, and Christianity in particular, make their not least significant attack on this universal human ethos by challenging our ultimate historical myth. They do present new laws; they do present to us new ideals. But beyond all this they make their impact on us by calling into question our whole conception of what is fitting—that is, of what really fits in—by questioning our picture of the context into which we now fit our actions.[46]

James Gustafson's theocentric ethics poses a similar realistic challenge to any moral teleology that focuses on human ends to the exclusion of these ultimate limits on our human projects. Any moral meaning we give to human action must take account of a universe which existed long before we—any of us—came to be, and which will continue long after we—all of us—are gone.[47] Paul Ramsey, elsewhere in his work, regards the moral significance of Christian eschatology as just this revision of our sense of why moral actions have meaning.

> Eschatology has at least this significance for Christian ethics in all ages: that reliance on producing *teloi*, or on doing good consequences, or on goal seeking, has been decisively set aside. The meaning of obligation is not to be derived from any of these ends-in-view in an age that is fast being liquidated. The Christian understanding of righteousness is therefore radically non-teleological. It means ready obedience to the *present* reign of God, the alignment of the human will with the Divine will that men should live together in covenant-love no matter what the morrow brings, even if it brings nothing.[48]

A public theology of peace which rests on something like this theological realism of Niebuhr, Gustafson, and Ramsey cannot endorse Walzer's concept of the supreme emergency. If the threat of annihilation renders traditionalist moral restraints meaningless, it is not clear from a realist perspective how they could be meaningful in the first place. That is not to say that the circumstances of supreme emergency, the imminent threat of the destruction of a community and the moral tradition it sustains, do not constitute a very special case in ethics. We would want to construct an international ethic in which the threat, to say nothing of the execution, of that destruction was categorically prohibited. We would insist that rights of sovereignty and autonomy that are ordinarily almost inviolable should yield to active intervention to forestall that destruction and break the power of the forces that were attempting it. But the point of that way of treating a supreme emergency is precisely to formulate a notion of moral rules that is adequate even to these exigencies, not to suspend the rules for the exigent situation. We gain nothing in that effort by adopting a perspective which suggests that the actions of the community directly under the threat of destruction lose their moral meaning unless the community survives.

The problem of supreme emergency thus reveals a discrepancy between the inclusive traditionalist position, carried through consistently, and the considered theological position of some religious thinkers who have also adopted elements of inclusive traditionalism as a point of entry into public discourse. The happy thought that we might be able to treat a version of the American-Jewish-Christian-Western-democratic tradition as a working moral consensus, relegating all theological differences to the "deep and unending controversy" over the "substructure of the ethical world,"[49] proves not to work. The substructure is, as it were, riveted to the normative superstructure at many points. The moral consensus cannot simply be shifted from one platform to another without alteration.

For some, perhaps, the realist position amounts to a declaration of *fiat justitia, ruat caelum*, a maxim that always strikes teleological moralists as pointless, since, as G. E. Moore put it, "those who would assent to the maxim . . . will generally be disposed to believe that justice never will, in fact, cause the heavens to fall, but will rather be always the best means of upholding them."[50]

The point for the realist, however, is the need for an account of morality that penetrates deeply enough into reality to be able to distinguish between the fall of the heavens and the collapse of one's own sacred canopy.

## SUPREME EMERGENCY AND SUPREME CRISIS

The inclusive realist approach to public discussions of war and peace, then, conceives its principal moral task as the articulation of standards that can provide meaningful limits on the use of force when a community is threatened with the loss of its way of life as a whole, as well as in the face of the less complete, though still grievous, losses that accompany less than total war. In the end, those who are unable to sustain an idea of moral action that remains meaningful even under a fairly immediate threat of annihilation are apt to find that it loses meaning in the face of lesser threats as well. The calculation of consequences for oneself and one's community, which Walzer seeks to limit to the most narrowly defined extremity, may well instead become the only measure of meaningful action, at least when the actors are states and their military and political leaders.

If the threat of nuclear war leads us to see this problem more clearly than we have seen it in the past, and so to divide more sharply the realist from the traditionalist options in our ways of thinking about morality, that is one more measure of the pervasive impact that these weapons and their possibilities have had on our life since 1945. The Second Vatican Council spoke of the threat of nuclear war as "a moment of supreme crisis" for the whole human race.[51] The "crisis" here has not just the medical or political senses of a decisive turning point in the course of events, but also the theological sense of judgment. What is at stake is not only whether we shall survive this supreme emergency of our own making, but whether we can do so *within* a framework of values that give meaning to our actions, and not *in spite* of it.

## Notes

1. Augustine, *The City of God*, XIX, 25.

2. Karl Barth, *Church Dogmatics* (Edinburgh: T. & T. Clark, 1957), 2/2, 543. This modern disillusionment with moral reasoning is by no means exclusively Christian. It is reflected, too, in a strand of recent Jewish theology which questions whether there can be ethics outside of the *halakah*. See, for example, Aharon Lichtenstein, "Does Jewish Tradition Recognize an Ethics Independent of Halakah?" in Marvin Fox, ed., *Modern Jewish Ethics* (Athens, Ohio: Ohio State University Press, 1975), 62-88.

3. See George A. Lindbeck, *The Nature of Doctrine* (Philadelphia: Westminster Press, 1984).

4. The attentiveness to the realities of history and political experience which marks various forms of political realism establishes a point of connection

between political realism and the realism explicated here, which is an under-standing of meaning and use of religious language. Realists in this sense may be proponents or opponents of political realism, though I will suggest that Reinhold Niebuhr, the paradigmatic "Christian realist" in politics, was also a realist in my sense. The connection between these two senses of 'realism' is explored further on p. 180 above. In this essay, 'realism' without qualification refers to the position which grounds the meaning of moral ideas in common human experi-ence, in contrast to the traditionalism that relates those meanings more closely to the discourse of particular communities and ways of life. For more on contem-porary political realism, see Robin W. Lovin, "Introduction" to *International Ethics and the Nuclear Age*, ed. Robert J. Myers (Lanham, Md: University Press of America, 1987), and also George Weigel's essay in this volume.

5. Robin W. Lovin and Frank E. Reynolds, eds., *Cosmogony and Ethical Order: New Studies in Comparative Ethics* (Chicago: University of Chicago Press, 1985), 31.

6. Many contemporary realists hold a more pragmatic view of how language is shaped by reality. These authors reject the metaphysical realism of classical "correspondence" theories of truth, but they insist nonetheless that our languages are constrained by a reality that is not infinitely plastic to human conceptual schemes. For a general discussion of these issues, see Hilary Putnam, *The Many Faces of Realism* (LaSalle, Ill.: Open Court, 1987).

7. John Courtney Murray, *We Hold These Truths: Catholic Reflections on the American Proposition* (New York: Sheed and Ward, 1960), 99.

8. H. Richard Niebuhr, *Radical Monotheism and Western Culture* (New York: Harper and Row, 1970).

9. Reinhold Niebuhr, "Augustine's Political Realism," in *Christian Realism and Political Problems* (New York: Scribner's, 1953), 119.

10. Paul Ramsey, "Love and Law," in Charles W. Kegley and Robert W. Bretall, eds., *Reinhold Niebuhr: His Religious, Social, and Political Thought* (New York: Macmillan, 1961), 82.

11. The sectarian position is historically associated with the churches of the "Radical Reformation," whose withdrawal from secular social obligations and benefits is exemplified today in the pacifism of the Mennonites and the Church of the Brethren, and in the more rigorous rejection of public education, social insurance, etc. by the Old Order Amish. The "Two Kingdom" position is historically associated with Lutheran theology and churches.

12. John Howard Yoder, *The Christian Witness to the State* (Newton, Kans.: Faith and Life Press, 1964); also his *The Politics of Jesus* (Grand Rapids, Mich.: Eerdmans, 1972) and *The Priestly Kingdom* (Notre Dame, Ind.: University of Notre Dame Press, 1984).

13. Stanley Hauerwas, "Abortion: Why the Arguments Fail," in *A Commu-nity of Character* (Notre Dame, Ind.: University of Notre Dame Press, 1981), 212-29.

14. Stanley Hauerwas, *Against the Nations* (Minneapolis: Winston Press, 1985), 11-12.

15. Morton White, *What Is and What Ought to Be Done* (New York: Oxford University Press, 1981), 42-43.

16. See Carl Sagan, "To Preserve a World Graced by Life," *Bulletin of the Atomic Scientists* 39 (January 1983), 2-3.

17. For a careful discussion and critique of this noncognitivist position in theology, see Janet M. Soskice, *Metaphor and Religious Language* (Oxford: Oxford

University Press, 1987), 142-61. Soskice herself defends a realist account of theological language.

18. Michael Walzer, *Just and Unjust Wars* (New York: Basic Books, 1977), xvi.

19. Walzer, xv, 44. Walzer is something of a realist when he does give thought to the justification of the moral principles that govern warfare. He says that "morality refers in its own way to the real world" (12), and he assumes, in fact, that all of us do live within that one moral world: "Perhaps there are other worlds to whose inhabitants the arguments I am going to make would seem incomprehensible and bizarre. But no such people are likely to read this book" (Walzer, 20). A realist in the stronger sense that I have given that term would, however, appeal to reality not only at the point of justifying morality, but also in the course of determining the norms themselves.

20. One thinks especially of Maritain's suggestion that people trying to draw up a list of internationally recognized human rights should just agree on the contents of the list and not explain *why* they think human beings have those rights. See David Tracy, "Religion and Human Rights in the Public Realm," *Daedalus* 112 (Fall 1983), 237-54. Note also John Langan's emphasis on casuistry and "the broad consensus that can be drawn in support of mid-level moral principles . . ." in his essay in this volume.

21. Paul Ramsey, *War and the Christian Conscience* (Durham, N.C.: Duke University Press, 1961).

22. Paul Ramsey, *Speak Up for Just War or Pacifism* (State College: Pennsylvania State University Press, 1988).

23. See Richard McBrien, *Caesar's Coin* (New York: Macmillan, 1987), for an up-to-date restatement of this distinction between moral and religious questions.

24. John Courtney Murray, *We Hold These Truths*, 109. Murray may himself have moved toward a more consensual understanding of the natural law, according to the interpretation of his work presented by Leon Hooper, *The Ethics of Discourse* (Washington, D.C.: Georgetown University Press, 1986), 93-99.

25. National Conference of Catholic Bishops, *The Challenge of Peace: God's Promise and Our Response* (Washington, D.C.: United States Catholic Conference, 1983), par. 79.

26. "Over the centuries, three classical positions developed among Christian thinkers and church bodies: pacifism, 'just war' doctrine, and the crusade. While this threefold division never fully reflected the diversity of Christian views, it is particularly outmoded and inadequate for clarifying the ethical dilemmas of the nuclear arms race. Nevertheless, proponents of those classical positions have seriously addressed these dilemmas. Here we sketch the three traditions in briefest outline before addressing the central nuclear issues and proposing a new and more varied ethical spectrum." *In Defense of Creation*, 30.

27. See, for example, Richard John Neuhaus, *The Naked Public Square* (Grand Rapids, Mich.: Eerdmans, 1984), 145-47.

28. Morton White uses the term "non-reductive naturalism." P. F. Strawson speaks of "liberal" or "catholic" naturalism (using the latter term in a nontheological sense and the former term in a nonpolitical sense, of course). See White, *What Is and What Ought to Be Done*, 104-5; and F. Strawson, *Skepticism and Naturalism: Some Varieties* (New York: Columbia University Press, 1985), 1.

29. For an examination of the knowledge claims in traditional beliefs and rituals, see John Skorupski, *Symbol and Theory* (Cambridge: Cambridge University Press, 1983).

30. Hilary Putnam, *Reason, Truth, and History* (Cambridge: Cambridge University Press, 1981), 119-25.

31. Reinhold Niebuhr, *The Children of Light and the Children of Darkness* (New York: Scribner's, 1944).

32. Ramsey, Walzer, and the Catholic bishops, for example, arrive at different assessments of the morality of deterrence within the just war tradition. Walzer (278-83) has explicitly challenged Ramsey's justification of the limited use of nuclear weapons as a deterrent threat. Richard Miller has analyzed a wide range of theological literature on deterrence and concluded that the just war tradition, taken by itself, is not sufficient to provide a moral evaluation of deterrent threats to use nuclear weapons. Richard Miller, "Nuclear Deterrence and Just War Tradition: A Study in Loyalty, 'Realism,' and Risk" (unpublished Ph.D. dissertation, University of Chicago, 1985).

33. H. Richard Niebuhr, *The Responsible Self* (New York: Harper and Row, 1963), esp. 106-7.

34. James M. Gustafson, *Ethics from a Theocentric Perspective*, 2 vols. (Chicago: University of Chicago Press, 1981, 1984).

35. Where religious thinkers turn their attention to questions of means, their contribution will probably be in the limited but important area of showing that the means we propose sometimes require levels of competence or altruism that are incompatible with what we know about human fallibility and selfishness.

36. Council of Bishops of the United Methodist Church, *In Defense of Creation* (Nashville, Tenn.: Graded Press, 1986).

37. This is more true in the American setting than in Europe, where Protestants, at least, are more skeptical of the relevance of just war criteria as a way to frame the issues relating to nuclear weapons.

38. Walzer, xv.

39. Gilbert Harman, "Moral Relativism Defended," *Philosophical Review* 84 (January 1975), 3-22.

40. Walzer, 251-68.

41. Walzer, 254.

42. Ibid.

43. See, for example, Bryan Hehir's essay in this volume.

44. There are, of course, religious thinkers who would readily employ nuclear weapons in defense of American and/or Christian values, but they tend to speak of these uses as the fulfillment of a moral imperative, not the overriding of it.

45. See Ramsey, *Speak Up for Just War or Pacifism*.

46. H. R. Niebuhr, *The Responsible Self*, 109.

47. Gustafson, *Ethics from a Theocentric Perspective*, vol. 1, 87-114.

48. Paul Ramsey, *Deeds and Rules* (New York: Scribner's, 1967), 108-9.

49. Walzer, xv.

50. G. E. Moore, *Ethics* (New York: Oxford University Press, 1977), 75.

51. Quoted in *The Challenge of Peace*, par. 1.

# THE CONVERSATION

John Langan began his commentary on Robin Lovin's paper by observing that the moral justification of a course of action involves an appeal to shared values or premises. Thus, Lovin's search for an all-encompassing grand theory of moral justification may be difficult in the extreme, given the radical diversity of values among people and the near impossibility of discovering premises held in common by, for instance, Marxists, Islamic fundamentalists, Christians, and American military leaders of the Sherman/Patton type. The pluralism of the world suggests that ethicists need a strong dose of humility, and a lower set of expectations about the fruitfulness of theologically or philosophically based methods of relating ethics to politics.

Langan added that ethical theories, whether designed to regulate conflict between communities or resolve moral issues across cultural lines, can be found in two different forms. The "thin" form, highly abstract and formal, focuses on the possibility of discovering common principles among reasonable people in different cultural communities. An example of this is H.L.A. Hart's argument, in *The Concept of Law*, for a minimum content to the natural law: any kind of society will agree on a few basic principles, such as the right of self-defense. One problem with "thin" forms of ethical theory, though, is that they cannot support a detailed casuistry sensitive to the facts of particular cases; so, "thin" forms have limited utility.

There are also "thick" forms of ethical theory, rooted in an intellectual soil that is historically, philosophically, and theologically rich, and developed over time as casuists apply classic principles from the tradition to detailed circumstances. "Thick" theories also have their own problems; they are more vulnerable to historically conditioned factors, and they have difficulty in adapting to changes in the intellectual, social, or technological environment.

In Langan's view, the most one can hope for, in terms of the ethics of international politics, is agreement on a few key principles in a "thin" theory. The moral issues raised by "thick" theories should be left for each tradition to work out, with an eye open to a degree of convergence among the traditions in the long term.

Langan questioned Lovin on two further points. Lovin's use of the term "realism" was unclear, even perplexing. Lovin's "realism" involves an appeal to a wide range of cognitive sources (like history) and certain kinds of psychological hypotheses. But there is a different kind of "moral realism" which focuses on the question of what values are most important. And there is yet another kind of realism, of the "political" variety, which seeks a radical reordering of values which Christians view with considerable skepticism. How does Lovin deal with the differences among these kinds of realism, and what exactly does he mean when he employs the term?

Langan also wished to clarify Lovin's interpretation of Michael Walzer's notion of "supreme emergency" in *Just and Unjust Wars*. One way to understand this concept is to say that there ought to be, within the context of meaningful moral restraints to war, a contained exception in the form of nuclear deterrence. Meaningful moral constraints are not necessarily exceptionless. Does this mean, though, that moral claims do not have an overriding status, and if so, how does one reconcile this with Walzer's contention that moral principles are good from God's perspective and are not to be overridden by human commitments to various projects?

Lovin replied that he would not describe "supreme emergency" as a contained exception within Walzer's moral system. Walzer tells us that a moral system is composed of a series of deontological constraints on the use of force. When a "supreme emergency" arises, the decision maker sets these aside and resorts to utilitarian criteria. But this raises the question of whether Walzer has a coherent ethical system. For one of the characteristics of a coherent system is that any action taken in its name must fit within its logical and moral boundaries. It is, at the least, strange for Walzer to say that under certain threats to his moral system the decision maker must step outside that system and resort to a different calculus in order to determine a morally compelling course of action.

Lovin added that the weakness of traditional political realism is that it does not consider any moral principles overriding. He preferred to describe his own "realism" as a form of "ethical naturalism," grounded in a strong sense of the way in which traditions of language and discourse are formed—which precludes its accepting the notion that we live in radically different and incommensurable linguistic and moral communities.

John Langan noted that war presents a particularly acute challenge to any community of moral discourse, even when the war is between two parties sharing the same moral tradition. With reference to Walzer, Langan stood by his earlier claim that his "supreme emergency" was a contained exception and part of an effort, albeit a partly incoherent one, to restrict the slide into utilitarianism. Ultimately, Walzer ends up recognizing the subordinate character of just war theory to other religious and moral considerations; for he crafted his "supreme emergency" argument in the context of Israel's moral dilemma before its neighbors and its right to protect its identity and way of life.

Michael Novak sought to bridge the gap between Lovin and Walzer on the issue of overriding moral principles by citing the ancient legal maxim, *salus populi suprema lex.* In his critique of Catholic collaborators in Vichy France, Yves Simon appealed to this principle in order to show that it was morally necessary to step outside the law and support the resistance, even to the extent of taking lives. By the "people" Simon meant, not the France of the majority, but that France which was true to its authentic republican traditions and which respected personhood: not simply the French people but the French moral achievement or moral tradition. When that tradition was under fundamental assault, the struggle for its survival overrode other moral considerations, because if the tradition were destroyed, there would be no moral dialogue. Thus, we can say that we always live in an *implicit* condition of supreme emergency. Our freedom to be true to the best in our moral traditions rests on the preservation of those physical and political conditions within which the exercise of freedom and moral choice is possible. The defense of a free and just political order is thus a morally compelling goal of the highest degree precisely because outside this order the rule of might takes precedence over right, and moral action is terribly difficult, if not impossible.

Lovin conceded that this might be a way of dealing with the conundrum posed by Walzer, but that the success of such an attempt hinged on the definition of the *populi*. It is not clear that the supreme value should always be the survival of *this* particular people or *this* particular tradition.

Todd Whitmore argued that Walzer's "supreme emergency" argument was empirically and theoretically problematical. Empirically, the Allies continued to devastate German cities up to the very end of the war, that is, well past the point when Germany posed a deadly threat to their societies. And this, in turn, helped Allied decision makers to condone the atomic bombing of Hiroshima and Nagasaki. The Western moral tradition is concerned over the effects of certain acts on an agent's moral character. A perpetual condition of "supreme emergency," such as Walzer claims underlies nuclear deterrence, means that as individuals and as a society our moral character may be affected, even altered, by our willingness to commit the grossly immoral acts implied in the threat to use nuclear weapons.

George Weigel replied that actions taken under the "supreme emergency" justification are not always morally coarsening. Michael Novak's earlier allusion to the French resistance was quite relevant to this point, as was the personal experience of Albert Camus, who emerged from his involvement in the resistance much more reflective and morally mature than before.

Michael Novak also disagreed with Whitmore, noting that the "supreme emergency" required of its participants the kind of fortitude that Thomas Aquinas considered one of the highest virtues: fortitude exercised over the long term.

William O'Brien reminded the group that, in the Catholic tradition, political society is not viewed as an agglomeration of individual lives and values but as something good and morally necessary in itself. A threat to this society, therefore, is more than a material threat to individual lives. It is a threat to a very valuable human good, and this gives society the right to defend itself.

James Turner Johnson wanted to challenge the assumption shared by some members of the group, including Robin Lovin, that just war theory is purely deontological. According to Johnson, just war theory contains an important utilitarian or consequentialist element. The processes of moral reasoning enjoined by the just war tradition contemplate the inclusion of both deontological and consequentialist considerations as the decision maker ponders what course of action he should take.

Johnson suggested that the "supreme emergency" situation posed a basic conflict between the principles of discrimination and proportionality. In the Middle Ages, "discrimination" and "proportionality" were defined by a concept of justice grounded in a transcendent reference point. In modern times, however, discrimination has come to be viewed solely in terms of an immanent reference point: the rights inherent in noncombatants. Johnson thought it was appropriate to take as our foundation a transcendent reference point, and from it look at the question of whether noncombatant rights are absolute, or whether they are grounded in a lower-order value and thus might, under certain circumstances, be subordinate to a moral principle above and beyond themselves.

Johnson also drew attention to an earlier conception of a theology of peace that has direct relevance for policy makers today. This was the medieval understanding of society as "rightly ordered" only when it ensured justice; this justice becomes, in turn, the most solid foundation for peace. This concept of the relationship of order-to-justice-to-peace is the heart of the just war tradition.

Johnson's appreciation of that tradition also led him to reject Lovin's critique of "traditionalist" politics. A "traditionalist" model, argued Johnson, is adequate for a pluralistic society if it eschews sectarianism and adopts a more denominational approach in which traditions tolerate one another in spite of their differences.

Lovin did not want to rule out unequivocally the "traditionalist" approach. But he thought that "traditionalists" had no way of dealing with the problem of incommensurability between different systems of moral discourse—and the resulting impasse usually resolved itself into sectarianism. By offering a different way to think about disagreements, Lovin thought his "realism" offered a way out of the "traditionalist" dilemma.

Michael Novak cautioned against making too much of the difficulty of reaching consensus. Even at the United Nations it is possible to reach limited forms of consensus. Certain moral atrocities such as the Holocaust and the Cambodian genocide help define the outlines of moral consensus among diverse traditions.

John Cooper brought the discussion back to the issue of "supreme emergency" by noting the awful moral dilemma an American president would face if told that, according to U.S. radar screens, a first strike had been launched against the United States and he had only fifteen minutes in which to order a retaliatory attack before his land-based missiles were destroyed. This would be a "supreme emergency" at its direst, especially given the fact that the president would have to rely solely on information from computers.

Robert Gessert thought that Cooper's scenario forced us to think about how to avoid putting a president in that kind of situation. Paul Nitze has long argued that we should structure our nuclear strategy and weapons so that if an American president were confronted with the kind of scenario described by Cooper, his first option would be a defensive one. The Strategic Defense Initiative might be such an option, as would be more discriminate weapons systems with greater accuracy and control, weapons that could be used against Soviet weapons while reducing collateral damage to noncombatants. People who want to make nuclear war more controllable would be in agreement with Nitze's position. Those who thought that the best way to strengthen deterrence is to make nuclear war so uncontrollable and destructive as to make it unthinkable would oppose Nitze's position, even though their course of action would leave the president with no meaningful moral option in case deterrence ever breaks down.

R. James Woolsey wanted to qualify Gessert's observation by challenging its outward moral elegance. Gessert's proposed solution would work if the West held nuclear weapons solely for the purpose of deterring nuclear war. But in fact, the West is also prepared to use nuclear weapons in response to certain forms of conventional aggression. Hence, we could be the first to use nuclear weapons, and this might touch off an escalatory reaction in which distinctions between defensive and offensive weapons would quickly disappear. Woolsey did not disagree with this "first-use" strategy, because he thought that on balance it had worked in discouraging Soviet aggression against Western Europe. But it certainly made Western nuclear strategy less morally elegant than Gessert seemed to claim.

Michael Novak pointed out that neither systems analysis nor theoretical moral analysis can provide a complete answer to the question of how a president ought to, or would, react if placed in John Cooper's scenario. A very important variable is likely to be the decision maker's character. And character is a matter of virtue and inner strength.

John Langan wondered what the relationship of Lovin's conception of "realism" was to the kind of moral realism proposed by John Finnis, Germain Grisez, and Joseph Boyle in *Nuclear Deterrence, Morality and Realism* (1987). These scholars argue that nuclear deterrence is unacceptably immoral because it rests on the threat to destroy millions of innocent lives; moreover, the threat is not only immoral itself, but it also corrupts those who wield it. Lovin replied that his conception of "realism" differed in that it recognized that a situation cannot be morally evaluated to the fullest extent on the basis of a hypothetical "what if" question. Deterrence may look *as if* its substance is the threat to do something grossly immoral, but that is not necessarily what it is about.

In closing the discussion, Lovin emphasized that the kind of culture we can create is a key to whether we will be able to discuss these moral issues freely and reflectively. And without a "realistic" understanding of our philosophical theologies and their limitations, we can slide into a situation in which our fragile cultural consensus fragments into a series of sectarian discussions in which we are unable to communicate across our differences.

JOHN P. LANGAN, S.J.
AND HAROLD H. SAUNDERS

# Refocusing the Ethical Agenda: Political Settlement as an Alternative to the Use of Force

## THE NEED TO CRYSTALLIZE AN ETHICS OF POLITICAL SETTLEMENT

A world plagued by hunger and poverty and weighed down by the cost and danger of highly destructive weapons demands that nations resolve conflicts peacefully. This requires a historic rethinking of familiar concepts used to explain how nations relate and new attention to processes of conflict resolution. In the nature of things, these processes will necessarily be political; given the current condition of the world, there is overwhelming need for them to be peaceful. The situation further demands renewed attention to the ethics of resolving conflict both justly and peacefully.

Ethical reflection about international relations has long taken as given a choice between just war—albeit as a last resort—and negotiation. It has also dealt with a stark contrast between two approaches to the conduct of international relations: First was the supposed "realism" of state institutions providing security by translating economic resources through military technology into the ability to have one's way by force if need be or by forcing negotiation if possible. Second was a so-called "idealistic" approach that assumed the actions of nations should be constrained by some moral considerations and that interaction among nations should be governed by internationally accepted principles, which were to be as enforceable as possible.

Changes in today's world make it misleading to think any longer that such either/or choices exist. As whole human beings, we are at the same time realists and idealists. The difference has become a matter of emphasis. The world today demands a wider range of ways to generate change peacefully and a new integration of ethical thought to assure justice.

Familiar concepts of international relations often do not provide an accurate picture of how today's world works. Familiar instruments of statecraft do not reliably produce the results expected of them. This is not to say that states are fading from existence or that either force or economic power has become irrelevant; these factors still create a framework within which international life takes place, but their nature and relative importance are changing. It is now clear that we have not paid adequate attention to a wide range of possibilities for generating change politically and peacefully.

Consider experience in the past half-century—a world war followed by "the long peace." Military and economic power have been needed to confront a Hitler, a Stalin, a Pol Pot, or a Saddam Hussein. Reflections on "the long peace"—as well as on whether World War II could have been prevented—focus on words like containment, deterrence, and quarantine. Behind the shield established by containment and deterrence, creative change in Western Europe actually came from human reconciliation between Germans and their former enemies, from a Marshall Plan that rebuilt friend and foe alike, from the vision of individuals who imagined a new Europe based on political and economic community. Change in Eastern Europe and the Soviet Union that ended the Cold War came about as people saw more clearly and vividly the dramatic disparity between their system and that of the Atlantic Community. When change came, it came because leaders decided they could not sustain an empire based only on military power; it came when those with no raw power demanded an end to regimes that had no legitimacy.

We do not have such conclusive examples from the Third World, but the point is also valid there. Arabs and Israelis recognize that neither can impose a resolution of their conflict by force of arms; when peace comes, it will come through a political process of changing relationships. On the other side of the world, the Association of Southeast Asian Nations (ASEAN) showed that it is possible to build a community among nations with divergent traditions. Conflict in Nicaragua has not been ended by a decisive victory in battle but has been slowly transformed through a political process.

We must devote much more attention to the political processes that produce change peacefully. In that effort, we need a sustaining body of ethical thought. Students of ethics in this field face three challenges.

The first is to identify and rethink ethical principles that have been built around the behavior of nation states and the traditional instruments of statecraft but are not adequate guides to action in today's world. Some of them no longer probe deeply enough to guide the conduct of relationships among nations in our highly interactive and interdependent world. Some of them may even block creative thought about the peaceful resolution of conflict.

A second challenge is (a) to recognize the wide range of political actions between war and negotiation that can help change relationships and resolve conflict peacefully and (b) to elaborate a body of ethical norms to assure justice in those actions. Much more attention has been given to the question of when war is just than to the ethics of negotiating processes and political settlements.

A third challenge, as interactions among nations become more intricate, is to rethink together across cultures—east, south, west, and north—the principles governing those relationships. For what seems just in one tradition may often seem unjust in another.

This essay begins to respond to these challenges. It is important to underscore that we are not rejecting work done in the past; we do say that a great deal of previous ethical thinking about international order and conflict has not probed deeply enough. We also recognize the possibility of a continuing need to use force against aggression by states. But direct aggression will probably not be the source of most of the conflicts that will plague the world. In many racial, sectarian, and ethnic conflicts, political settlement may provide the only hope of ending violence. Our purpose is to offer a way of developing our ethical understanding of international conflicts in a way that will provide appropriate guidance in a vastly changed situation.

Reorganizing our thinking about how nations relate and the ethical foundations of those relationships is not an abstract theoretical exercise. How governments and people picture what they do heavily influences how they do it. So this is not a discussion about theories and theologies but about how leaders will achieve justice through different instruments that bring about destruction, peacemaking, and economic progress.

## OUR CHANGING WORLD REQUIRES REFOCUSING THE ETHICAL AGENDA

For four hundred years we have pictured nation-states as rational institutions with leaders amassing military and economic power to pursue supposedly objective interests in strategic zero-sum contests with other states. The underlying metaphor has been the chess game. We have pictured problems being resolved by the use or threat of power or by forcing formal negotiation.

That picture alone does not fully explain how nations relate today, if it ever did. This chapter begins from a contrasting observation: *Rather than visualizing a strategic chess game, we increasingly see relations among nations today as a political process of continuous interaction among whole bodies politic. That dynamic process may be called "relationship."* If power is the ability to influence the course of events, power today may emerge at least as much from the political ability to conduct those overall relationships effectively as it does from wielding military or economic power or being an unyielding negotiator. If power lies in the conduct of relationships, we need to understand the ethics of its use in that function.

### Changes in today's world

Our rethinking of relationships among nations starts from three related observations about how nations interact in today's world.

First, we see more and more problems that no one state can deal with alone. This is true partly because these problems cross borders and partly because more centers of influence affect events today. We find ourselves reflecting more and more on the nature and limits of state power and the ways in which this power is exercised outside formal contacts with other states.

Nuclear weapons began to transform our thinking. We realized that the effort of one state to achieve absolute security might increase insecurity in another nuclear state and provoke a preemptive nuclear attack. Late in the 1970s the idea of "common security" emerged, paradoxically affirming that governments may not be able to provide security for their people without the cooperation of potential adversaries. In the economic field, the world needs to rethink its concepts of competition and cooperation. No one nation can prosper alone, and threats to economic security reach across borders in the form of ecological dangers as well as in the more traditional areas of trade and international monetary practices. Even human rights—once the exclusive province of individual governments— affect international relationships.

Second, we find a growing need to pay more attention to the political energies and interactions of communities of people rather than concentrating merely on states and governments. More people now interact more immediately, so there is greater need to take the human factor into account both within and among nations. With broadening popular participation, change often seems to swell from the bottom up rather than to come from the top down. Even in authoritarian governments, we are more conscious of popular movements outside and inside the government that shape policy making.

Increased popular involvement results partly from far-ranging revolutions in communication, transportation, and information. Problems of governance now concern people around the world; analysis is moving beyond the institutions of government and state to the collections of human beings who constitute and run those states. Leaders are beginning to realize that solutions to problems lie not only in the power and proficiency of government but in the genius of political movement and organization that combines popular energy with governmental coordination and direction. Politics lags behind technology. On the international stage, what one leader says or does will be heard, seen, and assessed within hours by another leader's constituencies. Peoples in many nations are more aware of each other as human beings and not as distant and abstract adversaries. The relationships among nations are increasingly determined by public agendas that are no longer shaped in relative isolation.

Experience demands new awareness of the human roots of interests, and the conflicts among them. Fear, mistrust, suspicion, rejection, hatred, and misperception are often greater obstacles to peace between nations than inability to resolve technically definable problems.

Third, traditional instruments of statecraft often do not reliably accomplish what is expected of them. As we observe the broadening involvement of publics, we need to focus on political instruments that can be used to change political environments so that publics will encourage and sustain new approaches.

We have normally thought of the instruments of statecraft as including the exercise of various forms of military and economic power to gain what nations want as well as a nonviolent alternative, negotiation. In more recent times, we have come to recognize the potential of those opinion-shaping programs which fall under the rubrics of "information" or "propaganda."

Today, the most powerful weapons the world has ever known cannot be used by leaders of conscience. Even when force is used, it does not produce the expected or desired results. The U.S. and Soviet experiences in Vietnam and Afghanistan are not unique. Israeli military superiority has not quelled Palestinian nationalism, and changes in the Israeli-Palestinian relationship since 1988 have come not from the armed power of a state but from the unarmed resistance of a popular movement.

Negotiation depends more on political leaders changing the political environment than on the skills of negotiating teams in finding technical solutions. The following observation is as relevant to summit talks between Soviet and U.S. leaders as to the Arab-Israeli peace process: Negotiation does not initiate change. Change is initiated and shaped in the political arena. Negotiation may define, capture, crystallize, and consolidate change that has already begun. But until political leaders have transformed the political environment, negotiators are unlikely to succeed. Even if they do reach a technically sound agreement, it may not be fully implemented or have the intended consequences.

### The need for conceptual change in historical perspective

These global changes require us to develop new concepts, as well as to rethink familiar ones. Both tasks may be easier if we reflect on how we came to our familiar concepts—and to our uneasiness with them—in the perspective of the last five centuries.

The rise of the sovereign nation state produced a world with no central authority where each national unit relied on its own power to pursue its interests and to protect its security. The practice of seeking a balance of power became the essence of the system in order to block aggression, limit war, and regulate competition. In this state system, rulers and philosophers sought some "objective" order. To curb the most destructive uses of power, statesmen developed "rules of the game" from experience over time. Philosophers of law and moralists proposed principles to define just and unjust uses of national power.

In the twentieth century, two "world" wars and the experience of nuclear weapons' unprecedented destructive capacity caused men and women to question whether it can be right for nation states to use power unilaterally to pursue their interests. People increasingly refuse to accept the view that the world can work only through the clash of power. We do not yet see the fading of sovereign states into a world federation. But many observe that national sovereignties are increasingly limited in what they can accomplish by themselves and argue that genuine influence in the decades ahead will not come from the use of raw power. An increasing number argue that a "great power" will steadily decline over the next century not only because it has became militarily or economically overextended but if it does not recognize that the nature of power and influence has changed.

Recognition of Soviet-U.S. nuclear parity in the late 1960s caused leaders on both sides to see that military power could not be used to settle differences between the two nations. Their answer in the period of détente in the early 1970s was to "substitute negotiation for the use of force" in resolving disputes, but that approach did not go far enough.

Leaders did negotiate important arms control agreements. But détente did not founder in the negotiating room. Détente foundered on military deployments in Angola, in Ethiopia, in Europe, in the Middle East, and eventually, in Afghanistan. It foundered for lack of a sound overall relationship that may well have been impossible to achieve with then current Soviet leaders.

Now in the 1990s, with the winding down of the Cold War, our reflections are many. The most important lesson of the century may not be found in the experience of defeating aggression in two world wars but in struggling with the question of why those wars were not prevented. It may lie even more in the experience of containment and in pondering the collapse of totalitarian governments and centrally managed economies in Europe.

Substituting negotiation for force can be an important step toward a more peaceful world, but the even more important step is to know how to shape political environments that generate the changes that can then be crystallized in negotiated agreements. Advancing technology will be essential to improving the quality of life on this earth, but making technology usable will depend on bringing whole human beings back into the process of generating and guiding change. In foreign affairs, that requires concepts that incorporate the politics and ethics of international relationships.

### The concept of relationship

The concept that seems best to capture the interactive human processes we are experiencing is the concept of "relationship." At first hearing, "relationship" is such a commonplace word that we hardly notice it. But when we stop to think about relationships that sustain us as human beings, we can begin to feel the power, depth, and dynamism of this deceptively simple notion.

"Relationship" combines five important elements: (1) the existence of interests and needs—both practical and psychological—of two parties in a shared situation; (2) whatever the character of the interests and needs that bring parties together—whether in conflict, competition, or cooperation—a pattern of interaction develops as a political process in that situation over time with its own methods of communication; (3) as interaction between parties becomes more complex, there is an increasing need for setting boundaries and regulations in sensitive areas so that the parties can determine when each is respecting or threatening the other's interests, identity, and deeper needs; (4) in the interaction, power is a factor but it can take many different forms; (5) eventually, the evolving pattern of interaction between the partners provides a context within which an inter-dependence of interests is defined and which can generate problem-solving action together that both partners value as an extension of themselves.

"Relationship" applies to nations as well as to people. Nations—despite some institutional characteristics—are communities of people. In a relationship, each party thinks and acts differently because of the other. Leaders building relationships around interdependent interests and human needs will act differently from leaders maintaining a balance of power or attempting to exercise power at others' expense.

Protecting one nation's identity and security, for instance, may not be possible outside a relationship embracing both allies and adversaries who share a common security problem and its solution. Cooperating, resolving conflict, or curbing confrontation requires probing underlying interests and needs that define what is vital to each party. Instead of negotiating on specific issues, leaders concentrate on what grows in the space between them if they define a problem as affecting common interests and if they work together over time on solutions. A relationship begins to grow, the political environment changes, and the parties can do more than they first thought possible. They need not surrender individual identities; to the contrary, the relationship may enlarge their potential. As time passes, the relationship itself acts as a brake against purely self-centered action.

The change that comes from altering conflictual relationships and building problem-solving relationships is the politically powerful experience we need to study, teach, and develop in practice. Building and conducting a creative relationship—among nations as among human beings—can be a transforming experience that produces fundamental change, as for instance in Western Europe after World War II.

To rely on relationships is not utopian; rather, it is inevitable. An interdependent world locks nations into relationships with others whom they may not trust or like, but all-out contests of force between them are no longer—if they ever were—an effective, responsible, or secure way of conducting those relationships. In so many unregulated conflicts, each side loses more than it must and gains less than it might.[1]

### Ethical implications

A key step in refocusing the ethical agenda in the light of this concept of relationship is to reassess the standard judgments that have been made about the traditional instruments of statecraft. The morality of nuclear deterrence has already been pointedly examined, but little attention has been given to political approaches to the peaceful resolution of conflict.

Before that work can proceed, work comparable to the moral debate on the rightness of nuclear war must be done on the political interactions among nations. Taking off from the familiar view of nation states as self-contained rational actors, international lawyers, diplomats, and philosophers have written elaborate codes of behavior to protect the integrity of the state. They have developed principles of nonintervention and noninterference in the internal affairs of other states and on the limits of behavior in war and the rules of diplomatic practice. Theologians have written about the ethics of a contest of power and what constitutes a just war. Some of these principles as usually stated are no longer precise enough guides to behavior in the interdependent, interactive, nuclear world described above, and may even be seriously misleading.

Extending our focus beyond state institutions to the political process of interaction among whole bodies politic enlarges thought and practice in two directions. First, it increases the range of political instruments available for peaceful resolution of conflict that must be addressed by ethicians. Second, it broadens and deepens the body of ethical thought that can be brought to bear on relationships among nations.

Assuming that peaceful settlement is ethically preferable to using force, the question is: What ethical issues are raised in using that wider range of political instruments? What ethical principles are appropriate in the political process of continuous interaction among whole bodies politic as contrasted to the strategic chess game between self-contained states?

We lived for centuries, for instance, by the principle that one nation should not interfere in another's internal affairs, but in today's world that is not possible. Cross-border interactions among constituencies on many levels are daily facts of life. No government controls the everyday flow of people, data, pictures, education, investment, money, joint ventures, markets, services, thinking, and perceptions across borders.

An ethical principle of noninterference is well intentioned, but its essence can be preserved only if we identify more precisely the ethical touchstones for protecting each party's identity and integrity in an often intense interaction. Some interactions across borders may indeed be insidious, but some offer opportunities for guiding change peacefully, with respect for others. Understanding the political process of interaction can suggest imaginative approaches to common problems. It is not sensible to go on saying that such interaction violates the principle of noninterference. In fact, a sensible approach is to build relationships in which conscious mutual respect keeps political interaction within limits that protect the identity and integrity of each partner.

As we examine the dimensions of these relationships among groups of human beings in whole bodies politic, we open the door to a richer and more usable body of ethical thought to guide us. Where might those ethical touchstones come from?

Ethical thought on civil and political rights and in such UN documents as the Universal Declaration of Human Rights may provide a more realistic guide for relationships among nations than an ethics built around state institutions run by governing elites. Saying this is not just an instance of Americans imposing their standards of human rights on others. To be sure, there has been much of that. The point here is that thought about protecting human identity and rights must be part of the ethics of how nations relate in a world where whole bodies politic interact.

A second body of ethical thought that may provide insight, since we are looking beyond states to human beings in their bodies politic, has to do with the ethics of interpersonal relationship and of community.

Thinking of relationships among nations as a political process among bodies politic greatly enlarges the arena for peaceful and just resolution of conflict. We can now think not of a choice between war and peace as the only alternatives but of a choice from along a wide spectrum of actions between war and formal negotiation that can change relationships peacefully.

The widened space between war and negotiation—the space for political settlement—requires much more attention from students of ethics as well as from students of international relationships. As we examine what goes on in that space, the door opens to a wider range of ethical thought. Since what goes on in that space is part of the larger political—and therefore human—process through which nations interact, it becomes legitimate to draw insight from the ethics of interpersonal and community relationships.

We recognize that nations have characteristics of their own, but we do not accept the assertion that states are separate from the people who constitute and run them as grounds for declaring interpersonal ethics out of bounds in the study of relationships among nations. If states face problems they cannot resolve without attending to the connections and possibilities that we have considered under the concept of relationship, a body of ethical thought built solely on the assumption of a sovereign state deciding alone is not a realistic or complete ethical guide for those human beings who govern.

## Political settlement and the negotiating process

Some students and practitioners of negotiation have already begun to enlarge that space by recognizing that negotiation is not just what happens around the table but depends on the larger political environment in which it takes place. For at least two decades some have been speaking of the "negotiating process" so that it includes what must be done in the political arena to build relationships needed for successful negotiation and the effective implementation of negotiated agreements.

Talk about "political settlement" now takes that work further. Political settlement emerges from the process of changing a conflictual relationship to one in which the parties can resolve differences peacefully. It may or may not involve formal negotiation, but many functions of the negotiating process broadly conceived are also inherent in the political processes that change relationships and vice versa. Those functions are simply among the ways human beings conduct and change relationships.

The distinction between the negotiating process and political settlement at this point is imprecise, and it may have to remain so. To the extent that a distinction can be drawn, it grows from the fact that political actions may pave the way for negotiation, or they may help change a relationship so fundamentally that negotiation, if it is needed at all, will deal only with details of new arrangements. Put another way, a policy maker with a problem to solve may start down a political track to redefine a problem or to cause constituents to see their interests in a different light and support a change of course. The policy maker may then decide that negotiation would be useful or that the situation can be changed for the better simply by a series of interacting political moves. The fact that exploratory exchanges can play a role in either negotiation or political settlement will continue to blur the line.

One way to deal with the hazy boundary between political settlement and the negotiating process here is to start by enlarging our understanding of negotiation, since it is the more familiar and more explicit activity. At some point, it is subsumed in the larger process of building, conducting, and changing relationships. In fact, some problems may be resolved politically without formal negotiation.

It is not our task here to define precisely the boundaries between the negotiating process and political settlement; that work goes on elsewhere. Our purpose is to broaden thinking about activities involved in peaceful resolution so as to refocus ethical dialogue on the issues they raise.

## A broader view of the negotiating process

Negotiation has been pictured traditionally as a discrete, formal series of exchanges in which constituted authorities working from conflicting positions and interests try to reach agreement. Behind that bargaining, the relative power of the parties—including the threat of violence—often affected the outcome. The result of negotiation against such a background of power could be just or unjust. More often, it would be assessed according to whether it seemed to serve national interest as leaders defined it.

Experience in international relationships suggests that even formal negotiation often depends heavily on political action to initiate change in the political environment that will make negotiation possible and agreement lasting. Conventional negotiation theory was inadequate because it dealt with what happens in the negotiating room and did not pay enough attention to the period we now call "prenegotiation." That is why we need a larger theory of negotiation. It is also possible to understand those foundation-building stages in the negotiating process as part of the larger political process of changing relationships. We maintain that the outcome from a negotiation embedded in a larger political process or a relationship changed through such process is more likely to be just than one arrived at by leaders or negotiating teams acting alone. It will be based on the participation and consent of a wider range of people; it will be more sensitive to the variety of interests and forms of power; it is less likely to be distorted by a preoccupation with short-term gains or by the desire to make the most of temporary advantages.

A broader theory of negotiation begins with realization that the negotiating process encompasses two different experiences—one that precedes actual negotiation and one that starts when negotiators try to produce a specific agreement. Theorists and diplomats have concentrated on identifying the formulas, techniques, exchanges, and transactions useful in the negotiating room. They have paid less attention to the time before negotiation. That is sometimes a long and complicated stage when parties are deciding whether or not to commit themselves to a settlement at all—or at least to explore the possibility of negotiating. The key task of this period is building political foundations for changing relationships in ways that could either solve a problem without formal negotiation or that would initiate change that could be crystallized in a negotiated agreement.

Even when parties reach the negotiating table, carrying on serious negotiation, overcoming obstacles, breaking logjams, and advancing new proposals may require leaders to move back and forth between the negotiating room and the political arena. It is in the political arena that the pressures to negotiate seriously are generated and that the problems under negotiation are often reconceptualized in politically more supportable ways. Implementation of one agreement can change the political environment and can open the door to negotiation of even more difficult issues.[2]

### A human process

To enlarge our understanding of the negotiating process adequately, we need to reach beyond theory into the human roots of the negotiating experience. We need to think of negotiation first not in terms of skill and technique in bargaining but as a different way of thinking. Even those who theorize about negotiation increasingly describe it less as a contest and accommodation between different or opposing positions and more as a shared process for resolving common problems.

Negotiation in a broad sense is so pervasive in life that we can be tempted to say that every human transaction is a negotiation of sorts. While eventually we need to define negotiation more narrowly, it is instructive to begin by looking at the broad picture.

Negotiation—like speaking prose and unlike skiing—is one of those things that we human beings do with very little sense that it is a special activity. It is a natural part of learning another's interests and needs in any human relationship. We learn it at mother's knee, and we develop our skills in the nursery and on the playground. From this early on, our experience of "negotiation" is shaped by demands, threats, offers, alienation, and reconciliation. It is contrasted to settlements imposed by command, with fighting things out, and with surrender and withdrawal. This is one end of the scale of activities we call "negotiation."

On the other end of the scale, negotiation can be a highly conscious, organized, and complex series of activities. Governments, corporations, unions, or associations may participate. Batteries of lawyers, advisors, and staff may hammer out agreements that run into hundreds of pages and cover remote contingencies and technical details about which the senior representatives of the parties may have only the haziest ideas. Even in such a setting, teachers of negotiation today maintain that lasting effectiveness lies not in a contest of power but in the search for common solutions.

Obviously, there are many intermediate steps on this scale, and many different factors may influence the shape and the outcome of a negotiating process. Negotiations may be public or private; they may involve large social entities, or be direct deals between two individuals; they may be highly ritualized, or be quite casual. Indeed, in our culture matters so different as selling real estate, writing labor contracts, making trade agreements, deciding the length of prison sentences, making and dissolving marriages, ending wars, settling civil suits, freeing hostages, and merging businesses will normally involve some element of negotiation.

In all these diverse activities—whether we call them "negotiation" or political or peaceful resolution—there are some standard features that we should notice before we take up the ethical dimensions of peaceful resolution of conflict. All are not necessarily present in every instance, but they are normally present and their absence requires explanation. It is these features that root negotiation or political settlement in the context of human—and therefore political—interaction. It is these features that give us the basic ethical shape of the process of peaceful resolution even before we consider the substantive outcome of the process.

## A process conducted in time

Negotiation is an activity carried on by human beings in time. It is not merely an event or a set of formal meetings producing a specific agreement, but an ongoing process.

In formal negotiation, the past can hang heavy over the discussions. Whether or not negotiators talk explicitly of the past, they and nations or organizations they represent are living with fears, hopes, and perceptions shaped by the past. They work from pictures of the other side and of the problem shaped in past experience. They pursue interests that experience has taught them are important in protecting their security and well-being. They may fear outcomes or seek solutions colored by analogies with a historical place and period they never experienced directly.

The present—negotiation itself—develops a certain rhythm, a life, of its own which can bring fascination or boredom and which is experienced differently by the different participants.

The present—the political context of the negotiation—is a moment in the evolution of a situation. Negotiators can analyze that moment in terms of whether a dispute has become "ripe for resolution." The success or failure of a negotiation often depends on whether circumstances and judgments about them in the political arena on both sides of a conflict have made the participants ready to accept a negotiated change in the situation.[3]

The shadow of the future is present in several ways. To begin with, negotiation is an instrument of change—an instrument for creating a future different from the present. If leaders choose to negotiate, the agreement—the characteristic product of negotiation—will be judged by the conformity of the future behavior of the parties to the terms of the agreement. Negotiators will behave differently when they are shaping a future relationship rather than trying to solve one problem with a party they will not see again. The experience of negotiating to produce a preferable common future may itself teach behavior in the relationship that will help to change a hurtful situation.

Finally, while negotiation is a continuous and cumulative process over time, it is itself part of an overall relationship. Not only do relationships between negotiators grow; more important, relationships between parties grow. It is the nature and quality of change and growth in that overall relationship over time that should be the first appropriate focus of ethical reflection.

## An interactive process

Negotiation is an interactive process in which two human parties face a harmful situation that each concludes can only be improved by cooperation with others.

*First:* Negotiation and political settlement are both increasingly seen as shared problem solving. They are processes in which the parties probe their own interests, seek to understand the interests of others, recognize common interests, and look for cooperative solutions when interests are damaged. Two parties begin to build a limited relationship to deal with problems which they recognize as in some way common. This view differs markedly from the traditional view of two parties bringing interests and positions to the table to be accommodated by bargaining. It reflects a different way of thinking—as relevant in politics generally as in negotiation specifically.

Each party to a conflict has a plurality of relevant interests that can be brought into the settlement process even when the dispute is apparently about a single good, e.g., a piece of property or territory. One simple way of doing so in that instance is by offering money—an instrumental good which the other party can use to pursue its interests as it sees fit. A more complex way is to probe beneath ostensible interests to find common ground where the less obvious interests of both sides in some ways overlap.

Each party makes independent judgments on how to manage its plurality of interests. It determines the menu of satisfied, postponed, renounced, or combined interests that shape its negotiating positions and judges what would be an acceptable agreement, partly in the light of changing possibilities determined by the context and by the moves of the other side. The precise shape of this menu is often unknown even to the party itself, since it can involve answers to hypothetical questions that may never have been clearly stated. Assessments of interests and of ways to satisfy them have to be explicitly formulated among those charged with articulating and managing the party's interests. The party then functions as an intelligent center of assessment and decision about the relative weights or priorities of various items on the menu. Achieving clarity can be a complex task requiring time and internal political discussion, but it can reasonably be expected to enhance a party's ability to make well-informed decisions.

Achieving clarity about the other party's interests—whether by intelligence gathering, analysis, or direct communication—and how it integrates its interests can be a powerful instrument, whether one approaches negotiation in an empathetic or manipulative spirit. Mutual recognition of the plurality of their interests makes it easier for both parties to grasp the range of possible exchanges and to understand that an outcome may be positive for both, particularly if the areas in which interests conflict are given less weight than those in which interests converge.

Since defining interests on a national level requires political decisions, one party's actions—deliberate or inadvertent—can reshape the other's debate. Political strategy for changing relationships can include actions to alter perceptions, options, and estimates of what is possible.

*Second:* Political settlement and negotiation are processes in which two parties learn to know each other well enough to understand what they have in common and what they can expect of each other. The process of building understanding may be distant and analytical to begin with, but in the end its best chance of growing is in face-to-face interaction.

Political settlement and negotiation presuppose a certain relationship between the parties. That relationship has sometimes been characterized as a rough equality, but a better word might be "mutuality." Enormous disparities in wealth and power can exist between negotiating parties. Such factors as love, conscience, respect for human rights, or willingness to accept a wider or narrower range of outcomes can enter the balance in unquantifiable ways. Such "equality" may even have certain constructed or fictitious elements. What is essential is that participants seek a solution from a relationship of mutual respect.

Political settlement and negotiation involve a process of deepening communication. In the negotiating room, this is overwhelmingly verbal, but in the political arena it is often true that "actions speak louder than words." Even nonverbal actions are transformed into verbal statements through questions about "what they mean by doing that." Gestures and actions, even the body language of the parties, can play a significant role in the process, but the capacity to explore what lies behind statements of interest and policy through extended and honest verbal communication is essential in any problem-solving relationship in the political arena or in the negotiating room.

Since the interests and intentions of the parties are not fully transparent to each other and since negotiation aims at achieving mutual consent to an agreement between the parties, negotiation calls forth characteristic virtues and vices. Thus when a party bargains with no real intention of reaching agreement, we judge that the party is not negotiating in good faith. When a party shows no serious regard for the other party's conception of its own interests and needs, we judge that the first party lacks a sense of fairness. When a party fails to adhere to the terms of an agreement that it has consented to, it is lacking in faithfulness to its commitments. The special virtues required in any process of resolution then are good faith, fairness, and faithfulness to one's word or commitments—principles that are also central in assessing any relationship.

As a relationship grows through collaboration on a vexing problem, each party begins to see through the other's eyes and even learns common perceptions. One's own moves are modified by estimates of the likelihood of particular responses. The other side is taken as an independent source of activity, capable of initiating its own proposals and of seeing things in new ways. Here we may notice that political settlement and negotiation differ from persuasion, in which the other side is assigned a more passive role and need only give consent to arguments and proposals. In negotiation, there is a common responsibility for developing a common solution. At some point, the common interest in preserving the ability to work together toward common solutions acquires a value of its own.

As interest in the problem-solving relationship grows, since it cannot be carried on by one side alone, it is possible for one party to put that relationship in jeopardy by breaking negotiations or by conducting them in a way that makes agreement a remote prospect at best. Negotiation can be replaced by silence, by a unilateral move to create a fait accompli, by an imposed settlement or Diktat, or by recourse to arms. An important corollary of this point for purposes of ethical assessment is that the moves of one party in a negotiation are normally to be assessed in relation to the actions and possible responses of the other party in the negotiation, as well as in terms of conformity to ethical rules or virtues.

*Third:* The option of moving out of the negotiating arena and back into the political arena underlines the fact that negotiation is always part of a larger relational context. In public affairs, it is part of an interactive political process—both within each body politic and between bodies politic. A comprehensive view of the negotiating process rarely separates what happens in and around the negotiating room from the relational or political environment in which the decision to negotiate was made and in which the outcome of the negotiation will be judged and implemented. Keeping in mind the interaction between the negotiating and the political arenas opens the door for creative trade-offs, for a redefinition of problems, and for new political scenarios containing new options.

Interests were traditionally seen as rationally defined in relation to objective circumstances. Today we recognize that interests include human needs—psychological as well as material—and that they are defined and given priorities in the political arena. The complex task of determining exactly what one's interests are varies with circumstances, with pressures and constraints that may alter the range of options and that may give certain items a special urgency. Individuals and societies can reasonably expect both needs and preferences to alter with time. These points set up the likelihood of complex patterns of divergence and convergence between the interests of parties in a settlement process and the virtual certainty of such shifts when the parties have long-term relationships with each other, which in the case of nation states will last over lifetimes.

Negotiators continuously interact with their environment, which itself is in constant change. While the persons in a negotiating process are themselves complex and variable, they are set within a context that is itself liable to change in many ways under the influence of creative political leaders. Social movements, demographic shifts, economic activities, intellectual and scientific discoveries, political decisions, ecological changes may alter the context for negotiations between individuals, between organizations, and between states. A negotiator stymied in the negotiating room has the option of moving outside that room to see whether he or she can take advantage of elements of change already at work to speed or to shape change so that the issues under negotiation can be seen in a different context.

It is at this point that a leader considers whether a political move can reconfigure a situation to give negotiation a fresh chance—or perhaps can change the situation without negotiation. A classic recent instance was Egyptian President Anwar al-Sadat's historic visit to Jerusalem in 1977. Sadat perceived that a major obstacle to restarting negotiation was not the inability to write terms of reference for a negotiation which the parties could accept. It was that few Israelis believed that any president of Egypt would make peace with them. He did not take a new negotiating position to Israel; his purpose was to demonstrate, in a way that would transform the Israeli political environment, Egypt's readiness to make peace. While acts such as Sadat's may be few, politicians daily take steps designed to change people's perceptions of a situation and of their needs and options. Sadat's act eventually led to two negotiated agreements, thanks to the political acts of U.S. President Jimmy Carter in inviting Sadat and Israeli Prime Minister Menachem Begin to Camp David in 1978 and in going to the Middle East in 1979 to salvage flagging negotiations on the Egyptian-Israeli peace treaty.

When we speak of political settlement of conflict apart from negotiation, we are speaking of efforts to initiate the course of change that may sometime later be defined and crystallized in negotiation. The ideal is for two parties to move forward together within some explicitly or implicitly agreed framework, but if the relationship cannot yet support that kind of dialogue, some political acts can have a catalytic effect not unlike the shock of using force but at much lower cost. In underscoring this point, we are emphasizing that negotiation is not the only peaceful alternative to the use of force in resolving disputes and changing situations. A range of political actions is usually available.

## Ethical implications: A process for achieving mutual consent

Since peaceful resolution—whether in political settlement or negotiation—involves parties that are independent centers of understanding, assessment, and decision, an inherent objective in any resolution process is obtaining mutual consent. Pressures may be brought to bear so as to elicit consent, which may well fall short of a paradigmatic situation of free choice. One of the parties may feel that he or she is in the situation of Aristotle's storm-tossed merchant who throws the cargo overboard in order to save the ship.[4] Both parties may feel that if they had their druthers, many things would be different. Consent may be reluctant, half-hearted, feeble. But if mutual consent disappears totally, then we are dealing with something other than political resolution or negotiation.

Characteristically, the aim of formal negotiation is to produce a written agreement, a meticulously formulated statement expressing the conditions under which the parties will deal with each other in the future. This may include omissions as well as actions. The agreement restricts the range of legitimate possibilities of action and constitutes a commitment by both parties to act or refrain from acting in specified ways. It must be precise enough to avoid misunderstanding that could later undermine the relationship. A further outcome of negotiation which is more difficult to define but which may be even more important is the political environment created around the negotiation. That environment will determine the character of the relationship as it grows in implementing the agreement.

While there is an inherent morality in the negotiating process, it does not follow that the results must be just. There is some presumption in their favor because they are produced by consent, but parties can negotiate and collaborate in doing things that are unjust. The Hitler-Stalin pact of 1939 is a clear example. Even when we are not thinking of criminal conspiracies, or of agreements corrupted by force or fraud, the terms of any given agreement are only one way of making general norms of justice specific and involve judgments that are open to moral questioning.

An agreement or change in relationship that emerges from a larger political process may well have a greater chance of meeting standards of justice and fairness. Negotiation is a particular moment in a relationship when the parties try to reach a precise agreement on some aspect of their relationship. When it involves a shared effort to find a common solution to a common problem and grows out of an evolving relational context, the mutuality in the process and in the outcome is the central feature in understanding the ethics of peaceful settlement. The concept of mutuality draws on the ethics of changing interpersonal relationships and the ethics of interaction within community to generate change. It takes us to the core of what shapes and changes human perceptions in relationships. But it also takes us to religion and theology.

## THEOLOGICAL FOUNDATIONS OF DIALOGUE AND PEACEFUL SETTLEMENT

If our thinking about how nations interact focuses on the relationship between whole bodies politic, we must include the whole human beings who make up those bodies politic. For vast multitudes their relationship to God is basic and will remain so. Philosophers, theologians, legal and political theorists have all argued about our ability to reach a common understanding of moral norms without relying on specific religious traditions. For many people in today's world, religion appears as part of the problem and not as part of the solution. Indeed, religion has often exacerbated political conflict and has given rise to bitter divisions within and between communities. We can all think of Christian, Jewish, Muslim, and Hindu extremists who have been conspicuous for their zeal in opposing the enemies of God and for their impatience with more conciliatory approaches. But religion is simply too important and too fundamental an aspect of human life for policy makers and negotiators to dismiss it to a purely personal realm or to treat it with contempt and fear. Rather, both those leaders who want to achieve political settlement of disputes and to arrive at peace through just agreements, and those counselors and colleagues whom they employ in this task need to have a carefully thought out set of principles that will ground their preference for political settlement. Such a set of principles will have to be something that can be integrated with different religious outlooks and traditions and that can be defended against the more intransigent and bellicose proponents within a particular religious tradition.

### The ethics of force versus peaceful settlement

We start from one of the classic conditions established over the years in Western thought to justify war or the use of force—that arms must be a last resort. This condition reflects the view that peaceful instruments for achieving justice are morally preferable to instruments of force. It requires that peaceful ways of settling a dispute have been tried and have not been successful.

Success in this type of situation is not merely a matter of preventing war. That can be done by surrender. Success also includes preserving what each side holds as essential values to which it has a claim in justice. If it is important to prevent war while preserving values essential to each side, then it is morally imperative to broaden the range of means for achieving a just settlement peacefully.

Given widespread presumptions about the limited efficacy of peaceful means, states that believe fundamental interests are challenged feel compelled from time to time to choose between negotiating and fighting. In some cases (the Middle East is a prime example), they may choose to do neither but may remain in permanently envenomed enmity. In others, negotiation and fighting are blended, as in the later stages of the Vietnam War, when negotiations were conducted in order to end fighting. Even without actual fighting, negotiations may take on a highly coercive character, when one side has overwhelming power or is much more willing to use force. Conversely, one side may fight in order to negotiate, that is, use force to precipitate negotiation or to achieve an advantageous basis for negotiation.

These possibilities indicate that we are not confronted with a simple dichotomy between negotiation and the use of force. Sometimes they may not be sharply distinguished in either time or purpose. Further, they are not to be contrasted to each other simply as good and evil. Even though they are distinct forms of behavior, the intentions and attitudes that shape the conduct of war and of negotiations can overlap, though they also exhibit characteristic differences. There are situations in which one would be willing to fight, others in which one would negotiate, others in which one would do either, and still others in which one would do neither.

Nevertheless, the Western moral and legal tradition has consistently preferred negotiation over fighting. Churchill reflected this in his dictum, "It is better to jaw, jaw than to war, war." Precisely because the choice is often ambiguous and because the presumption is that peaceful settlement is morally preferable, it is important to develop ways to peaceful resolution.

## The ethics of choosing political settlement or negotiation

In the ideal case, two parties in a significant dispute who make contradictory claims as a matter of justice, come through dialogue and negotiation to understand each other's needs and find a way to satisfy the demands of justice through voluntary acceptance of mutually satisfactory terms. Such an outcome eliminates the need and the negative consequences of using force and the damage to moral character which the use of force frequently produces. The evils of war are avoided, and the demands of justice are met, since the mutuality and the voluntary character of the agreement seem to ensure that injustice is not being done to either party. This accords with Aristotle's dictum that "being unjustly treated is not voluntary."[5]

Needless to say, not all instances of peaceful settlement fit into this ideal pattern. The choice to try to reach a peaceful settlement is not always easy or clear-cut.

Even an agreement that seems voluntary may not produce a just outcome. For one thing, some state leaderships can act against the interests and norms of behavior common among their constituents and accept terms of agreement that do serious injustice even to their own citizens. Leaders of a government that enters into an agreement can be replaced by opponents of the agreement who do not accept its justice. Damage may also be done to third parties, whose interests may be adversely affected, as, for instance, when the interests and rights of Czechoslovakia were gravely damaged at Munich in 1938. Some issues may be left unresolved at the end of a negotiating process. Demands for justice may be left unsatisfied because it is felt that they cannot be met at the time or because one or both parties give higher priority to other considerations. The agreement, especially when one side has a clear preponderance of resources, may be less than fully voluntary. Later developments may cause it to have negative consequences which had not been adequately foreseen or evaluated.

But the possibility that an outcome will be judged unjust should not cause us to dismiss the prima facie connection between voluntary agreement and the just, negotiated settlement of conflicts and disputes. That connection is worth affirming for two reasons. First, the departures from the ideal model of negotiation are widely recognized in our understanding of international relations. Second, in many international and other disputes parties may hold significantly different conceptions of justice. Disputes arise between political communities that have rich but divergent heritages of norms about justice and more or less sophisticated accounts of how the present contentious situation arose. These communities are not living in some premoral or amoral state of nature or behind a veil of ignorance about their histories, needs, and aspirations.

The prospect of voluntary or mutual agreement serves as an alternative to the effort to settle a dispute by applying only one side's conception of justice to the facts as that side understands them in order to arrive at a conclusion or judgment about what is to be done. For what we call the internal resolution of the dispute—that is, its resolution by appeal to norms and beliefs that are internal to one side—may be conscientiously arrived at by political leaders on that side in such a way that it does indeed conform to the demands of justice as seen from their perspective. But it still may strike proponents of the other side as not meeting the demands of justice as they understand it and as manifesting the distorting influences of ideology and interest on what should be a fair and impartial judgment.

## Overcoming ethical objections to peaceful settlement

Even voluntary agreement on mutually accepted terms may strike some proponents of either side as a "sellout," a deviation from the demands of justice as they understand it. A negative reaction is likely to be especially vehement when the disregarded claims of justice are seen as having a religious character. This means that they are linked in various ways with what has ultimate reality and worth; and so it may well become more difficult to accept the possibility that these claims may be overridden or compromised. This is even more likely to be a problem when in the political community and its religious traditions there is a tendency, either explicit or implicit, to deny that outsiders or people adhering to another tradition can in principle have legitimate claims against our community. A religious or ideological interpretation of the demand for justice may then make negotiation on the basis of mutuality an unacceptable alternative.

Is the only answer to religious intransigence a movement to secularization of outlooks in order to make possible the settlement of otherwise interminable disputes? This is an unattractive prospect for several reasons. It seems to involve yet another imposition of Western liberal values on other peoples and traditions and to imply yet another reduction in the influence of religious values in the world. It also seems to involve begging the question in such a way that just demands conceived and articulated within a particular religious tradition are devalued or even totally discredited. This is a difficult theoretical problem in a pluralistic world; and it has many negative practical aspects. For instance, if leaders of a political movement or government enter into agreements which a dominant religious community brands as falling short of the demands of justice, prospects for the durability of a settlement go down and costs for the political leaders who support it go up, perhaps even to catastrophic levels.

But the problem should not be allowed to remain at the level of a theoretical impasse. Three types of considerations can push us forward, even when we are dealing with states and movements that claim a specially privileged status for their judgments about what justice requires.

First, considerations arise from the status accorded in a given religious or ideological tradition to those outside that tradition. Some considerations that fall under this heading may well seem to make matters worse; e.g., Marxist denunciations of bourgeois morality as well as of divergent social-ist groups, or some portraits that Christian and Muslim apologists have drawn of each other over the centuries. But when groups in contention have had to deal with each other over generations, they have usually developed a subsidiary and corrective tradition which gives a more favor-able assessment of the adversaries and establishes the possibility that the adversaries can make at least some claims raising serious issues of justice. Such considerations can also be integrated with more general considera-tions about the dignity of human beings created in the image of God or as manifesting fundamental aspects of our common human nature.

Most religious traditions have some doctrinal perspective on the moral obligations of the community and its members toward those outside the community. Christians are familiar with this sort of perspective from Romans 2:12-16, where Paul acknowledges that the Gentiles have the law written on their hearts. Jewish tradition has elaborated an account of the Noachian commandments which bind all.[6]

These doctrinal perspectives should not be equated with a theory of natural law which is rationally accessible to all human persons, even though there may be a substantial identity of content between the precepts of natural law and the moral norms affirmed by the religious tradition as binding on all. For such an equating of the two sets of norms could well cause us to forget that the important norms in question are affirmed from within the religious tradition and so may not be dismissed by adherents of the specific religious tradition as alien positions which restrict their faithfulness to the divinely willed requirements of justice.

It may be true that these more universalist moral norms do not have the "thickness" and definiteness needed for people to reach conclusions with regard to particular cases or even to express clear disagreement within a specific community of moral discourse. But they still provide an important resource for beginning construction of a secondary or deriva-tive moral community—a community which draws together people from divergent and even adversary communities. Such a community may be thought of as an ad hoc creation for settlement of a given dispute or con-flict; but it may also develop a broader and more durable character. It becomes a continuing relationship of the type that we argued earlier in-creasingly characterizes life among nations today. These norms also pro-vide a barrier against the worst kinds of dehumanizing treatment which groups may be tempted to mete out to their adversaries, or at least an internal basis for criticizing such treatment.

Second, within a given community defined in religious or ideological terms, there will be norms which enjoin mutual consent as a means for the settlement of disputes. These make an important and even necessary contribution to the stability and order of the community. The crucial step of universalizing these norms and of applying them to alien groups and individuals is never easy in practice and may seem to involve an idealistic and moralistic simplification of the problems presented by international and intergroup conflicts. But even after we acknowledge the theoretical and practical difficulties that lie in the way of such an approach, we can still point to the existence of these norms as evidence of the value that a community attaches to the voluntary and peaceful settlement of disputes.

It is important, however, to recognize two distinct ways in which voluntary consent resolves disputes. One, explicitly endorsed in Christian tradition, involves the renunciation of one party's claim for the sake of higher goods and presupposes a conversion of heart which is less likely—and not always appropriate—in the international forum. The second, which is the path of negotiation, presupposes that parties remain attached to their interests and even more to what they regard as their rights or justified claims, but that they may ultimately be willing to renounce or modify them if such action is judged to be necessary or advantageous. This view does not presuppose that interests and rights are accorded an absolute status or that they cannot be redefined in important ways; rather, it assumes that they continue to be taken seriously and are overridden only with great difficulty. (They can be overridden by appeals to moral or legal considerations, by compensatory offers, or by threats of greater harm.)

The second way, the path of negotiation, is the one that is usually thought to be operative in the decisions of states; but the boundary between shifting priorities among interests in the political arena and backing away from a course of action for the sake of a higher good is not well defined. The path of conversion and voluntary renunciation may be open to individuals and to "moral men," but not to states and "immoral societies," as Reinhold Niebuhr argued more than fifty years ago. The appeal to conversion has indeed been a prominent element in religious denunciations of nuclear deterrence and in calls for the total renunciation of nuclear weapons. While these appeals have special force within the religious community and some limited effectiveness outside it, senior policy makers are not immune to changes of heart, especially when moral argument and compelling circumstances converge to make a new course of action attractive.

Continuing attachment to one's interests and the interests of one's community has mixed consequences when we look toward the negotiated resolution of disputes. On the one hand, it can erect insurmountable barriers to agreement and can prevent people from seeing the issues in dispute from any standpoint other than their own. On the other hand, it can make one or both parties sensitive to a wider range of threats and sources of harm that can be effectively dealt with only on a cooperative basis. On the level of confrontations between states with nuclear weapons, it points to the desirability of establishing a stable regime of arms control and to various measures of common security. More broadly, it provides the basis for a further way of arguing for the desirability and the moral worth of ways of settling disputes through voluntary agreement rather than through violence.

Religious and ideological traditions will generally use standards of judgment about benefits and harms that rely to some extent on common views shared across religious and ideological divisions. The lives of children, the stability of families, the opportunity to share in food and drink, the simple joys of serene prosperity, the careful pursuit of craft and learning are counted as goods in the life of any stable community. They are goods which are compatible with conflicting religious and ideological traditions and which are likely to be damaged by resorting to force. This fact can be the basis for a considered preference for negotiation over force without stepping outside the boundaries of one's own given religious or ideological tradition. Esteem for these goods may not be high in certain decision-making elites, but it will normally be present in democratic communities.

Third, among ways of dealing with an impasse between two traditions unable to communicate across a perceptual or moral divide, is the possibility of adding options for informal dialogue on practical steps toward political settlement in order to avoid an either/or choice between war and formal negotiation. Establishing or restoring dialogue is integral to building or changing relationship. In crisis, we need to focus on defusing an immediate confrontation in ways that will allow us to lay a foundation for working on the resolution of differences over time. In such a situation we may encounter the paradox of marshalling force not to use it but to contain a threat and to create a standoff that can open the door to dialogue and to political settlement. We have become familiar with words like "containment" and "quarantine." The art in such approaches is to build in time for dialogue seeking mutually tolerable steps away from confrontation without compromise of basic values.

## Reflections

We have argued that within religious and ideological traditions that champion conflicting conceptions of justice and authorize using force to protect justice and other moral-political values, there are and must be grounds for preferring peaceful settlement to force in resolving conflict. This argument in a sense recapitulates an important aspect of the development of just war theory, which has long had to reckon with the possibilities that issues of justice within a conflict situation could not be sorted out definitively and that each side would have not merely contradictory intuitions about the right way to resolve a dispute but also differing theoretical accounts of how the diverse claims of justice are to be subordinated one to another so as to give a coherent and practical statement of what justice requires in the political community.

The claim that negotiation is preferable to war is bound to strike most contemporary Westerners as a truism which does not need much argument. In our century we have had sufficiently bloody reminders of the costs of war to convince us that we must try to prevent its outbreak and that the great powers should live under a regime of restraint and even self-denial with regard to the use of force in response to what in earlier ages would have been regarded as unacceptable provocations.

There are some who think that this lesson has been learned too well and that some of our allies, at least, exhibit an excessive willingness to move too quickly from armed confrontation to a process of negotiation. This view should not be dismissed out of hand. It does have certain ironical aspects, for it usually involves Americans urging Germans and Japanese to greater readiness to take up arms. But it also reminds us of how difficult it can be to sustain the preferability of peaceful settlement once a serious case is granted for defense of political values by force. For in such a situation we have to deal with values of the first importance to the security of the political community and with a serious, proximate threat to these values. Where fighting is thought to be justified, negotiating may well be portrayed as the course preferred by those who lack the strength and clarity of mind to face issues squarely or the vigor and courage to pay the price of defending values against attack. There is also the danger that a determined and skillful adversary may gain by negotiation what could not have been gained by the use of force.

Are we then to conclude that the presence of a serious, proximate threat overturns the general thesis that peaceful settlement is preferable? Or do political settlement and negotiation always remain the preferable course? We might well be tempted to the second alternative if we direct our concern primarily to the possibility of superpower confrontations. But we also think that it cannot be correct to generalize from a nuclear situation in which the stakes are unprecedentedly high. We ask, for instance, whether it would have been morally wrong for the Western powers to fight Hitler in August and September of 1938, rather than negotiate. (We can also ask whether preventive measures before 1938 would not have been the most moral approach.)

The decisive considerations that can overturn the presumption in favor of peaceful settlement have to do with the behavior and intentions of the adversary. These are matters on which there is often considerable uncertainty and about which fear and bias can strongly influence judgments. These judgments are not arrived at by reflecting on general moral truths, but by making a reasonable estimate of the likely effects of alternative courses of action on cherished values. Disagreement in these judgments can exist among people who espouse the same moral principles. The judgments that the use of force is indeed the last resort or that negotiations with a determined adversary are futile and even dangerous are rarely achieved with the kind of deductive rigor or evidential clarity that will satisfy all persons of good will and that will thus terminate the moral debate.

Because conflict is increasingly costly, the affirmation that peaceful settlement is normally preferable to war is still relevant even when it is overridden in a given situation. More practically, unless we pay full attention to the widening range of political instruments to defuse crises and resolve conflict, we cannot argue in good conscience that we are resorting to arms "as a last resort." Unless we blend the threat of force with an all-out political effort to prevent war and open the door to peaceful settlement, we do not have the right to argue that the use of force is justified. Put another way, have we done all we can—politically as well as militarily—to prevent war? Have we done all we can to develop a political option between war and negotiation?

What has been said thus far about the moral role of negotiations from the standpoint of just war theory has been written with an eye on two ways of construing just war theory: (1) as a set of specific moral and legal norms governing the relations between states; and (2) as a set of moral norms which, when stripped of those elements that are peculiar to the historical development of international relations and military practice in the West, formulate the response of reason to social disputes in which claims of justice are in conflict and in which there is likelihood of one or both sides resorting to force.

As we have argued in this paper, the assumption that the parties in dispute in the contemporary world are discrete sovereign entities with no necessary interest in collaboration has largely lost its hold and must be replaced by a new paradigm of international relationships. But even for those who believe that adoption of some new paradigm is not yet well founded and that this world still contains many familiar obstacles to the attainment of justice and peace that are best dealt with by relying on well-established paradigms for the management and resolution of international conflict, there are still strong reasons for affirming the preferability of peaceful settlement to war, and these reasons apply, although not always conclusively, even across religious and ideological divisions.

A CONCLUDING WORD

In a world that could make each human being more secure, better nourished and educated, healthier, and more fulfilled, it will be criminal for leaders to rely mainly on contests of economic and military power to achieve goals defined only from self-centered interests. Shifting focus to the process of interaction among bodies politic—and to the instruments of resolving conflict peacefully—introduces into the agenda of ethical thinking about how nations relate, traditions of thought that have often been said to be inappropriate among states. It becomes more difficult to assign to states a different code of ethics from the code that governs the human beings who constitute and run those states. States will continue to have characteristics of their own, but it is increasingly difficult to ignore the ethics of relationships among the peoples and groups who define them.

In this joint essay we have explored a territory or a set of possibilities that fall between the general religious demand for peace and the well-defined categories of the just war tradition. These possibilities for the peaceful and political settlement of disputes and for the building of a network of long-term relationships among nations are increasingly likely to be important and actual in the changed world that lies ahead of us. But we are convinced that our ethical understanding of these possibilities and of the political instruments and decisions that will make them real needs to be made much more precise. We think that exploring these possibilities is particularly important in bringing us beyond the impasse between idealism and realism within which so much thinking about international conflicts has been confined. Because of its orientation to a newly emerging international reality, our work is unavoidably tentative and incomplete. It is also work that for its completion has to draw together both theorists and practitioners, both those who are actively engaged in shaping a new international reality and those who are pondering how to define and maintain the moral character of this reality. For ethicists, this will require an approach that is attentive to the meaning of the empirical details in disputes and their settlement, as well as to the diversity of religious and intellectual traditions with which we are involved.

## Notes

1. Harold Saunders first developed these observations on our changing world and the concept of relationship in two papers: (1) "Beyond 'Us and Them'—Building Mature International Relationships," a draft monograph prepared in 1987-88 under a grant from the United States Institute of Peace in

collaboration with the Kettering Foundation; (2) an early version of that paper published as a work in progress, "Beyond 'We' and 'They'— Conducting International Relationships," in *Negotiation Journal: On the Process of Dispute Settlement* 3. 3 (July 1987), 245-77. The observations were refined under a grant from the Carnegie Corporation of New York for "The Arab-Israeli Conflict in a Global Perspective," in John D. Steinbruner, ed., *Restructuring American Foreign Policy* (Washington, D.C.: The Brookings Institution, 1988), chap. 8. A fuller discussion of that conflict appears in *The Other Walls: The Politics of the Arab-Israeli Conflict in a Global Perspective* (Princeton, N.J.: Princeton University Press, 1991). The concept of relationship was developed with the support of the Ford and MacArthur Foundations as "An Historic Challenge to Rethink How Nations Relate," in Vamik D. Volkan, Demetrios Julius, and Joseph V. Montville, eds., *The Psychodynamics of International Relationships, vol. 1—Concepts and Theories* (Lexington, Mass.: Lexington Books, 1990), chap. 1. This approach is also applied to "The Soviet-U.S. Relationship and the Third World," in Robert Jervis and Seweryn Bialer, eds., *Soviet-American Relations after the Cold War* (Durham, N.C.: Duke University Press, 1991), chap. 6. In each case, these observations and the concept of relationship are stated in more or less the same—often verbatim—form as the necessary starting point for analysis of a particular question. Each publisher has agreed to this practice.

2. The ideas about the politics of preparing and sustaining negotiation are developed more fully in Harold H. Saunders, "We Need a Larger Theory of Negotiation: The Importance of Prenegotiating Phases," *Negotiation Journal* 1. 3 (July 1985); in *The Other Walls: The Politics of the Arab-Israeli Peace Process in a Global Perspective*, op. cit. (especially chapters 1, 2, 9, 10, and Epilogue); and in Cecilia Albin and Harold H. Saunders, *Sinai II: The Politics of International Mediation* (Washington, D.C.: Foreign Policy Institute, Paul H. Nitze School of Advanced International Studies, Johns Hopkins University, 1991).

3. The concept of "the ripe moment" or "ripeness" has been most fully stated by I. William Zartman and Maureen R. Berman in *The Practical Negotiator* (New Haven and London: Yale University Press, 1982), 50-57, and by Dr. Zartman in *Ripe for Resolution: Conflict and Intervention in Africa* (New York and Oxford: Oxford University Press, 1985).

4. Aristotle, *Nicomachean Ethics*, III, 1, 1110 a 8-12.

5. Ibid., V, 9, 1136 b 6-7.

6. For a brief philosophical presentation of the significance of this theme in Jewish and Christian teaching, see Alan Donagan, *The Theory of Morality* (Chicago: University of Chicago Press, 1977), 4-8.

# THE CONVERSATION

George Weigel began the discussion by posing a series of questions to John Langan and Harold Saunders. The first of these had to do with the issue of whether all moral languages contain "corrective and subsidiary traditions" that make transcultural moral discourse possible. Is this true, for example, of Leninism, or of the more tough-minded forms of Islam? Are there "subsidiary" traditions, in these two volatile worlds, which actually prescribe normative negotiation with the capitalist adversary or with the "infidel"? Weigel also wondered whether the "goods" enumerated by Langan and Saunders were as universally validated as the authors suggested. Some of these goods did not seem to be operative in Beirut, Belfast, or the Korean peninsula.

Weigel then asked about the paper's reading of international relations history and theory. Was it entirely accurate to suggest that the "Melian dialogue" or ultrarealist paradigm was the only mode of statecraft pursued by Western governments today, or over the last five centuries? The paper's reference to the evolution of postwar Western European politics suggested that there were in fact practical, nonadversarial alternatives to the stark "Melian dialogue" paradigm. Second, did the "old paradigm" of international politics really reduce "power" to military power, as Harold Saunders suggested? Didn't many advocates of the "old paradigm" understand that power had many dimensions, the resort to violence being only one of them? Third, do the changes taking place in today's world really justify adopting the "new paradigm"? Or is this another situation in which the American penchant for therapeutic solutions to political problems is asserting itself? Finally, Weigel cautioned against the manipulation of negotiations by adversaries eager to exploit Western good intentions and naiveté and ready to use negotiations as part of a psychological warfare strategy. The "new paradigm" should include an "ethic of relationships" that could help prevent negotiations from becoming an instrument of manipulation.

Michael Novak drew attention to the many possible meanings of the terms "new paradigm" and "relationship." Langan and Saunders seemed to assume that the "new paradigm" was morally superior to the "old paradigm"; but this ought to be explored in more critical detail. The term "relationship" also needed further clarification. Novak suggested that what the authors had in mind was the Aristotelian concept of political friendship: the exercise of hard-headed realism by two or more parties in pursuit of a common good, combined with an awareness of the interdependent nature of their interests and goals. This kind of "relationship" is possible between states and statesmen, but it differs sharply from the "touchy-feely" or California concept of "relationship."

Harold Saunders agreed with Novak's semantic caution, and emphasized that whether one adopted the term "friendship" or "relationship," what was meant in this context was distinct from interpersonal relationships. Indeed, Saunders's diplomatic experience had taught him to be wary of the tendency of some statesmen to pursue personal relationships with their counterparts as the all-purpose solution to the problems of international politics.

John Cooper thought that, in refining his definition of "relationship," Harold Saunders might consider three political-ethical criteria. The first was legitimacy: were the parties to the relationship legitimate representatives of their respective constituencies? Did they have legitimate moral agency? Not all governments in the international system represented, or were accountable to, their people. The second criterion was truthfulness: did both parties have an equal commitment to transparency and good faith, and were they prepared to refrain from manipulating the negotiations in order to undermine the opposite side? The third criterion was consent to the relationship, and this consent had to be grounded in equality. The kind of Aristotelian political friendship described by Novak was a relationship among equals. Only when these three criteria were satisfied was a relationship capable of an "ethic of responsibility" that enables the parties to recognize claims to justice transcending their own interests.

Thomas Reese thought that the concept of "friendship" was not helpful because it invariably connoted a "personal" or affective relationship. Since there were few nation-states which Americans were prepared to deal with on that basis, Saunders's concept was not very relevant to those knotty conflicts of interest that characterized international politics. Reese thought that the Gospel norm of "love," radical though it was, might serve better. The Scriptures admonish us to love our enemies, not to like them or trust them. Love implies a relationship in which we respect the other party and want what is best for him, regardless of our feelings toward him.

Saunders responded that, while he was personally committed to the "love" principle articulated in the Gospel, he was aware of the political difficulties of incorporating it into the policy process. Did the concept of "love" capture the elements of realism, suspicion, and guardedness that were essential to his concept of "relationship" as "putting oneself in the other person's shoes"? Ultimately, what he had in mind was something like the kind of "businesslike" relationship that most Americans favor toward the Soviet Union. Far from being static, such a relationship can be highly dynamic and provide opportunities for imaginative, mutually beneficial compromise.

Saunders wanted to make it clear, however, that even though the character and quality of the U.S.-Soviet relationship might vary, one could not deny the existence of the relationship itself. As in many situations in life where we find ourselves locked into relationships with people we don't like, the United States and the USSR were locked into a relationship as a result of their possession of nuclear weapons. Although we might not admire or trust the Soviets, we had an obligation to turn this inescapable relationship into something more constructive than a perpetual standoff.

Saunders added that he was well aware that the "old paradigm" was still the guiding logic of international politics. No statesman could or should ignore the critical role of the balance of power. Hence, Saunders did not seek an immediate replacement of the "old paradigm" by "the new"; for now, both paradigms would continue to coexist as images of different but interrelated aspects of world politics. The question was whether policy makers, who pride themselves on their realism, were prepared to accept the legitimacy of the "new paradigm" in its complementary role. In other words, were they ready to add to the "old paradigm" a new dimension of understanding, reflective of ongoing changes in both the empirical structure and normative requirements of international politics, so that over the long run the "old paradigm" might give way to the new?

Michael Novak pointed out that the impersonal character of Saunders's "businesslike relationship" was actually one of its advantages. The Founding Fathers thought that a "businesslike" relationship was a good image for America's conduct of its relations with other states, as it combined political detachment, realism, and a dynamic search for common interests. Saunders was right on another point: the best "relationship" was one which went beyond necessity and aimed at a creative, future-changing, productive interaction. But this, contrary to the "California model," involved human beings working together at the peak of their capacity for realism.

Responding to earlier queries by Weigel and Novak, Saunders argued that the "new paradigm" was indeed ethically preferable to the "old." The latter saw states as rational actors using power to pursue national interests with little regard for others. The "new paradigm," on the other hand, posits reconciliation as one of the goals of negotiation. And reconciliation, whether of God to man or man to man, could only take place in the context of relationships.

At this point, George Weigel cautioned against a repetition of Hans Morgenthau's dubious assertion that the only real "ethics" was the ethics of interpersonal relationships—from which Morgenthau concluded that politics was essentially amoral. Social ethics, Weigel argued, had its own distinctive moral logic based on the distinctive ends of politics. Moral reasoning about international relations did not necessarily have to confuse statecraft with friendship.

Paul Seabury brought Clausewitz's concept of war as a contest of wills for the attainment of a political end into the discussion. Understanding the relationship of negotiations to conflict means understanding the underlying political wills. Sometimes a party's interests will be served best by refraining from negotiations, or by continuing a state of indirect warfare during negotiations. Sometimes wills are so hardened that it is impossible to carry out meaningful negotiations unless one party's will is altered, or broken, through a massive defeat. Scholars of "conflict resolution" look askance at the concepts of "defeat" and "victory." Yet even in the twentieth century, victory or defeat can create the political and military conditions for a lasting settlement, as it did with Germany after World War II.

Anthony Quainton was troubled by the paper's assumption that parties enter negotiations in order to preserve essential values and to settle conflicting claims of justice. But in today's world, there are parties (of various ideological and religious persuasions) who want to expand and propagate their values, not simply preserve them, and who want to restructure the world radically in order to impose on others their particular vision of justice. In places like the Middle East, it is difficult to isolate negotiation from ideology; the opportunities for the development of transactional, "businesslike" relationships are fewer than Saunders seemed to suggest.

Samuel Lewis also questioned Saunders's reading of contemporary world politics. The "new paradigm" may be morally preferable, but it is not necessarily going to triumph. Moreover, Lewis suggested, George Weigel was correct in arguing that the "new paradigm" was not so new after all. The Concert of Europe, the League of Nations, and the United Nations were efforts at creating a structure of constructive, nonadversarial relationships similar to Saunders's "new paradigm."

In the contemporary world, if one bracketed European integration and the Gorbachev-inspired Soviet rapprochement with the West, it was difficult to find much evidence of a "new paradigm." It was certainly not operative in Indochina, the Middle East, or Africa. And where the nation-state was not the predominant institution, Seabury's clash of wills took the form of ethnic and nationalist conflict, religious wars, and struggles rooted in ancient historical and cultural animosities.

Lewis did agree with the paper's measured appreciation of the role played by the personality of leaders and their relationships to one another (their "interpersonal chemistry") in driving negotiations forward or stalling them. It was important, of course, not to overestimate the contribution that personal relationships can make to the solution of inter-state conflicts. Yet in most of the Third World, where regimes tend to be based on a leader's charisma and personality, a leader's personal qualities and his relationships with his counterparts can shape the prospects for international violence or its amelioration.

Saunders tried to reduce the apparent differences between Lewis's position and his by agreeing that the "new paradigm" does not describe the world as it is today. But it does describe some aspects of international politics that have become significant over the last twenty years. Interdependence has grown more complex and multidimensional; state boundaries are more porous and subject to erosion by the flow of people and ideas through them; modern technology continues to increase the incentives for greater political and economic cooperation and integration among states. While the "old paradigm" describes the dominant mode of interaction in world politics, it cannot by itself give us either an accurate and comprehensive view of what is happening, or a valid normative framework for responding to change.

Saunders readily admitted that the "new paradigm" had both empirical and normative dimensions. It not only claimed to describe a new, vital aspect of international politics. It also suggested a different way of acting in response to these empirical developments. Thus, the "new paradigm" contained an empirical assertion and an ethical vision.

George Weigel wanted two questions clarified. First, how much of the truly substantive aspects of contemporary international politics were described and explained by the "new paradigm"? Second, how significant was the danger of construing adversarial relationships as if they were amenable to the "new paradigm" when in fact they were not? Were there not serious consequences in such an error? Did prematurely assuming the existence of qualitatively different relationships, and acting on that assumption, risk impeding the development of a new form of international politics?

Robert Lehman disliked Michael Novak's emphasis on the "business-like" or "impersonal" nature of a political relationship, arguing that the term "relationship" necessarily implied ethical obligations and a qualitatively different way of approaching the world. The adversarial model of ethics and international relations posed the question, "What are our obligations toward the foreigners?" in a dichotomous "we/they" form. A relational model, on the other hand, recognized the existence of what Martin Buber called "space" between parties, and the obligation not to treat the other as an object.

George Weigel asked Lehman whether his critique did not presuppose that there were other parties willing to be related to in the way he described. That was the critical empirical question which the paper had not resolved.

Harold Saunders suggested that it was not important whether most of international politics conforms to the "new paradigm"; indeed, it does not. What matters is that, even as we continue to operate in a world dominated by the "old paradigm," we open our minds to the possibility that a "relational" way of thinking will occasionally give us opportunities for constructive action. The "new paradigm" gives us an open window through which we can discern new dimensions of world politics.

Alberto Coll argued that two key factors had facilitated the emergence of a "new paradigm." One was global capitalism, which has set the context for the kinds of interdependent economic relationships in which states see it to their benefit to open their borders and their economic and political systems, and to relate to other states along the lines of the "new paradigm." If the predominant economic system in the world became statist socialism, we would see a sharp reversal of the trend detected by Saunders. The second factor was the successful maintenance for four decades of a military balance of power favorable to the coalition of liberal states known as the "West." Under the security umbrella provided by this preponderance of power, there has been room for the growth of the interactive processes encompassed by the "new paradigm." The preservation of a balance of power favorable to the West, and the continued sway of global capitalism, were thus essential requirements for the future viability of the "new paradigm."

Agreeing with Coll, Samuel Lewis pointed to two contradictory trends in today's world. One was toward more intense technological, economic, and cultural interaction; these seemed to give greater empirical and normative weight to the "new paradigm." The other trend, visible in some parts of the world, was toward more obscurantism, isolationism, and ideological or religious fanaticism; in facing these, we would be well advised to apply the "old paradigm."

Paul Seabury noted that the German political philosopher Karl Schmidt drew a distinction between two types of animosity, expressed in the Latin words *hostis* and *inimicus*. *Hostis* is a formal animosity, often characteristic of groups struggling for tangible objectives, which dissolves as soon as their conflict ends. *Inimicus* denotes a more deep-seated hostility, arising from sometimes unfathomable depths of cultural, historical, or religious animosity, and which is far from easily resolvable. Contemporary religious traditions, especially in the West, have difficulty understanding the nature, or the implications for international politics, of the many varieties of *inimicus* present in the world.

Michael Novak agreed with Saunders that substantive changes taking place in the world required a revision of the "old paradigm." The old dichotomy between ideas and realpolitik had lost much of its force. In an age of instant telecommunications, personal computers, and a global mass media, ideas have great power to affect political developments. The Chilean generals had learned that, no matter how militarily powerful they were, their disregard for human rights had cost them vital political and economic support in the United States and elsewhere around the world. The Polish Communist leaders had learned a similar lesson: a closed society was increasingly difficult to maintain except by the costliest and most extreme means of coercion. No realist statecraft could ignore the power of ideas.

In closing the discussion, John Langan agreed with Michael Novak that what the Marxists call "the forces of production," including modern technology and communications, were changing the character of international relations. The very definition and sources of international political power were changing. This, in turn, meant that new anxieties and uncertainties would arise as statesmen and citizens alike reevaluated the "old paradigm" and searched for ways of incorporating into it elements of the new.

# DAVID HOLLENBACH, S.J.

# The Role of the Churches
# in
# the American Search for Peace

The 1980s have been a decade of intense debate and significant development in the areas of United States policy concerning matters of war and peace. These debates and developments have touched on a broad range of issues: the arms buildup and nuclear freeze movement of the early years of the decade; U.S. policies in Central America and the Middle East; the Strategic Defense Initiative; the U.S.-Soviet treaty eliminating intermediate-range nuclear forces; the significance of *glasnost* and *perestroika*; the possibility of deep cuts in strategic nuclear weapons and reduction of conventional forces by both the Warsaw Pact and NATO. Especially since the Reykjavik summit meeting between President Reagan and Secretary Gorbachev in 1986 and the INF treaty of 1987, the possibility of a new military relationship between the superpowers has been entertained by informed observers with a growing seriousness. The 1989 elections in both the USSR and Poland have also raised hope that a new, post-Cold War political relationship between East and West is at least imaginable. At the same time, the possibilities of genuine political change in Communist societies are precarious, as the response of the ruling powers to the democracy movement in the People's Republic of China once again demonstrated. The dangers that would attend any military conflict between the superpowers continue to remain extremely high.

Each of these matters of political and military policy has important moral dimensions. The Christian churches in the United States have been active participants in the effort to place the moral aspects of these questions on the agenda of national discussion. The demands of Christian morality, of course, have led Christian communities to reflection on the legitimacy of warfare and on peaceful alternatives to it throughout history. But the range and depth of this reflection have varied considerably from one historical period to another. The 1980s have unquestionably been a time of intensified engagement with these questions by the churches.

In particular, church leadership bodies have issued a number of pronouncements on war and peace matters for the guidance of their members and in order to contribute to the larger public debate. The best known of these church statements is the 1983 pastoral letter of the U.S. Catholic bishops, *The Challenge of Peace: God's Promise and Our Response.* Other examples include: the statement of the 1985 General Synod of the United Church of Christ, "Affirming the United Church of Christ as a Just Peace Church"; the study commissioned by the Presbyterian Church (U.S.A.) entitled *Presbyterians and Peacemaking: Are We Now Called to Resistance?;* the statement of the 1988 General Assembly of the Presbyterian Church, *Christian Obedience in a Nuclear Age;* the United Methodist Council of Bishops' *In Defense of Creation: The Nuclear Crisis and a Just Peace;* the National Association of Evangelicals' program on "Peace, Freedom and Security Studies"; and a report prepared for the Episcopal Diocese of Washington, D.C., on *The Nuclear Dilemma; A Christian Search for Understanding.* Most recently, the U.S. Catholic bishops have issued a *Pastoral Reflection* and a *Report* reassessing and updating the conclusions of their earlier pastoral letter in light of policy developments from 1983 to 1988.[1]

The purpose of this essay is to highlight three factors that shape the ethical analyses of U.S. defense policy found in these church statements: (1) the way the international political and military situation is interpreted both empirically and theologically; (2) the status of the just war tradition and the understanding of the nature of a just peace in the moral reasoning advanced by the documents; (3) the bridge question of how religious, moral, and political points of view should be related to each other in approaching public policy. The approaches to these three themes will be reviewed in order to learn where the possibilities and pitfalls for future church participation in the search for peace may lie.

The documents considered have notably different purposes and different levels of authority within the church communities that produced them. Therefore they will be taken as emblematic of certain trends in the discussions going on among Christians, not as definitive or exhaustive representations of the range of Christian opinion. Neither a comprehensive history of church involvement in the search for peace over the last decade nor detailed textual exegesis of the documents will be provided. Rather, the purpose here is to offer a broad-gauged interpretation of the strengths and weaknesses of recent church involvement in this search. It is hoped that this will lead to an increased measure of wisdom as Christians address emerging questions of war and peace from a moral point of view in the 1990s.

## I. INTERPRETATION OF THE CONTEXT

In all the recent church teachings on war and peace, an empirical description of the contemporary international situation sets the context for the ethical analysis they contain. The understanding of this context is also influenced by the way these empirical descriptions are interpreted theologically. These empirical and theological considerations jointly determine how the churches understand the meaning of the events to which they are responding and thus directly affect their moral recommendations.

All of the church statements recognize that the rivalry between the United States and the Soviet Union is central to the structure of the entire international situation today. But this rivalry is understood in three notably different ways. First, some of the church statements argue that both the United States and the USSR are equally to blame for international tension and conflict. A second interpretation places the onus primarily on the global aspirations and repressive nature of Communist regimes. A third view argues that the mutual vulnerability of the superpowers to nuclear destruction and the changes currently underway both within the Soviet Union and in U.S.-USSR relations may open the way to a basic transformation of the global political order.

The first of these analytic frameworks is present in the Methodist bishops' 1986 statement. The claim that the United States and the Soviet Union deserve equal blame for international tensions is defended by parallel sketches of the abuses committed by each side in recent history. The Methodist bishops acknowledge that the USSR lacks a tradition of democratic liberties, defines human rights in a way that emphasizes economic and social security, and has been historically repressive of public protest. They note Soviet intervention to close access to Berlin in 1948, deployment of missiles in Cuba in 1962, suppression of the Hungarian uprising in 1956 and the Prague Spring in 1968, hostile policies toward Israel since 1960 together with harsh restrictions on Jewish emigration, violations of the Helsinki accords of 1975, degradation of détente by the deployment of new missiles in Eastern Europe in the late 1970s, and finally, the invasion of Afghanistan in 1979.[2] They provide a similar list of the shortcomings of the United States. The Methodist bishops are distressed by a "constant and extreme magnification of the United States-USSR differences to the point of demagoguery and even utter dishonesty" in American public discourse.[3] This arises, in their view, from a failure to acknowledge that the behavior of the United States has given the USSR ample cause for grievance: intervention on Soviet soil during the revolution of 1918; refusal to recognize the Soviet government for fifteen years; refusal of a Soviet request for postwar reconstruction assistance in 1945; the U-2 overflights that led to the collapse of the 1960 summit meeting; failure to ratify the SALT II treaty.

The Methodist bishops add a religious perspective to strengthen their case against portraying the U.S.-Soviet relationship in a stark us-them fashion. They place considerable emphasis on the presence of "tens of millions" of Christians within the Soviet Union. Though the Methodist document notes the restriction and persecution that religious believers have undergone in the USSR, it goes on to comment that "this endurance of religious faith and practice seven decades—and three generations—after the Bolshevik Revolution is one of the most remarkable spiritual triumphs of modern history."[4] Conflict and confrontation between the superpowers, therefore, would include conflict and confrontation among Christians. Ecumenical bridges between the churches in the United States and churches in the Soviet Union point the way toward greater mutual understanding between the two nations.

In other words, the Methodist bishops' description of the superpower rivalry seeks to undercut extreme forms of anti-Soviet fear as well as excessive confidence in the American cause. And their stress on the presence of Christians within the boundaries of the Soviet Union introduces the theme of ecumenical ties that should unite all Christians to reinforce this perspective. I think it is fair to say that both their presentation of the historical record of the two countries and their use of the ecumenical appeal to the unity of Christians provide a picture of the situation that is, at best, uncritical and one-sided.

Dana Wilbanks and Ronald Stone make the same point in a more extreme and questionable way in a study paper prepared for the Presbyterian Church. This is not an official statement of the Presbyterian Church. Indeed, some of its conclusions aroused strong opposition within the Presbyterian Church and were not included in the official statement approved by the Presbyterian General Assembly in 1988. But the Wilbanks-Stone study does represent one current of opinion found in the churches. It suggests that the driving force in contemporary international conflict is "the identification of other peoples and nations as enemies."[5] The very notion that the Soviet Union is an enemy of the United States is at the root of the superpower conflict. By applying the label "enemy" to the USSR, the United States is itself a major cause of international danger. Though Wilbanks and Stone acknowledge that there are genuine conflicts between the United States and the Soviet Union, in the same sentence they observe that there are similar conflicts between "the

United States and Japan or New Zealand or the Federal Republic of Germany or Mexico."[6] The beginning of the solution to the superpower rivalry, therefore, is to cease the psychological and rhetorical escalation of the conflicts that exist between the superpowers to the status of an elemental struggle between right and wrong, good and evil, friend and enemy.

In a rather astonishing theological heightening of the stakes, Wilbanks and Stone go on to suggest that "Perhaps the key biblical insight is that we are our own worst enemy. The sin is in us. The chief builders of walls of hostility are ourselves. Perhaps we are even God's worst enemy as we pervert God's humanizing intention for the world into a rigid division of the world into friends and enemies."[7] I call this statement astonishing because it simply inverts the attitude of anti-Soviet fanaticism the authors reject and replaces it with unilateral American guilt. It is certainly true that Christian faith demands that adversaries recognize each other's common humanity and seek just reconciliation with each other. It is also evident that the United States has not always lived up to these obligations. But recognition of common humanity and the pursuit of reconciliation will not be accomplished by smoothing over the really pointed conflicts that do exist between the U.S. and USSR social systems or by placing all the blame for these conflicts on the United States. This is, I believe, fundamentally misguided both politically and theologically. Politically, one need not descend into crass jingoism when one recognizes the repressive and aggressive character of the policies of Lenin, Stalin, and Brezhnev. Theologically, one ignores at one's peril the mixture of good and evil in all historical undertakings that has been evident to theologians from Augustine to Reinhold Niebuhr.[8]

A second interpretation of the dynamics of the international situation sees Soviet-bloc threats to both justice and peace as the principal engine of conflict. Such analysis is found in the *Guidelines on Peace, Freedom and Security Studies* published by the National Association of Evangelicals. The NAE states that the notion that the evils fostered by the democratic West and by the Communist world are morally equivalent is "flatly contradicted by history and current events."[9] The fear that arises from contemplating the dangers of a military conflict between the superpowers should not be allowed to obscure the crucial differences in their ideologies and political systems. The NAE argues that the adoption of approaches like those of the Methodist bishops or of Wilbanks and Stone provides evidence that some religious leaders "in the name of overthrowing tyranny . . . [have] become handmaidens to even more complete and profound forms of oppression."[10]

From this forceful negative judgment, the NAE goes on to describe the context for the church's actions as one that calls for positive efforts to secure together the interrelated goals of peace, disarmament, U.S. security, and the advancement of democracy. It affirms that democracy and the rule of law are, in fact, the principal means for the nonviolent resolution of conflict both domestically and on the international stage.

This political claim is backed up theologically. Both tyranny and war are the results of human sin. Redemption from sin and the mitigation of its effects are possible only through union with Christ. But the church's mission is not to proclaim the possibility of reconciliation between persons and their Creator in an individualistic way. The ministry of reconciliation also extends to seeking reconciliation of human beings with each other, including reconciliation on the societal and political levels. In a fallen world the perfect elimination of all conflict is impossible; it will come only when God acts to establish the Kingdom in its full glory. Until that day, however, Christians have the responsibility to work for that degree of reconciliation and peace that can be achieved in social life. Democracy and the rule of law are the surest means to this end.

Thus the NAE argues that Christians should work to broaden the influence of Western democracy throughout the world and to oppose or even roll back Marxist socialism wherever possible. They set the following central goal for Evangelicals in public policy discussions:

> We will demonstrate a commitment to the values and institutions of a free society and we will support those in other societies who wish to build those values and processes into their own future. We will uphold the idea that peace and the advancement of human rights, especially religious liberty, are inextricably linked.[11]

Such a goal entails commitment to the defense and security of democratic institutions and increased efforts to change the international and domestic behavior of the Soviet Union to make it more responsive to democratic aspirations. The NAE *Guidelines* also call for pursuing these democratic objectives nonviolently. Doing so will call for the creation of new international institutions of conflict resolution. This, the NAE maintains, "is not a utopian dream; it is a matter of wise and steady work building a foundation for political community across national borders."[12]

There is much appeal in this vision. Some of its elements have parallels in the Roman Catholic bishops' pastoral letter on the nuclear question. For example, the Catholic bishops emphasize that the defense of justice and human rights must be at the foundation of any genuine peace. In their words: "The obligation for all of humanity to work toward universal respect for human rights and human dignity is a fundamental imperative of the social, economic, and political order."[13] The Catholic bishops are also unambiguous in their critique of the policies of the Soviet Union that violate this imperative. A few citations are illustrative:

The fact of a Soviet threat, as well as the existence of a Soviet drive for hegemony, at least in areas of major strategic interest, cannot be denied. . . . Many peoples are forcibly kept under communist domination despite their manifest wishes to be free. . . . NATO is an alliance of democratic countries which have freely chosen their association; the Warsaw pact is not. . . . The facts simply do not support the invidious comparisons made at times, even in our own society, between our way of life, in which most basic human rights are at least recognized even if they are not always adequately supported, and those totalitarian and tyrannical regimes in which such rights are either denied or systematically suppressed.[14]

These statements are a clear indication that the Catholic bishops firmly reject an interpretation of the international context that places equal blame for injustice and violence on both superpowers, even though they do not entirely absolve the United States of failures to live up to its own ideals.

There are also analogies in the Catholic bishops' letter to the NAE's call for the creation of international institutions of conflict resolution and for the expansion of the democratic rule of law. In fact, such "world order" considerations have very strong roots in Roman Catholic tradition. They were developed in an especially clear way by Pope John XXIII in his encyclical *Pacem in Terris*. Both John XXIII and the Catholic bishops, however, are much more explicit in their recognition that war remains both a possibility and a reality in the contemporary international situation, even as they urge the development of structures of world order to minimize its likelihood.[15] Therefore their moral analysis seeks to address not only the problems raised by the political conflict between democratic and nondemocratic regimes but also the military and strategic dimensions of this conflict.

The NAE, on the other hand, does not discuss these military questions in any detail. For example, it states that the church should "encourage American initiatives to alter the current Soviet agenda and to develop pressures—both coercive (yet nonviolent) and persuasive—on and within that system."[16] It urges vigorous promotion of democracy by the United States in regions such as Central America. But the risks of war this may provoke are not addressed. George Weigel, a principal advisor to the NAE, maintains that the churches are too sensitive to these risks. He writes that the churches have been led astray by "a narrowly focused identification of 'intervention' with U.S. military action."[17] It is true enough that not all intervention need be military. But Weigel and the NAE do not address the conflicts between maintenance of peace and the promotion of democracy today. The simultaneous pursuit of peace, security, and freedom is a highly desirable goal, and efforts to create domestic and international institutions and legal systems that make these goals more compatible are urgent. In advocating such an approach, the NAE has made an important contribution. But the international system as we know it is defined by the absence of institutions and laws that are adequate to this task in many circumstances. When peace, security, and freedom conflict, priorities must be established among them. The NAE does not provide guidance that could help establish such priorities in a prudent way. Without an analysis of the possibilities and dangers that accompany different decisions about these priorities, a vigorous effort to promote democracy could end up endangering all three objectives of peace, security, and freedom itself. If the Methodist and Presbyterian documents are naive about the depth of conflict between the U.S. and the USSR, the NAE and Weigel minimize the dangers involved in pressing forward in this conflict in a highly interventionist way. More careful analysis of these tradeoffs is needed for an adequate understanding of the political and military context.

A third perspective on the context for moral argument is found in the pastoral letter and 1988 report of the Roman Catholic bishops and in the study of *The Nuclear Dilemma* prepared for the Episcopal Diocese of Washington, D.C. These documents are concerned almost exclusively with the nuclear level of U.S. foreign and military policy, but their analyses have considerable relevance to other levels as well.

Both the Roman Catholic and Episcopalian documents argue that the relationship between the United States and the Soviet Union is shaped by two factors. The two nations are political and ideological adversaries. But their security and well-being are also increasingly linked by the mutual threat of nuclear destruction and by a growing global web of economic interdependence.

The Episcopalian report argues that "the crux of the nuclear dilemma lies in the state of the relationship between the superpowers."[18] While the report is convinced that misperception, erroneous perspectives, and ethnocentric attitudes dangerously distort understanding on both sides of the superpower rivalry, it denies the notion that the superpower conflict is simply a matter of a misunderstanding of the intentions of the USSR by the United States or vice versa. "This conflict comes from major differences in the international goals of the two nations, in the interests which they pursue, and the values in which they believe."[19] Thus the Episcopalian committee explicitly rejects the view that threats to peace and justice by the United States and the USSR are morally equivalent. Precisely because the conflict is so real and the stakes are so high in the nuclear age, it is imperative that both sides come to understand themselves and each other as clearly as possible. The Episcopalian report seeks such a rational understanding of the conflict, not the dissolution of the conflict simply through a change in psychological attitudes or rhetoric.[20]

But the report also insists that the international context cannot be adequately interpreted as a traditional conflict of nation-states with different ideologies and political objectives. The existence of nuclear weapons and the threat of destruction they embody have transformed the rivalry into something unimagined in the prenuclear era. This transformation is a fact that deeply affects the effort to address the political and military situation from a moral point of view. "Neither superpower can enjoy the kind or degree of security that was available in pre-nuclear days. Security itself has become mutual. The protection and survival of each nation depends on the restraint and cooperation of the other."[21]

The Roman Catholic bishops presented a similar argument both in 1983 and 1988. In their more recent report, they made it clearer than they had perhaps done in 1983 that the qualitatively new moral issues of the nuclear rivalry must be understood in light of *both* the political relationship between the United States and the USSR *and* the technological nature of the weapons they possess.[22] They point out that the classical moral problems of international politics continue to shape the context today: preventing aggression; building international relations on the basis of justice and freedom; protecting human rights within states and among states; protecting weaker nations from stronger ones. However, nuclear weapons have changed the way these problems must be understood:

> The moral problem of the nuclear age arises when the classical political questions are joined to the contemporary technological prospects of a nuclear war. . . . Nuclear war remains a possibility, but it is increasingly seen as devoid of the rational political purpose and moral limits which have made war a justifiable activity in the past. Nuclear weapons threaten to destroy the very objectives which once provided the political and moral justification for using force.[23]

In other words, the problem to be addressed from a moral point of view has been fundamentally altered by the interconnected empirical realities of politics and technology in the nuclear age. An inadequate understanding of the context for moral reasoning will result from either an exclusive focus on the political rivalry of the superpowers or exclusive attention to the dangers of nuclear weapons themselves. This rivalry and these dangers are interconnected realities that structure the international situation today. The Episcopalian report summarizes the issue this way:

> The world's nuclear predicament has been formed by two interdependent factors:
>
> — The nature and existence of nuclear weapons; and

— The profound distrust and antagonism embedded in the U.S.-
Soviet relationship.

Each poses agonizing issues. Each constantly interacts with and affects the other. Neither can be dealt with independently of the other.[24]

In the view of the Episcopalian report, the political relation between
the superpowers is a more fundamental source of danger than is the existence of nuclear weapons.[25] This is true in the sense that, if there were no
antagonism between the United States and the Soviet Union, there
would be little reason to fear the use of nuclear weapons in a war
between them. At the same time, the existence of the nuclear threat
demands a transformation of our way of thinking about their political
rivalry. For nuclear threats and counterthreats themselves intensify interstate political antagonisms and can only be managed and reduced by
political means.

This recognition of the interconnection between the political and
technological-military aspects of the superpower relationship has opened
up the possibility of imagining U.S.-Soviet relations in fundamentally
new ways. Most of the church documents, for obvious reasons connected
with the time of their composition, have little to say about how Gorbachev's agenda of *glasnost* and *perestroika*, as well as the signing of the INF
treaty, will influence the interpretation of the context for moral analysis.[26]
All of them, however, express a strong wish that the antagonisms and
dangers of past U.S.-USSR relations might be reduced in the future,
while the prospects for human rights and freedom are simultaneously
advanced. As the Catholic bishops put it in 1983:

To believe we are condemned in the future only to what has been
the past of U.S.-Soviet relations is to underestimate both our human
potential for creative diplomacy and God's action in our midst which
can open the way to changes we can barely imagine.[27]

When this statement was written, of course, it was an expression of
hope rather than an analytic description of the state of superpower
relations. The United States was in the midst of a major military buildup,
Yuri Andropov was Secretary General in the Soviet Union, the Soviets
were fighting in Afghanistan, Poland was under martial law and Solidarity
was outlawed. The Catholic bishops stated that they did not intend to
encourage illusions that the future could be without tensions. But they
did want to warn against the idea that the future could only be as conflict-ridden and dangerous as the past.

Significant developments have, in fact, proven possible. Since 1983
there have been major developments in both the political and military
aspects of superpower relations. Even analysts noted for their "realistic"
approach to international affairs accept the view that we are entering a

new phase in East-West relations that calls for the development of a new policy agenda.[28] Mr. Gorbachev has stated that "A turning point has come, indeed, in the development of world events," and Mr. Bush has said that NATO now may be able "to move beyond the era of containment."[29] It would be naive, of course, to think that all tension and possibility of war has somehow disappeared. It has not. Nevertheless, both the Episcopalian report of 1987 and Roman Catholic report of 1988 argue that a fundamental shift in U.S.-Soviet relations is in the making, and that this calls for a different contextual framework for moral analysis than was the case in the early 1980s. They share this view with a growing group of secular policy analysts. It should be noted that this emphasis is not based simply on a moral affirmation that the superpower relationship ought to be less conflictual and dangerous. Rather, it contends that political and military realities are evolving in directions that make this realistically possible. The Episcopalian report stated that it found the 1987 environment "for improved relations as propitious as it has ever been in the long history of US-Soviet competition," though the document rightly remained quite sober in its stress on the fact of continuing competition.[30] The Catholic bishops pointed out that the new situation presents the superpowers with an opportunity, not a certainty. Grasping the present opportunity will depend on the overarching vision of the governments of the United States and the Soviet Union, as well as the informed action of the citizens in this country.[31] Such vision and action must be structured by an understanding both of the moral limits on military competition, and of the demands of a morally acceptable regime of peace in our time. This drives analysis from the level of the interpretation of fact to the level of moral reasoning and normative judgment.

## II.  JUST WAR AND JUST PEACE

Ethical assessment of policies in this area concerns both the demand that states act with justice toward their own citizens and those of other nations, and the demand that justice be pursued by peaceful means. This raises the classic question of how to conceive the relation between the values of justice and peace. Any person of good will, of course, hopes that justice can be secured peacefully and that peace will be built on justice. But when these values tragically conflict, the need for a moral doctrine to establish priorities is plainly evident.

In practice, there are only two possible answers to the question of the relative moral priority of justice or peace. Either justice is taken as the more fundamental value or peace is. The just war tradition argues for the first alternative. It sees the obligation to defend justice and human rights as a precondition for genuine peace, and it is therefore willing to grant legitimacy to the limited use of force to secure justice in some circumstances. Peace that is not built on justice is not true peace at all but rather a sort of violence. Thus, absolute refusal to resort to force does not ensure a peaceful existence but may lead to the loss of both peace and justice. John Courtney Murray stated the core of the just war tradition this way:

> The single inner attitude that is nourished by the traditional doctrine is a will to peace, which, in the extremity, bears within itself a will to enforce the precept of peace by arms. But this will to arms is a moral will; for it is identically a will to justice.[32]

An ethic of nonviolence reverses this priority and insists that resort to lethal force is never legitimate. There are a number of different types of the ethics of nonviolence, including a form that follows Jesus' command "resist not evil" literally, one that struggles actively for justice though in a nonviolent way, and one that is based on a secular hope that enlightened reason and persuasion will make war unnecessary.[33] But common to each of these forms of pacifism is the conviction that killing human beings in the pursuit of justice is itself an injustice. Thus, just war ethics and an ethic of nonviolence are ultimately incompatible stances. No one can be both a just war thinker and a pacifist at the same time.

In the recent church documents, however, there seems to be a desire to blur the distinction between the just war ethic and pacifism. For example, the Catholic bishops state that just war thinking and the ethic of nonviolence are "two distinct moral responses having a complementary relationship."[34] The nuclear revolution has caused a qualitative transformation of the realities that moral analysis must address. Because of this transformation, the Catholic bishops maintain that

> Both the just-war teaching and non-violence are confronted with a unique challenge by nuclear warfare. This must be the starting point for any further moral reflection: nuclear weapons particularly and nuclear warfare as it is planned today, raise new moral questions. No previously conceived moral position escapes the fundamental confrontation posed by contemporary nuclear strategy. . . .[35]

This challenge leads them to conclude that just war teaching and nonviolence are "distinct but interdependent methods of evaluating warfare," and that this interdependence is rooted in the fact that both traditions "share a common presumption against the use of force as a means of settling disputes."[36]

The Episcopalian report maintains a similar view that nuclear weapons raise new questions about the adequacy of received tradition. It states that "The traditional doctrine of 'just war,' part of early Christian thought, is applicable to, but inadequate for the nuclear age."[37] The Methodist bishops make a parallel observation about the limits of just war thinking. But they also oppose the view that this tradition should be jettisoned and replaced by an absolute commitment to nonviolence.

> A just-war ethic is never enough. Our churches must nurture a *new theology for a just peace*. . . . We are also persuaded that just-war morality provides too narrow a base from which to discern many of the most salient issues of the nuclear crisis. We cannot agree, however, with those who claim that nuclear weapons have simply nullified the just-war tradition altogether.[38]

The National Association of Evangelicals adds the following perspective:

> We accept, therefore, that good men may differ on the morality of war. Our appeal is that all, whatever their views on the use of national military power in a particular instance, join in action to develop alternatives to reliance on war for justice or security.[39]

What is going on beneath the surface of these statements? In some of the recent pronouncements from the churches, this way of thinking has a tone and a lack of analytic rigor that results from refusing to face the conflicts that can and often do exist between justice and peace. The United Church of Christ's pronouncement that it now sees itself as a "just peace church" is developed in a way that sounds like little more than a statement that the UCC is for all good things and against all bad things.

In some cases, this lack of realism has a religious or theological source. For example, the Methodist bishops and the Presbyterian General Assembly move very rapidly from a description of the *shalom* of the eschatological kingdom of God to the peace that is historically achievable. The Methodist bishops write that "*Shalom* is positive peace: harmony, wholeness, health, and well-being in all human relationships. It is the natural state of humanity as birthed by God."[40] Though this statement may accurately portray how Christians understand the human condition "before the fall," the "wholeness" of justice and peace is precisely what has been shattered by human sin. Paul Ramsey has strongly criticized the Methodist bishops for failing to take seriously the difference between the Christian eschatological hope in God's restoration of this full *shalom* at the end of history, and an eighteenth century belief in the possibility of eliminating both war and injustice through rational enlightenment and historical progress.[41] The Methodists, in Ramsey's view, ignore both the persistence of human sinfulness and the radical discontinuity between history and the kingdom of God. These theological distortions lead to ethical confusion. They minimize the tensions between justice and peace and the real distinction between the just war

and pacifist traditions. They also make the Methodist bishops' attempt
to develop a new "theology for a just peace" too easy a task.

The case of the Roman Catholic bishops is somewhat different.
George Weigel has criticized the Catholic bishops for falling into the same
theological error of too closely identifying the *shalom* of the kingdom of
God with the peace and justice that are achievable within history. He
maintains that this error appears when the bishops write that

> We must recognize the paradox we face as Christians living in the
> world as it presently exists; we must articulate our belief that love is
> possible and the only real hope for all human relations, and yet accept
> that force, even deadly force, is sometimes justified and that nations
> must provide for their defense.[42]

In Weigel's view, this passage implicitly identifies "peace" with
"love," and in doing so minimizes the importance of working for the
morally worthy peace of a rightly ordered political community that can be
achieved "prior to the world's final conversion" at the eschaton.[43] I think
this misreads not only the passage Weigel explicitly criticizes but also the
overall argument of the Catholic bishops. In fact, in the very same paragraph that contains the sentences that agitate Weigel, the Catholic
bishops quote these words from John Paul II:

> Christians know that in this world a totally and permanently peace-
> ful society is unfortunately a utopia, and that ideologies that hold up
> that prospect as easily attainable are based on hopes that cannot be re-
> alized. . . . Christians are convinced, if only because they have learned
> from personal experience, that these deceptive hopes lead straight to
> the false peace of totalitarian regimes. But this realistic view in no way
> prevents Christians from working for peace; instead it stirs up their
> ardor, for they know that Christ's victory over deception, hate, and
> death gives those in love with peace a more decisive motive for action
> than what the most generous theories about man have to offer.[44]

This passage clearly distinguishes eschatological *shalom* from the peace
that Christians work for in history. Weigel has to ignore it, and other pas-
sages like it, to make his critique of the Catholic bishops even plausible.

The "paradox" that the Catholic bishops refer to has a different
meaning than the one Weigel gives it. In saying there is a paradox
between the Christian conviction that "love is the only hope for human
relations" and the possible justification of the use of deadly force, the
bishops are, in fact, echoing one of the most influential interpretations of
the Christian ethic of participation in warfare in recent generations, that
of Paul Ramsey. Ramsey has argued that the root of a Christian just war
theory is the obligation to love one's neighbors, even if these neighbors
are enemies. The paradox arises from the fact that when one of these

neighbors is engaged in aggression against another, love can demand that the innocent neighbor be defended against the one who is the aggressor. And *if* such defense is possible only by the use of deadly force, then war can become a work of Christian love. That, on the face of it, is surely a paradox. But it also shows why Ramsey so insisted that the same duty to love one's neighbor that could provide just cause for participation in war simultaneously generates strict moral limits on warfare (discrimination, proportionality, last resort, etc.).[45] The Catholic bishops develop exactly this sort of argument in the paragraphs following their reference to the "paradox" of the demands of love and the legitimacy of participation in war, and Ramsey's work is explicitly cited.[46]

This discussion of the roots of a Christian just war theory in the ethic of love of neighbor provides a framework for understanding the Catholic bishops' assertion that just war theory and an ethic of nonviolence are interdependent and complementary stances. They are interdependent the way two branches of the same tree are interdependent. They both spring from the same religious-moral root: the obligation to love one's neighbor. This obligation, the Catholic bishops state, leads to a common "presupposition which binds all Christians: we should do no harm to our neighbors; how we treat our enemy is the key test of whether we love our neighbor."[47] This demand of love is at the basis of all Christian ethical approaches to war, both pacifism and just war theory.

Thus, I think Paul Ramsey's claim that the Catholic bishops have erred when they maintain that an ethic of nonviolence and just war theory have this common presupposition departs from his own argument that love of neighbor is the foundation of justice, and therefore of the just cause criterion in just war theory. In Ramsey's view, in just war theory *"the presumption is to restrain evil and protect the innocent."*[48] True enough. But I would call this the proximate presupposition of just war theory. It is itself rooted in the deeper presupposition of the obligation of neighbor love. This deeper presupposition means that even in a fallen and unjust world, there must be a presumption against the use of lethal force, even in the defense of the innocent. This presumption is common to both just war theory and pacifism. Were it not, just war theory would fail to be faithful to the obligation to "do no harm" to one's neighbor (even one's enemy), and the *ad bellum* norms of proportionality, last resort, etc. would become superfluous. Where just war theory and pacifism part ways is on whether this deeper presupposition they share is an absolute, exceptionless obligation, or whether love of an innocent neighbor can sometimes demand doing harm to a neighbor who is perpetrating injustice.[49]

It is for theological reasons that the two traditions within Christian ethics reach different conclusions about the absoluteness of the presumption against the use of lethal force. Both just war ethics and an unsentimental form of pacifism, such as that expounded by Stanley Hauerwas or John Howard Yoder, are fully aware of the brokenness of the world and of the conflicts that can occur between justice and peace. The two traditions, however, have different theological understandings of Christian responsibility in the face of such conflicts. It is often said that this difference is between the just war tradition's conviction that Christians must be responsible participants in the effort to shape the life of the human community, and the pacifist's commitment to a life of witness to Jesus Christ through faithful discipleship. Paul Ramsey's careful study of the work of Yoder and Hauerwas, however, has convinced him that this distinction needs to be withdrawn.[50] It is condescending to genuine Christian pacifists by suggesting that they are irresponsible toward the neighbor. It is also unfair to just war Christians by implying that they seek to control history ("to run the world," in Yoder's terms) in a way that only God can do.

In Ramsey's recent analysis, the distinction between the traditions is between two kinds of responsibility and two kinds of witness. For the just war Christian, responsibility and witness are both to be lived within the sphere of statecraft, though without the illusion that one possesses God-like power to control the outcome of political affairs. For the pacifist, responsibility lies outside the sphere of the state, and witness consists in showing that government is not the final power that rules the world. Thus, each of the two traditions is a partial and realistic response to the call of discipleship in a world where political power is both necessary and always in danger of becoming demonic. The just war Christian shoulders the tasks of both responsibility and witness that flow from the necessity of government. The pacifist undertakes those responsibilities and forms of witness that follow from the limits of government and its temptation to usurp the place of God. Neither tradition has cornered the market on either effectiveness or fidelity. In Ramsey's words:

> We need to affirm the coeval, equally worthy, irreducible parting of the ways of Christian pacifists and justified-war Christians. Neither is able to *depend* on the consequences in the whole of their activities, or to discount the effectiveness of the other's witness. All this can be said, I believe, while holding that in the divine economy for this world just war is the meaning of statecraft, and that pacifism cannot be addressed to states. Still, these are equally Christian discipleships.[51]

They are, in other words, complementary ethical responses to the problems of both justice and war, as the Catholic bishops maintain. Ramsey's argument, however, helps clarify how this is so in a way that goes deeper than the Catholic pastoral letter. And Ramsey's analysis shows why it would be both theologically and politically naive to interpret this complementarity in a way that optimistically homogenizes the two traditions by looking for the gradual pacification of politics through progress and enlightenment. He charges the Methodist bishops with falling into this trap.

Does this mean that all the talk in the recent church documents about an ethic and international politics of "just peace" is really a manifestation of such a superficial belief in progress? Some of it doubtless is. But there are other lines of argument for an ethic and politics of "just peace" in the church statements that avoid this pitfall. They are based on sober analysis of the dangers and opportunities of the current international situation. In the contemporary context, Christian ethical reflection must not confine itself to a narrow focus on the morality of particular acts of war, but also move on to a consideration of systemic changes in the international military and political situation that have resulted from the nuclear revolution. These changes affect both the bipolar relationship between the United States and the Soviet Union and the global order as a whole.

For example, the National Association of Evangelicals recommends that Christian reflection should be concerned not only with debates about what acts of violent force may be justified in defense of human rights, but also with how to construct a new political framework that secures these rights nonviolently. The present challenge is to develop thinking within the churches about the moral meaning of what George Weigel has felicitously called "a *jus ad pacem*, a horizon of achievable human possibility against which questions of the *jus ad bellum* and the *jus in bello* could be argued."[52] Or in the alternative language of Stanley Hoffmann, the nuclear age challenges us to recognize that "today, in many instances, morality requires not only a *jus in bello* and a *jus ad bellum*, but a *jus* or rather a praxis—*ante et contra bellum*."[53]

This emphasis on positive obligations to secure peace has particular relevance today. As was argued above, a genuine opportunity to redefine the U.S.-Soviet relationship appears to be opening up today. It is by no means certain that this possibility will be actualized. And it is certainly not the case that we stand on the brink of the final elimination of the dangers of war and the reality of injustice. Nevertheless, the political and theological realism that is the basis of Christian just war thinking means paying careful attention to real possibilities for international reconciliation and not just to continuing dangers of conflict and injustice. Because of the presumption against violence that it shares with pacifism, just war thinking must always seek justice peacefully whenever this is possible. The present international situation may contain the potential of moving toward a greater degree of "just peace" between the U.S. and the USSR than has been the case up to now. To the extent that this is the case, the obligation to seek a just peace is realistic, not utopian.

Movement to actualize this potential for a more just peace is not simply a matter of changing psychological attitudes or political rhetoric. It will call for concrete political, military, and economic steps as well—what Hoffmann calls a "praxis *ante et contra bellum*." The Episcopalian, Roman Catholic, and Evangelical statements contain a number of specific suggestions that indicate what some of the steps in such a praxis may be.

First, there are *political* steps that can help improve the chances for a just peace. J. Bryan Hehir, citing the recent observations of George Kennan and Marshall Shulman, has suggested that the possibility exists of basing the political relation of the U.S. and the USSR on the classical model of big power competition and shifting it away from the more dangerous and more ideological pattern that has prevailed during the Cold War.[54] As noted above, both the Episcopalian and Roman Catholic documents argue that the key to this new political relationship is the fact that the security of the United States and that of the Soviet Union are interlinked and dependent on each other because of the dangers of nuclear war. Or to put the matter negatively, the United States and the Soviet Union are mutually vulnerable. Neither superpower is capable of assuring its own security on the basis of its own strength; each needs the cooperation of the other if it is to protect its own interests and even its own existence. The relationship between the superpowers is profoundly misunderstood if it is regarded as a zero-sum game, and regarding it as such may be the single greatest obstacle to the security of each. We need to find a way to break the horns of this "prisoners' dilemma" of unrelieved mutual hostility if we are to avoid an endless arms race and the disaster to which it will very likely lead.

The Episcopalian report argues that the way out of this cul-de-sac begins with the acknowledgment of the Soviet Union's status as a world power and functioning society that the United States is not intent on destroying.[55] This does not mean moral or political acquiescence in repressive or aggressive behavior by the USSR. Rather, it sets limits on how the superpower competition will be conducted. A just peace, by definition, must be based on respect for human rights. Mr. Gorbachev has made a number of encouraging promises in this regard and has taken steps to realize some of them. Western political policy toward the Soviet bloc should press for further evolution in this area and respond positively if and as it occurs. Such a political evolution in U.S.-Soviet relations would also provide a basis for building stronger institutions of world order for peaceful resolution of conflict in the future.

Improving the political relationship is directly linked with a second aspect of movement toward a more just peace, namely, the U.S.-Soviet military competition and arms control. Indeed, the political and military/arms control dimensions of the U.S.-Soviet relationship mutually condition each other. If security is necessarily common security, the United States should be intent on communicating to the USSR in word and deed that it is not seeking to gain an advantage that would enable it to dismantle the Soviet system through nuclear blackmail or actual attack. Communicating this must be one of the guiding objectives of U.S. strategy, force structures, declaratory policies, and weapons development and acquisition programs. This leads both the Roman Catholic bishops and the Episcopalian report to urge that the United States declaratory and operational policies should renounce the pursuit of nuclear superiority, first-strike-capable weapons, war-fighting strategies that go beyond the purposes of deterrence, and strategic defense measures that can be used as enhancements of a war-fighting capacity. The same recommendations, of course, apply to the Soviet Union.

The INF treaty is a first step toward mutual agreement in this area. It is a hopeful sign that cooperation to reduce the nuclear threat *can* occur. The Roman Catholic bishops, echoing the pope, state that the INF "treaty points beyond itself to other larger arms control questions."[56] They argue that the demands of common security call for vigorous pursuit of further progress, both on the level of conventional force reductions, in the nuclear and space talks (concerning both strategic nuclear weapons and defensive weapons in space), and in efforts to limit the proliferation of nuclear weapons to nations that do not now possess them.[57] This arms control agenda, the Catholic bishops note, is more modest than the total nuclear disarmament that they hold out as an ultimate objective. As work on this post-INF treaty arms control agenda goes forward, important new questions will have to be faced. Bryan Hehir recently noted some of them:

> Where do stability and security lie—in continuing reliance on nuclear weapons as the ultimate deterrent, in a new mix [of conventional and nuclear forces] that "lengthens the nuclear fuse," or in an effort to shift purely and simply to conventional deterrence in the European theater?[58]

Despite these questions, the Catholic bishops are convinced that arms control, even short of disarmament, is essential to movement toward common security and a just peace:

> Arms control can channel the superpower competition in the interim while other, more profound efforts seek to transform the political relationship. The fundamental importance of arms control needs to be reaffirmed in this evaluation. It is one way we take hold of our common nuclear future with the Soviet Union.[59]

This "just peace" framework, in other words, seeks to move beyond an exclusive focus on questions of *jus ad bellum* and *jus in bello*, to the *jus ad pacem* and *jus ante et contra bellum* that are so crucial to mutual security in the nuclear age. Indeed, this framework shows that the negative limits of just war thinking and the positive conditions of "just peace" thinking are inextricably intertwined with each other. Under present political and military conditions, negative moral limits on legitimate warfare, such as discrimination, proportionality, and reasonable hope of success, point to the positive conclusion that the peoples of the United States and the Soviet Union have a *jus ad pacem* in their competition with each other. Superpower relations— both political and military—must constantly press toward securing this right to peace by acting *contra bellum ante bellum*.

Of course, this does not settle all the questions that need to be addressed concerning superpower relations, or resolve issues such as the legitimacy of intervention in Central America, the Persian Gulf, or other regional conflicts. But it does provide guidance that is at once morally serious and contextually realistic for the central rivalry between NATO and the Warsaw Pact. It shows that the realism of just war theory, in our day, implies that common security and a just peace ought to be our moral and political objective. I think this ought to be a major emphasis of the churches as they seek to make their contribution to the search for peace in the 1990s.

## III. LINKING MORAL AND POLITICAL RESPONSIBILITY

A final observation on one other dimension of the churches' engagement in the current debates is called for. The framework I have proposed, like that of the Roman Catholic bishops and the Episcopalian Committee of Inquiry, is not likely to satisfy a number of participants in the current church discussions. Some will argue that to begin the discussion with an analysis of the relationship between the superpowers mutes the call of the gospel as a fundamental challenge to the current political and military situation.

For example, the Wilbanks-Stone study for the Presbyterian Church argues that U.S. military policy, particularly on the nuclear level, has in fact become a demonic force in opposition to the very sovereignty of God. Nuclear weapons place the power over all life and death on earth in human hands. Their possession is an idolatrous attempt at human "usurpation of the position of God."[60] Therefore Wilbanks and Stone suggest (though they do not definitively conclude) that Christians must go beyond efforts to reform military policy to a stance of fundamental resistance to it. They describe the contrast this way:

In a reformist stance, the church can say about nuclear weapons policies: "We can go along with them for the time being but will seek to change them." In a resistance stance, however, the church would say: "We cannot go along with nuclear weapons policies because acquiescence in them constitutes a betrayal of our faith. We shall not rest content with merely reducing the number of warheads on nuclear missiles but seek the transformation of national defense policies."[61]

This passage certainly has a radical ring to it. But on closer inspection, it is not entirely clear what it means.

Does "transformation of national defense policies" mean unilateral disarmament? Would deep cuts in the strategic forces of the superpowers—either with or without the deployment of strategic defenses—constitute the kind of transformation envisioned? Would the adoption of a "common security" master-concept, accompanied by the kind of changes in political and military strategies suggested above, be regarded as "going along" with nuclear weapons policies? Unless such questions are dealt with more seriously, statements like this have the effect of splitting Christian moral responsibility from the domain of political responsibility altogether. This may be appropriate if one stands with John Howard Yoder and Stanley Hauerwas in the traditions of Anabaptist theology, where both Christian responsibility and Christian witness are exercised outside the domain of statecraft. But such a position is at least unusual coming from two ethicists in the reformed tradition. Reformed ecclesiology is certainly compatible with resistance to the state in some circumstances. But the reformed tradition in ethics calls for a more careful analysis of just what is to be resisted before advocating such a stance. To fail to produce such an analysis threatens to undercut both responsibility and witness.

The Methodist bishops raise a less forceful but nonetheless significant objection to the framework being suggested here. They recommend an approach based on the notion of common security as the basis of a just peace that is in some ways similar to that I have just suggested. Their position on the issue of the continuation of some form of deterrence as part of a common security framework, however, lacks full conceptual clarity. They state that "deterrence must no longer receive the churches' blessing, even as a temporary warrant for the maintenance of nuclear weapons."[62] They believe that continuing acceptance of deterrence has the effect of politically and psychologically encouraging the continuation of the arms race. Therefore, reversing the long-term trends demands that the concept of deterrence itself be delegitimated.

The legitimacy of deterrence is frontally attacked by calling it a form of "idolatry" that tries to found security on an inordinate confidence that the rationality of governmental decision makers will prevent the failure of deterrence. One would therefore expect to find the Methodist bishops calling for immediate disarmament, even unilaterally. For if deterrence really is idolatry, a Christian would have no alternative but to insist that the idol must be smashed by those who erected it. As Paul Ramsey put it: "One thing Christian pacifists and just warriors have in common is that, if anything is shown to be *per se* a moral atrocity or to have no just cause *now*, it should be given Christian endorsement *no moment more*."[63] But this is not the Methodist recommendation:

> The rejection of nuclear deterrence, however, does not necessarily mean immediate, unilateral disarmament. Those who regard themselves as nuclear pacifists do not hold a fully responsible position if they only say No to nuclear weapons; they must also share in the difficult political task of working out a strategy of phased arms reductions.[64]

In the face of the momentum of the superpower competition which has driven the nuclear arms race for decades, one can be sympathetic with the Methodist bishops' effort to find a way to break the hammerlock that the concept of deterrence has on strategic thinking. But there are serious problems with the way they have tried to do it. Though Protestant theology has more strongly emphasized that every Christian is *simul justus et peccator* (justified and a sinner at the same time), any theology that acknowledges that human beings are saved by faith in God must rebel at the suggestion that even a little bit of idolatry can be part of a Christian's responsibility. Therefore one must conclude either that the claim that deterrence is necessarily idolatry is a rhetorical device, or that the Methodist bishops have fallen into an incoherent understanding of the relation between Christian faith and political responsibility. In either case, I do not think their challenge to the framework suggested here hits the mark.

An apparently more consistent critique is that of three Roman Catholic philosophers, John Finnis, Joseph Boyle, and Germain Grisez. They mount a sustained argument for immediate, unilateral, nuclear disarmament as a moral imperative.[65] This is accompanied by a systematic refutation of most of the ethical arguments that have been advanced to justify some form of continued reliance on nuclear deterrence during the interim period while the superpowers seek mutual, bilateral disarmament. The authors have no doubt whatsoever about what the West should do with its nuclear weapons and strategies: they should be dismantled and scrapped— today, not tomorrow.

Their argument for this conclusion proceeds with the inevitability of a logical syllogism. The first premise is that "common morality" absolutely forbids the killing of innocent human beings. Second, the intent to kill innocent persons, even a conditional intent to do so, is itself immoral.

Third, all deterrence strategies include such an evil intention. Fourth, therefore, all deterrence strategies are of necessity immoral. Fifth, and consequently, nuclear disarmament is morally required. Finally, since the likelihood of achieving immediate mutual disarmament by the superpowers is virtually nil, immediate unilateral nuclear disarmament by the West is a moral imperative. Q.E.D.

Unilateralist inclinations have been present in the religious and secular peace movements throughout the entire nuclear age, especially in West Germany and Britain during the 1980s. But they have rarely been stated with such conceptual clarity. What gives the work of Finnis et al. its really radical edge, however, is the fact that they believe that the most likely outcome of the recommended course of action will be the subjugation of the West by the Soviet Union. They regard this as a very bad prospect indeed. But because the good end of preserving the freedom of Western civilization may never be pursued through evil means, we must be prepared to risk domination rather than seek to prevent it through the immorality of nuclear deterrence. Morality demands, they suggest, that we should be willing "to accept anything, even martyrdom, rather than do wrong."[66]

The authors reinforce this philosophical argument theologically. They state that true "realism" will reject the false hope that the West can reliably defend itself through an immoral deterrent and will recognize that "the Christian way, if followed to the end, is sure to lead to suffering, and is likely to lead to disaster in this world, as it did for Jesus."[67] Therefore they reject a "false security theology" that implicitly identifies the peace and salvation of Christ with the safety and well-being of the West. Christ's peace and salvation are not of this world, so Soviet domination or even a nuclear holocaust is not the ultimate evil for Christians. Sin, even one venial sin, is a much greater evil than such physical catastrophes.

Response to the whole of the argument by Finnis et al. is impossible here. Let me simply observe that there are flaws in their argument on a number of levels. Each of these is a manifestation of an excessive confidence that they have achieved a degree of certitude simply not available to even the best intentioned and most well-informed participants in the war and peace debate.

First, in their strategic analysis the authors seem almost driven in their efforts to show that every conceivable form of deterrence rests on an intention to kill innocent persons. This aspect of their argument is marked by what I can only regard as a kind of lust to condemn. Though the question of intention is crucial in the moral debate about deterrence, it is more complex than Finnis et al. acknowledge. A strategy based on commitment to common security cannot be judged "murderous" in intent, as they claim every strategy but unilateral disarmament must be.

Second, for Finnis et al. moral and political wisdom exist in separate and airtight compartments. Such a split is profoundly contrary to the great tradition of moral and political philosophy in Roman Catholic thought and in the mainline Protestant traditions as well. It is defensible in the framework of Anabaptist theology, but it cannot be supported by philosophers who base their argument on a "common morality."

Third, this split follows from their conviction that consequences are irrelevant to moral reasoning; only intentions and actions count. Their polemic against "consequentialism" becomes a procrustean bed into which they try to force the entire nuclear debate. Their moral theory also makes a distinction between action and refraining from action that will not stand scrutiny. To regard maintaining some form of deterrent as an action for which we are responsible and unilateral disarmament as the cessation of an action for whose consequences we are not responsible radically denies the historical nature of human activity. Human moral agency—both in acting and in refraining from action—is much more deeply conditioned by the historical circumstances within which it is exercised than their view implies.

Finally, their theological argument that it is God, not human beings, who is finally responsible for the freedom, peace, and well-being of the world is certainly true. But it is brought to bear on the issues of deterrence in a simplistic way. Though humans are surely not God, we have been graced with the freedom and responsibility to share in God's providence. We must do this both with a sense of hope and with fear and trembling. Finnis et al. simultaneously imply that hope for the freedom and peace of the West is inevitably idolatrous under present historical circumstances, and also make fear and trembling in the face of decisions that could lead to disaster unnecessary. They seem almost smug in their confidence that they have found the one right answer to these earth-shaking questions. Roman Catholic ethics is deeply committed to the use of the full powers of human reason in the pursuit of the right way to live. But Finnis, Boyle, and Grisez provide a clear example of how reason runs amok when it lacks a sense of humility in the face of the complexity of our human condition and historical circumstances.

Despite the inadequacies of the recommendations of Wilbanks and Stone, of the Methodist bishops, and of Finnis, Boyle, and Grisez, the criticisms to which they subject the strategy of deterrence are not without moral force. Indeed, in recent years a growing number of secular policy analysts have suggested the deterrence doctrine has become part of the problem in international politics rather than part of the solution.[68] It is relatively easy to identify the problems—both moral and strategic— with the entire strategy of deterrence. The difficulty, of course, is to find an alternative that is both morally superior to what we have been living with for decades and also politically achievable. The Catholic bishops' 1988 report noted that this growing dissatisfaction was leading some strategic analysts to ask whether it might be possible to go "beyond deterrence." But the bishops noted the difficulty this involves: "All commentators, whether they are political analysts, strategists, or moralists, find it easier to propose going beyond deterrence than to prescribe the steps for accomplishing this task."[69]

Nevertheless, the Catholic bishops refused to regard this difficulty as grounds for an ill-defined stance of "resistance" as do Wilbanks and Stone. Nor do they let it lead them to the kind of inconsistent moral reasoning into which the Methodist bishops lapsed. Still less do they throw up their hands in moral anguish as do Finnis et al. Relying on their reading of the new possibilities opening up in U.S.-Soviet relations, they recommend seizing the opportunity to reshape the state of the question: "As long as nuclear weapons exist, deterrence will be an inherent fact of the superpower relationship. But improvement in the political atmosphere can, over time, reduce the significance of nuclear deterrence in the total relationship."[70]

This recommendation makes a claim about the demands of political responsibility today. But it also embodies a vision of moral and religious responsibility. It implicitly echoes the Episcopalian report's definition of the moral and religious basis for its policy recommendations: a conviction that Christ's redemptive mission "compels us to accept reconciliation as an essential element of our 'controlling vision' in public policy."[71] Reconciliation, of course, is not always politically possible in a broken world. But when it is—when justice and peace can be mutually supporting and enhanced together—the need to pursue it is simultaneously a political, moral, and religious obligation.

All this is not to maintain that we are on the verge of utopia (it should not be necessary to state this again in light of all the above). But there are clear signs that real progress is a possibility. The Catholic bishops' report makes a number of recommendations about how these possibilities might be seized in the areas of superpower politics, arms control, nuclear nonproliferation, conventional force reductions, economic development in the poor countries of the Southern Hemisphere. In my judgment, they are essentially on the right track. The situation is extremely fluid, so they do not claim to chart an absolutely certain course through all these waters. But they do provide a compass: the goal of common security and just peace. This compass will not solve all the problems or dispel all the ambiguities inherent in the search for peace in the context of our historical moment under the sun. But serious religious, moral, and political thinking like that in the Catholic and Episcopalian documents shows the way for the churches to grapple with these issues as they continue to place their final hope in something much better than we can ever achieve in history—the full peace of the Kingdom of God.

## Notes

1. National Conference of Catholic Bishops, *The Challenge of Peace: God's Promise and Our Response* (Washington, D.C.: NCCB/USCC, 1983); NCCB, *Building Peace: A Pastoral Reflection on the Response to The Challenge of Peace* and *A Report on The Challenge of Peace and Policy Developments 1983-1988* (Washington, D.C.: United States Catholic Conference, 1988); United Church of Christ, General Synod 15, *Social Policy Actions,* "Pronouncement Affirming the United Church of Christ as a Just Peace Church" (New York: UCC Office for Church in Society, 1985), 5-12; Dana Wilbanks and Ronald H. Stone, *Presbyterians and Peacemaking: Are We Now Called to Resistance?* (New York: Advisory Council on Church and Society of the Presbyterian Church [U.S.A.], 1985); 200th General Assembly of the Presbyterian Church (U.S.A.), *Christian Obedience in a Nuclear Age* (Louisville, Ky.: Office of the General Assembly, Presbyterian Church [U.S.A.], 1988); United Methodist Council of Bishops, *In Defense of Creation: The Nuclear Crisis and a Just Peace, Foundation Document* (Nashville, Tenn.: Graded Press, 1986); National Association of Evangelicals, *Guidelines: Peace, Freedom and Security Studies* (Wheaton, Ill.: National Association of Evangelicals, 1986); Committee of Inquiry on the Nuclear Issue, Commission on Peace, Episcopal Diocese of Washington, *The Nuclear Dilemma: A Christian Search for Understanding* (Cincinnati, Ohio: Forward Movement Publications, 1987). For a useful study of both Christian and Jewish involvement in these discussions in the early 1980s, see L. Bruce van Voorst, "The Churches and Nuclear Deterrence," *Foreign Affairs* 61 (1983), 827-52.

2. *In Defense of Creation,* 63-65.

3. Ibid., 63.

4. Ibid., 67.

5. *Presbyterians and Peacemaking,* 21.

6. Ibid., 22.

7. Ibid., 23.

8. This point is made by the Roman Catholic bishops in their discussion of the just war criterion of "comparative justice" (*The Challenge of Peace,* nos. 92-93). For an interesting discussion of why such distortions seem more frequent in some recent mainline Protestant social pronouncements because of their desire to be "prophetic," see Anne Motley Hallum, "Presbyterians as Political Amateurs," in Charles W. Dunn, ed., *Religion in American Politics* (Washington, D.C.: CQ Press, 1989), 63-73.

9. *Guidelines,* 22.

10. Ibid., 7.

11. Ibid., 27.

12. Ibid., 17.

13. *The Challenge of Peace,* no. 66.

14. Ibid., nos. 249-51.

15. Such world order concerns are also found in the Methodist bishops' document. Paul Ramsey has argued, however, that the Methodist document has too easily elided what can be expected from international institutions of conflict

resolution with the full peace of the kingdom of God. "Catholics know how to do 'world order' warlessness better than Methodists do. One can sense a flavor of *realism* in the Bishops' statement that I do not find in the analogous prospect of 'common security for the world community' . . . in the Methodist pastoral" (Paul Ramsey with Stanley Hauerwas, *Speak Up for Just War or Pacifism: A Critique of the United Methodist Bishops' Pastoral Letter "In Defense of Creation"* [University Park, Pa.: Pennsylvania State University Press, 1988], 139).

16. *Guidelines* 26; see also 15, 28.

17. George Weigel, *Tranquillitas Ordinis: The Present Failure and Future Promise of American Catholic Thought on War and Peace* (Oxford/New York: Oxford University Press, 1987), 378. For my response to Weigel's overall argument, see David Hollenbach, "War and Peace in American Catholic Thought: A Heritage Abandoned?" *Theological Studies* 48 (1987): 711-26.

18. *The Nuclear Dilemma*, 24.

19. Ibid., 65.

20. As Seweryn Bialer has put it, "Understanding each other as far as it is possible does not end the problem but leads only to its re-emergence on the rational level" ("The Psychology of U.S.-Soviet Relations." Extended version of the Gabriel Silver Memorial Lecture, School of International and Public Affairs, Columbia University, 14 April 1983. Cited in *The Nuclear Dilemma*, 65.)

21. *The Nuclear Dilemma*, 41.

22. George Weigel, among other critics of the 1983 letter, charged the bishops with neglecting the serious political differences between the United States and the Soviet Union in his *Tranquillitas Ordinis*. As the citations indicated on pp. 242-43 above indicate, I think this charge is wide of the mark. Nevertheless, the 1988 report addresses the interconnection of political and technological/military dimensions of the U.S.-USSR rivalry in a more explicit way right from the start. This is a useful clarification of the debate between the Catholic bishops and some of their critics.

23. NCCB, *A Report on the Challenge of Peace*, nos. 7-8.

24. *The Nuclear Dilemma*, 11.

25. Ibid., 44.

26. It is particularly surprising that the 1988 statement of the General Assembly of the Presbyterian Church has virtually nothing to say about these developments, since it was issued at a time subsequent to the INF treaty. One almost feels that the drafters of the Presbyterian statement were so bent on portraying the dangers of war vividly that they were reluctant to acknowledge that a positive step like the INF treaty had actually occurred.

27. *The Challenge of Peace*, no. 258. This passage is quoted with approval by the Episcopalian report, *The Nuclear Dilemma*, 83.

28. For example, see Valéry Giscard d'Estaing, Yasuhiro Nakasone, and Henry A. Kissinger, "East-West Relations," *Foreign Affairs* 68 (1989): 1-21; George Kennan, "After the Cold War," *New York Times Magazine* (5 Feb. 1989): 32ff.

29. Mikhail Gorbachev, Address to the General Assembly of the United Nations, 7 December 1988, in Foreign Broadcast Information Service, *Daily Report, Soviet Union* (8 December 1989), 11; George Bush, Opening Statement, news conference at the conclusion of the NATO summit meeting, Brussels, 30 May 1989, excerpts in *New York Times* (31 May 1989), A14.

30. *The Nuclear Dilemma*, 16.

31. *A Report on the Challenge of Peace*, nos. 27 and 28.

32. John Courtney Murray, *We Hold These Truths: Catholic Reflections on the American Proposition* (New York: Sheed and Ward, 1960), 268.

33. The just war and pacifist traditions are each really families of subtraditions. It is not relevant to my purpose here to make all the distinctions needed to understand the full richness of either set of traditions. On the just war family of traditions, see James Turner Johnson, *Ideology, Reason, and the Limitation of War* (Princeton: Princeton University Press, 1975); idem, *Just War Tradition and the Restraint of War* (Princeton: Princeton University Press, 1981). On the family of pacifist traditions, see Michael Howard, *War and the Liberal Conscience* (New Brunswick, N.J.: Rutgers University Press, 1978); James Turner Johnson, *The Quest for Peace: Three Moral Traditions in Western Cultural History* (Princeton, N.J.: Princeton University Press, 1987).

34. *The Challenge of Peace*, no. 74.

35. Ibid., no. 122.

36. Ibid., no. 120.

37. *The Nuclear Dilemma*, 20.

38. *In Defense of Creation*, 13, 32.

39. *Guidelines*, 26.

40. *In Defense of Creation*, 24.

41. Paul Ramsey with Stanley Hauerwas, *Speak Up for Just War or Pacifism*, 28-39. This critique is even more apposite in the case of the Presbyterian statement, *Christian Obedience in a Nuclear Age*, which states: "Shalom is the intended state of the entire human race. It involves the well-being of the whole person in all relationships, personal, social, and cosmic" (p. 8). All eschatological discontinuity has dropped out of this vision of *shalom*.

42. *The Challenge of Peace*, no. 78.

43. *Tranquillitas Ordinis*, 284.

44. John Paul II, "World Day of Peace Message 1982," cited in *The Challenge of Peace*, no. 78.

45. See Paul Ramsey, *War and the Christian Conscience: How Shall Modern War Be Conducted Justly?* (Durham, N.C.: Duke University Press, 1961), esp. chaps. 2 and 3; idem, *The Just War: Force and Political Responsibility* (New York: Scribner's, 1968), esp. chap. 6.

46. *The Challenge of Peace*, nos. 80-84. Ramsey's *War and the Christian Conscience* is cited in footnote 31.

47. *The Challenge of Peace*, no. 80.

48. *Speak Up for Just War or Pacifism*, 83.

49. From this it should be clear that I do not find Ramsey's critique of the way I have previously argued this point persuasive. See *Speak Up for Just War or Pacifism*, 108-10.

50. Particularly influential for Ramsey's creative rethinking of these issues are the following works by these authors: John Howard Yoder, *The Politics of Jesus* (Grand Rapids, Mich.: Eerdmans, 1972); idem, *Christian Attitudes to War, Peace and Revolution* (privately distributed by Co-op Bookstore, Goshen Biblical Seminary, 3003 Benham, Elkhart, Ind. 46517); idem, *The Priestly Kingdom: Social Ethic as Gospel* (Notre Dame, Ind.: University of Notre Dame Press, 1984); Stanley Hauerwas, *The Peaceable Kingdom: A Primer of Christian Ethics* (Notre Dame, Ind: University of Notre Dame Press, 1983).

51. *Speak Up for Just War or Pacifism*, 123.

52. *Tranquillitas Ordinis*, 357.

53. Stanley Hoffmann, *Duties beyond Borders: On the Limits and Possibilities of Ethical International Politics* (Syracuse, N.Y.: Syracuse University Press, 1981), 82.

54. Bryan Hehir, "Decade of Decision: Possibilities for the Nineties," *Commonweal* (16 June 1989): 362.

55. See *The Nuclear Dilemma*, 82.

56. *A Report on The Challenge of Peace*, no. 61.

57. Ibid., 62-70.

58. Hehir, "Decade of Decision," 363.

59. *A Report on The Challenge of Peace*, no. 75.

60. *Presbyterians and Peacemaking*, 16.

61. Ibid., 34.

62. *In Defense of Creation*, 48.

63. *Speak Up for Just War or Pacifism*, 62.

64. Ibid.

65. *Nuclear Deterrence, Morality and Realism* (Oxford: Clarendon Press, 1988). An earlier version of these remarks on Finnis et al. appears in my review of their book in *Theological Studies* 49 (1988): 766-68.

66. *Nuclear Deterrence, Morality and Realism*, 253, n. 8.

67. Ibid., 377.

68. For contrary assessments of the future strategic usefulness of deterrence doctrine, see Michael McGwire, "Deterrence: The Problem—Not the Solution," *SAIS Review* 5 (1985): 105-24; idem, "Dilemmas and Delusions of Deterrence," *World Policy Journal* 1 (1984): 745-67; Robert W. Tucker, *The Nuclear Debate: Deterrence and the Lapse of Faith* (New York: Holmes and Meier, 1985).

69. *A Report on The Challenge of Peace*, no. 74.

70. Ibid., no. 74.

71. *The Nuclear Dilemma*, 117.

# THE CONVERSATION

R. James Woolsey launched the discussion by noting that while he was pleased with David Hollenbach's reasonableness and his effort to balance the goals of peace and freedom, he disagreed with Hollenbach's endorsements of the Episcopal statement on nuclear weapons. In Woolsey's view, the Episcopal, Methodist, and Presbyterian statements were seriously flawed in varying degrees.

The Methodist assertion that the existence of millions of Christians in the United States and the Soviet Union changes the U.S.-Soviet relationship substantively is unpersuasive. In the last four centuries Great Britain, a Christian nation, waged war or threatened to do so against four Christian nations whose rulers attempted to overturn the balance of power and establish hegemony over the rest of Europe. The presence of millions of Christians in Spain, France, Germany, and Russia did not lessen the expansionist ambitions of Philip II, Louis XIV, Napoleon, Wilhelm II, Hitler, and Stalin, nor did the Christian faith of their peoples make the designs of these rulers any less dangerous to the freedom of other nations.

Even more problematic is the Presbyterian statement authored by Professors Wilbanks and Stone, which argues from the premise of original sin that the source of the U.S.-Soviet rivalry is *our* sin and *our* penchant for building "walls of hostility." Wilbanks and Stone then move to the astonishing conclusion that "the rivalry between the United States and the Soviet Union is much the same as contemporary conflicts between the United States and Japan or West Germany," thereby downplaying the need for military preparedness or any special reckoning of the threat posed by the peculiar character of the Soviet regime.

This curious interpretation of the political implications of original sin is in sharp contrast with the more cogent analysis offered by the American theologian Reinhold Niebuhr. For Niebuhr, man's universal sinfulness requires that power be balanced with power. This was also the view of James Madison who, in Federalist Paper 10, argued that a balance of power among competing factions is a prerequisite for domestic tranquility. At the foreign policy level, the pervasiveness of sin does not free us from the responsibility of distinguishing among degrees of relative evil and taking the necessary measures to deter aggressive regimes from harming us.

This was the approach taken by the National Association of Evangelicals' *Guidelines on Peace, Freedom and Security Studies,* which Woolsey considered the most responsible of recent religious statements on war and peace. The key theme of the NAE's *Guidelines* is that foreign and defense policy must be grounded in a proper balance between the ideals of peace and freedom: neither of these two moral goals can be absolute; policy makers should correlate them in a creative tension. This realistic approach avoids some of the more popular forms of moral escapism. One such escapism, present in the political left, is the belief that the Soviets pose no security threat to the United States; another, from the political right, is the claim that the Strategic Defense Initiative will rescue us from the practical uncertainties and moral ambiguities of nuclear deterrence. Woolsey disagreed with Hollenbach's contention that the general outlines of the Catholic bishops' pastoral on nuclear weapons were similar to the NAE's statement. Unlike the latter, the pastoral's support for nuclear deterrence was minimal, almost microscopic.

Woolsey found the Episcopal statement preferable to its Methodist and Presbyterian counterparts, especially in its recognition that the U.S.-Soviet rivalry is not simply a misunderstanding between two morally equivalent entities. Nevertheless, it had serious flaws, the chief of which is that it does not sufficiently highlight the distinction between the Soviet state and the Soviet people.

The interests of the Soviet people are not the same as those of the small ruling elite or *nomenklatura.* To say, as the Episcopal document does, that our security is interlinked with that of the Soviet Union masks this critical issue. So does the Episcopal assertion that it is folly to try to bring about the collapse of the Soviet regime. In fact, the present Soviet regime is highly unstable precisely because of its narrow political base; as long as this is the case, Soviet leaders will find it useful to paint a picture of the Soviet Union as a beleaguered state. As events in Poland and Eastern Europe have shown, there is much we can do to promote peaceful evolution toward a greater degree of pluralism and openness in the Soviet Union, and we should not hesitate to do so. Indeed, the only realistic hope for a long-term substantial improvement in U.S.-Soviet relations is that the character of the Soviet regime will change and that, as the USSR becomes more open and more accountable to domestic democratic pressures, it will follow a less threatening foreign and military policy.

According to Woolsey, the Episcopal statement's warning not to "hate the enemy" was irrelevant. The great majority of defense policy makers neither hate the Soviet Union nor desire to destroy it, but simply want to deter it. Deterrence is a morally complex enterprise because its objective is to prevent the outbreak of war, yet its instrument is the threat of massive nuclear destruction. Those uncomfortable with this situation have two options, neither one of which is entirely satisfactory. One is to deploy nuclear weapons that have a lower yield and are more accurate, so as to reduce their indiscriminate effects; yet many strategists think that these weapons make nuclear war more feasible and therefore likely. The other option is to rely entirely on conventional weapons, a course which would be both financially ruinous and strategically unreliable. The history of conventional deterrence and its recurrent failures suggests that this kind of system lacks the stability and certainty associated with nuclear weapons.

Woolsey concluded by suggesting that, in certain circumstances, direct and overpowering military intervention can be a morally sound policy. The American intervention in the Dominican Republic in 1965 illustrates the point. But anti-intervention sentiment within the American religious community and other segments of public opinion is so strong today that we wind up being only "moderately interventionist" or using just enough force to get involved but ultimately defeated, as in our policy of supporting the Nicaraguan *contras*. There are situations where, after examining all the relevant data and having decided to intervene, the use of overwhelming, decisive force may be the most strategically and morally sound instrument for achieving our goals.

In response, David Hollenbach pointed out that he did not disagree with Woolsey that deterrence involves serious moral and strategic dilemmas. His chief point, which was also made in the Episcopal statement, was that we need to develop criteria for distinguishing those forms of deterrence that are particularly provocative from those that are less so. In evaluating weapons systems, targeting policies, and other components of our overall system of deterrence, we need to reject those that might tend to transform deterrence into provocation. On the issue of intervention, Hollenbach thought that, again, the chief issue was the development of solid criteria that would enable policy makers to distinguish among different kinds of intervention, some more acceptable than others; and this was something which both Woolsey and the NAE statement failed to do.

Harold Saunders suggested that the ubiquity of power politics underlined by Niebuhr and other realists had to be taken seriously, but as a part of the picture of what politics is about. In today's interdependent world, many critical security, economic and environmental problems cannot be solved unilaterally. An increasing number of highly urgent problems can only be managed in the context of multilateral relationships in which the parties work toward "positive sum solutions" that benefit all involved, instead of "zero sum solutions" that benefit some at the expense of others. Such "positive sum solutions" are in the self-interest of all concerned because without them it would be impossible to enlist the support of states whose cooperation is essential to solving the particular problem. This approach to international problems is "realistic" in the highest sense of the term, but also in keeping with the theological imperative to seek reconciliation.

William O'Brien shifted the discussion by challenging the charge, made by some religious activists, that the United States has engaged in "nuclear blackmail." According to O'Brien, the purpose assigned to nuclear weapons in U.S. policy has been deterrence, not blackmail. But for James Woolsey the charge of "nuclear blackmail" was not a problem. Nuclear deterrence, argued Woolsey, is the name given to nuclear blackmail when employed by the good, the true, and the just. NATO's security has always rested on the threat to use nuclear weapons even in response to a Soviet conventional attack. The alternative, to rely on an exclusively conventional defense, is morally flawed because of its prohibitive cost and its strategic uncertainty and unreliability.

James Turner Johnson noted that the Catholic, Episcopal, Methodist, and Presbyterian statements on war and peace assumed that peace, understood as the absence of war, was the highest moral and political goal. This seemed strange to Johnson, because historically the Christian tradition has valued order and justice more than the absence of armed conflict. Christian theorists thought that a well-arranged political order was the essential precondition for justice, and the achievement of a just order was the basic foundation for peaceful relations within a community. At the level of international politics, a just order is difficult to attain because there is no authoritative supranational structure; hence the just war theory was developed in order to restrain international evildoers and prevent them from setting up an evil or unjust order. To define peace as the absence of war and make it the chief objective of both ethics and policy leads to a kind of monistic survivalism in which there is no room for evaluating policies in terms of their contribution to order and justice. The focus on peace as the primary goal also leads one to conceive deterrence as an end in itself (rather than a means to a positive good), and the just war tradition as a series of negative limits on the use of force (rather than as a normative framework within which it is possible, under certain circumstances, to use force to achieve positive moral objectives).

George Weigel argued that the *way* in which the churches had become involved in the peace and war debate was problematic. The churches claimed to come to the debate in a teaching and pastoral capacity. But they often wound up engaging in finely tuned policy analysis and prescription, a task for which they have no special competence. If the churches succumb to the temptation to try to micromanage policy, their moral authority will be diminished as people perceive that church statements have no greater claim to deference than those by other debate participants. Moreover, by immersing themselves in policy advocacy, the churches become partisan, thereby missing the opportunity to educate the American public on the forgotten skills of public moral argument. The churches' most valuable contribution is not their capacity to take positions on policy issues—anyone can do that—but their ability to teach the American elite the fundamentals of moral reasoning and its relevance to the policy process.

Finally, Weigel was concerned about the "flight to the psychological" apparent in many church statements, the tendency to drift from theological and political categories and analysis to psychological ones. This was another example of trendiness, and further distorted an already confused public debate.

Robert Gessert thought that most of the church statements were not only unrealistic and irrelevant, but also counterproductive. They operate on what Ernest Lefever called the "apocalyptic premise": the notion that nuclear weapons are so pregnant with the potential for doomsday that the just war tradition must be rejected and radically new ways of thinking devised. This apocalyptic mentality leads many church leaders to resist efforts to make nuclear weapons more controllable—selective response options, more flexible weapons systems, and more accurate targeting technologies—because these will "only make nuclear war more feasible" and hence will lead us to the very catastrophe we all wish to avoid. But the result of such resistance is weapons that are wholly uncontrollable and are a grossly immoral deterrent. Advocates of the apocalyptic premise not only perceive nuclear weapons as hopelessly uncontrollable, but also make sure that they remain that way.

Responding to Weigel and Gessert, Thomas Reese suggested that it was easy to accuse the church statements of being too general (and hence irrelevant), or too specific (and therefore outside the church's competence). Whenever it enters the political arena, the church has to strike the difficult balance between the proclamation of universal principles and their application to specific issues. During the civil rights struggles of the 1950s and 1960s, for example, the Catholic Church taught at the level of generalities, preaching against racism but not involving itself in specific issues, and thus failed to make a critical contribution worthy of its moral authority.

Weigel disputed both the historical accuracy of this claim, and Reese's implications in making it. There is a vast area for maneuver between general statements such as "racism is wrong," and highly specific policy prescriptions such as "the two-tiered minimum wage is right." There is no room for disagreement on the former; there is on the latter. The church does not have to speak only in vague generalities; but when it gets into the micromanagement mode it risks losing its distinctive character as a religious and moral teacher. Nor is there any evidence to suggest that the church's moral authority has been enhanced by its recent forays into the policy arena narrowly defined.

John Ahearne wanted to underline what seemed to him the unique contributions that religious communities can make to the war and peace debate. First, religious leaders can remind policy makers of moral questions they have ignored or to which they have not paid sufficient attention; no one else is likely to do this. Second, religious leaders can provide the laity a moral framework for addressing gritty political questions. Ahearne was not sure that the churches' statements on war and peace had cost them as much credibility as Weigel and Gessert suggested. In fact, he was prepared to argue that among many lay people, the bishops had gained a great deal of respect and authority precisely by addressing issues recognized by the average person as being of great importance.

James Turner Johnson was skeptical of the churches' ability to improve the quality of the public moral debate on war and peace. The Protestant churches, in particular, were in trouble and for several reasons. Many Protestant seminaries allowed candidates for the ordained ministry to graduate without a solid foundation in ethics; in many cases the teaching of ethics is reduced to "social ethics" without a serious study of the theological, philosophical, and historical foundations of Christian morality. Moreover, much of contemporary Protestant social and political ethics is anchored in a faulty reading of the experience of the civil rights movement in the United States and the assumption that this experience can be replicated and universalized in the context of international politics. The emphasis on *shalom* common to most of the denominational statements reflects this questionable assumption.

In closing the discussion, John Langan remarked that the churches' chief problem was not "micromanaging" so much as the lack of a more sophisticated casuistry, a more fully ordered way of analyzing the myriad details of policy issues in all their moral and practical ramifications. Within the group, Langan saw a sharp line of disagreement between those who think that church-based discussions of war/peace issues have certain characteristic weaknesses (such as the unwillingness to accept a degree of moral uncertainty or trade-offs), and those who are confident that the churches can handle issues of national security policy with the requisite sophistication and modesty. But there is a third view, which claims that the central problem with church interventions in policy matters is a kind of pathology, a deep-seated intellectual bias or blindness that prevents the churches from treating these issues with the same deftness as the Christian tradition has done historically. Langan thought that this question, explored by George Weigel in his *Tranquillitas Ordinis*

(1987), could be broadened to include the larger question of whether there is a pathology in the American religious experience itself which complicates the efforts of the American churches to address public policy issues responsibly.

# Afterword

In concluding the third and grandest book of his *Odes*, the Roman poet Horace congratulated himself on having produced a monument more lasting than bronze, a work that would stand in the way of his completely perishing. Four centuries earlier, one of the earliest and most acute observers of the ways in which moral considerations are bound up within political struggles, Thucydides the Athenian general and historian, affirmed that his work would be a possession forever. Both of these hopes were fulfilled in fact, but few contemporary scholars and writers entertain such grandiose ambitions. We have become accustomed to seeing the works of distinguished philosophers, theologians, lawyers, and social scientists pass into obscurity as new problems arise, as new methods of research and analysis are developed, and as the social experience of both scholars and their audiences changes. Even more do those scholars who examine the ever changing course of political events and who address the policy makers and public leaders as they attempt to ride that shifting stream of events have to be reconciled to having their analyses overtaken by events, sometimes even overwhelmed by them. At the same time, many scholars are consciously working within religious and intellectual traditions that have been fruitful sources of moral guidance over centuries. They are accustomed to see their work as providing applications of principles that transcend particularities of time and place or, alternatively, as providing continuity for a tradition precisely by developing modifications appropriate to a changed social and intellectual environment. They know that events of the past, both expected and unforeseen, have often refracted the light that comes from their traditional sources, and that traditions do not develop in a simple linear fashion.

The period after 1945 was marked by a profound questioning of both the legitimacy of warfare and the moral limits set on warfare by the major religious and philosophical traditions. This questioning was provoked by the development, use, deployment and limitation of nuclear weapons and their delivery systems. The established moral-political orthodoxy of nuclear deterrence with arms control, strategic parity for the superpowers, nonproliferation for small powers, and a system of alliances to protect vital interests and vulnerable friends may recently have begun to look archaic. But it is worth remembering that it is a system in which the basic moral principles are much older than the technology or the political configurations. The principles of just war theory had to be refracted through the events of 1945. These events included the collapse of the volatile political order of Europe, the beginning of the end of the Western empires, and the development of nuclear weapons. Great amounts of political vision and leadership, of moral argument and personal commitment were needed in order to fashion the very imperfect peace of the Cold War and to sustain the successive efforts to moderate its rigors and its irrationalities. The emergence at any time of a new kind of international order is not likely to require either a total rejection of the norms and policies appropriate to the previous order or an unquestioning and steadfast adherence to old principles.

The events in Eastern Europe during the last four months of 1989, which brought the collapse of Soviet-imposed Marxist regimes in East Germany, Czechoslovakia, Hungary, Rumania, and Bulgaria, constitute a particularly striking and unexpected example of change in the social and political environment within which scholars, reflective practitioners, and the general public raise moral questions about war and peace. These events have altered widely shared beliefs about the relationships between the superpowers, about the tenacity and irreversibility of Marxist regimes, and about the limited effectiveness of peaceful protest against such regimes. They have also overturned more controversial claims about the likelihood of nuclear war, about the economic sustainability of Marxist regimes, and about the depth and effectiveness of control in senescent totalitarian regimes. At a deeper level, these events have promised to bring about a lasting change in the shape of the international order and in what people take to be the paradigmatic forms of interaction and conflict in that order. The ensuing economic and political transformations have been rich in irony. Peaceful protests have had far more momentous results than conservatives or realists would have considered possible (though China has provided a concurrent example in which the hopes of pacifists and liberal idealists were rebuffed). Nuclear weapons have been less relevant to the maintenance of political order than their proponents have led us to expect and less destructive than their critics have predicted. The populations of Marxist societies and even significant fractions of Marxist parties have turned out to be more vehement critics of Marxist regimes than have many of their conservative or social democratic adversaries in the West. Marxism, which prided itself on being a scientific response to changing forces of production, has shown itself to be pitifully inadequate in shaping social and political forms appropriate to new technologies.

The events of 1989, of course, built on long-standing dissatisfactions within communist societies. They were preceded by the prolonged struggle of Solidarnosc in Poland, a struggle that for most of the last decade had to concentrate on sustaining a minimum level of organizational survival and public legitimacy; as well as by the open efforts of the Soviet and Chinese leaderships to restore a semblance of economic and political life to their moribund regimes. It was clear to all that the entire Marxist system of domination in Eastern Europe was in great difficulty. But no one with major responsibilities for analysis or for policy would have ventured to predict so rapid, so sweeping, and so peaceful a change as has in fact occurred.

This fact should serve as a salutary reminder of two very important points: first, the limited ability of experts to interpret and predict events, especially when they become really interesting; second, the large element of indeterminacy and incompleteness in our understanding of "the facts," particularly when these facts are complex social movements. The first point accords with Thomas Kuhn's interpretation of the difference between revolutionary science and normal science, a difference which does not allow for a steady predictability from one system to another. This is not a surprising conclusion, since it completes the analogical circle that begins with Kuhn's application of the political notion of revolution with its radical discontinuities to the history of science. The second point serves as a corrective to those who assume that indeterminacy in policy discussions originates solely on the side of values and who affirm that an otherwise clear view of the way things really are is easily obtainable and is only obscured by the nebulous fog of normative discourse. Acknowledging a large element of factual indeterminacy both about what is the case and about what is likely to happen should produce a certain modesty and skepticism in our own predictions and a charity in our assessments of the claims and predictions of others. It should also remind us of the continuing need for care in exercising the freedom of interpretation which accompanies that indeterminacy, and of the possibility that factual indeterminacy and uncertainty may even coexist with normative continuity and clarity.

The fact that the participants in our discussions did not foresee the events of 1989 in Eastern Europe, relevant though they were to our general topic, is an instructive illustration of the general limitations under which policy discourse has to be conducted, as well as a humbling reminder of the particular limitations and blindnesses that mark our own work. These memorable events occurred during the period between the end of our discussions in December 1988 and the preparation of the seminar papers for publication in this volume. So these events, whose meaning and consequences are still very much in dispute, could not be taken as material for reflection.

But there is an interesting premonitory discussion of these matters by James Woolsey in his comments on David Hollenbach's paper on the contributions of the churches to the debate on peace and security. In assessing the Episcopal statement, Woolsey made the following perceptive and indeed prescient remarks:

> In fact the present Soviet regime is highly unstable precisely because of its narrow political base; as long as this is the case, Soviet leaders will find it useful to paint a picture of the Soviet Union as a beleaguered state. As events in Poland and Eastern Europe have shown, there is much we can do to promote peaceful evolution toward a greater degree of pluralism and openness in the Soviet Union, and we should not hesitate to do so. Indeed, the only realistic hope for a long-term substantial improvement in U.S.-Soviet relations is that the character of the Soviet regime will change and that, as the USSR becomes more open and more accountable to domestic democratic pressures, it will follow a less threatening foreign and military policy.

Woolsey here uses the mode of conditional analysis rather than the mode of prediction; but the course of events supports the correctness of the analytical connections he proposed back in the fall of 1988. In fact, even if events had taken a very different course in 1989, most of what he said would still have held true. For careful analysis can enable us to see the underlying connections, tensions, and contradictions that mark the relationships between political and social movements and structures, on the one hand, and on the other the values, norms, and decisions that shape our making of policy and our living of the moral life. Not all of these connections, tensions, and contradictions will be actualized. The forests of international relations and national security policy are as full of roads not taken as is the yellow wood of Robert Frost's solitary traveller.

The road that America will be taking for the last decade of the second millennium will not be the same road we have been on for the last four decades—the decades of the Cold War, NATO, divided Germany, the sullen captivity of Eastern Europe, Soviet truculence in demanding obedience and refusing cooperation. These familiar landmarks are gone or are vastly changed. But any path we take into the future will have to proceed by some long-standing features of the landscape—the continuing strength of ethnic and religious rivalries, the economic disparities between Western Europe and both Eastern Europe and the developing countries—as well as more recent but very powerful transformations such as the irreversible potential for mass destruction that is inherent in contemporary technology, the demonstrated success and attractiveness of transnational and supranational forms of economic organization, and the permanent need to protect the ecological basis for safe and productive human life in advanced industrial societies.

There is enough continuity of features between the old situation and the new way forward to warrant a reasonable belief that most of the basic ethical and religious considerations advanced in our discussions will continue to be relevant and applicable, as well as to sustain the view that many of the political dilemmas and military possibilities will recur in ways that are transformed but are also partly familiar. My own expectation is that it will take some time for us to develop a shared understanding of the implications of a new set of paradigms of interaction and conflict in the post-1989 world. In the meantime, we will need to search for the elements of this shared understanding by scrutinizing the positions and theories of the recent past with a careful eye to their continuing applicability. It is my conviction that both the experience of reflective practitioners and the normative discourse of the academy and the religious traditions, which we have presented in this volume, will be found to contain many, though not all, of the elements we need for a new shared understanding of the requirements of a just and secure peace for the early years of the third millennium. More modestly, it is my hope that both the limitations and the accomplishments of these discussions may provoke others to carry on the rewarding debate over the right way to proceed through the dangers and uncertainties of international affairs to the opportunities and satisfactions of a just and lasting peace. In this way the debates in our Washington community may stimulate and in some measure illuminate the broader American search for peace.

JOHN LANGAN

# The Participants

The "American Search for Peace" seminar, which generated the preceding essays and conversations, was cosponsored by the James Madison Foundation and the Woodstock Theological Center under a grant from the United States Institute of Peace. Participants in the seminar reflected a broad range of theological and political opinion on issues of ethics, war, and peace in the scholarly and policy communities.*

---

John Ahearne, Vice-President, Resources for the Future; former Chairman, Nuclear Regulatory Commission.

Victor Alessi, Director, Office of Arms Control, U.S. Department of Energy; former Chief, Strategic Affairs Division, U.S. Arms Control and Disarmament Agency.

Mark Amstutz, Professor of Political Science, Wheaton College.

Dean Brackley, S.J., Visiting Fellow, Woodstock Theological Center.

Herman Breulman, S.J., chaplain, *Kusanuswerk*, Bonn.

S.J. Burki, Director for China Country Development, World Bank.

James F. Childress, Professor of Religious Studies, University of Virginia.

Frank Cody, S.J., Associate Professor of Education, University of Detroit.

Alberto R. Coll, Professor of Strategy and International Politics, U.S. Naval War College.

James Connor, S.J., Director, Woodstock Theological Center.

John Cooper, Senior Research Fellow, Ethics and Public Policy Center.

Michael Cromartie, Research Associate, Ethics and Public Policy Center.

John Donahue, S.J., Professor of New Testament, Jesuit School of Theology, Berkeley.

R. Bruce Douglass, Professor of Government, Georgetown University.

Nick Eberstadt, Visiting Scholar, American Enterprise Institute; Visiting Fellow, Harvard Center for Population Studies.

Larry Fabian, Secretary, Carnegie Endowment for International Peace.

James Finn, Editorial Director, Freedom House.

Suzanne Garment, Resident Scholar, American Enterprise Institute.

Carl Gershman, President, National Endowment for Democracy.

Robert Gessert, Program Director, Logistics Management Institute.

Owen Harries, Editor, *The National Interest*; former ambassador of Australia to UNESCO.

---

* These identifications locate each participant during the seminar, which met from February 1987 through December 1988.

J. Bryan Hehir, Associate Secretary, United States Catholic Conference.

Kent Hill, Executive Director, Institute on Religion and Democracy.

David Hollenbach, S.J., Professor of Moral Theology, Weston School of Theology.

J. Leon Hooper, S.J., Research Fellow, Woodstock Theological Center.

Kenneth Jensen, Director of Research, U.S. Institute of Peace.

James Turner Johnson, Professor of Religious Studies, Rutgers University.

Douglas Johnston, Executive Vice-President, Center for Strategic and International Studies.

Charles Krauthammer, Senior Editor, *The New Republic*, and recipient of the 1987 Pulitzer Prize for Commentary.

John P. Langan, S.J., Rose Kennedy Professor of Christian Ethics, Georgetown University; Senior Fellow, Woodstock Theological Center.

Robert Lehman, Vice-President and General Counsel, Charles F. Kettering Foundation.

Samuel W. Lewis, President, U.S. Institute of Peace; former Assistant Secretary of State for International Organization Affairs and U.S. ambassador to Israel, 1977-85.

David Little, Professor of Religious Studies, University of Virginia.

Robin W. Lovin, Professor of Ethics and Theology, University of Chicago.

Gerald M. Mara, Associate Dean for Research, the Graduate School, Georgetown University.

Paul D. McNelis, S.J., Associate Professor of Economics, Georgetown University.

Richard John Neuhaus, Director, Center on Religion and Society.

David Newsom, Associate Dean of the School of Foreign Service, Georgetown University; former Undersecretary of State for Political Affairs.

Michael Novak, George Frederick Jewett Chair in Religion and Public Policy, American Enterprise Institute; former U.S. representative to the UN Human Rights Commission and U.S. ambassador to the 1986 Helsinki Review Conference on Human Contacts.

Joseph S. Nye, Jr., Professor of Political Science, Harvard University; former Deputy Undersecretary of State.

William V. O'Brien, Professor of Government, Georgetown University.

Allen Parrent, Associate Dean for Academic Affairs, Professor of Christian Ethics, and Vice-President, Protestant Episcopal Theological Seminary in Virginia.

Robert Pickus, President, World Without War Council.

Gerard Powers, Advisor, Office of International Justice and Peace, United States Catholic Conference.

Anthony Quainton, Deputy Inspector-General, U.S. Department of State; former U.S. ambassador to Nicaragua.

Thomas Reese, S.J., Fellow, Woodstock Theological Center; Associate Editor, *America*.

Harold Saunders, Visiting Fellow, The Brookings Institution; former Assistant Secretary of State for Near East and South Asian Affairs.

Thomas Schubeck, S.J., Visiting Fellow, Woodstock Theological Center.

Bruno Schüller, S.J., Professor of Moral Theology, University of Münster.

Paul Seabury, Professor of Political Science, University of California, Berkeley.

Amy Sherman, Assistant to the President, James Madison Foundation.

Peter Steinfels, Editor, *Commonweal*.

George Stephanopoulos, Staff Director, Office of Congressman Edward Feighan.

Anne-Marie Streyer, *Kusanuswerk*, Bonn.

Harry G. Summers, Jr., Contributing Editor, *U.S. News & World Report*.

James D. Watkins, former Chief of Naval Operations.

George Weigel, President, James Madison Foundation.

Bruce Weinrod, Director of Foreign Policy and Defense Studies, Heritage Foundation.

David Wessels, S.J., Professor of Political Science, Sophia University, Tokyo.

Todd Whitmore, research assistant, University of Chicago.

R. James Woolsey, partner, Shea & Gardner; former Undersecretary of the Navy.